"Ron Belsterling has been a respected voice among those of us who train college students for youth ministry for years. In this book he offers readers a gift of scholarship, passion, thoughtfulness, creativity, and encouragement. . . . If you *do* youth ministry, if you *care* about youth ministry, you need to read this book!"

—DUFFY ROBBINS
author of *Building a Youth Ministry that Builds Disciples*

"'Youth ministry as an experiment has failed.' So said the late, great Mike Yaconelli. . . . But for some of us, it really doesn't feel that way. . . . Ron speaks with the authority of one who has been there, done it, and collected the coffee travel mug 'lifer' award. He is passionate about youth and is a welcome voice in pushing back on those hunting for easy targets."

—ANDY DU FEU
Moorlands College, Christchurch, UK

"Ron Belsterling imparts seasoned and time-tested youth ministry wisdom that will help us well as we equip kids for a lifetime of passionately seeking, loving, and serving Christ. For the seasoned youth worker, this book will rekindle your passion by challenging you to think in new ways about youth ministry. And for those just starting out, Ron will help you build a strong ministry foundation that will serve you well."

—WALT MUELLER
author of *99 Thoughts for Parents of Teenagers*

"Ron Belsterling is a seasoned veteran of both youth ministry and of research on relationships and how they impact people's relationship with God. . . . He brings a deep understanding of how relationships develop, what hinders securely attached relationships, and how youth ministry ought to be done with youth who have different past experiences in relationships with their parents and with God."

—KEVIN LAWSON
author of *Supervising and Supporting Ministry Staff*

"Equipping the next generations to follow Christ is the highest calling of ministry. In this thorough overview, Ron Belsterling has captured this biblical vision and offered an inspirational call to youth ministry coupled with a practical, strategic guidebook. At a time when many communities are worried about the well-being of teenagers. . . . *A Defense of Youth Ministry* is a remarkably refreshing resource."

—**KEN CASTOR**

author of *Grow Down* and *Make a Difference*

"I hope this book is seen for what it is, an intense look at the needs and means of reaching and leading the next generation. . . . Ron is a peace-maker as defined by Jesus in Matthew 5, a true son of God fighting to see the world of youth ministry, families, and the church growing in partnership."

—**DALE PATRICK, SR.**

High School Ministry Pastor, Grace Church, Middleburg Heights, Ohio

"In this book Ron offers extremely helpful information. In youth min-istry, you see all sorts of attachment issues with both teens and parents. With an in-depth knowledge of the psychology of the teens who display these patterns in their youth or young adult groups, Ron . . . gives youth leaders insight, which I know has given me fresh perspectives on how to see and approach parents and their teens."

—**MARV NELSON**

author of *Unleash, Empowering the Next Generation of Leaders*

"This book answers my questions about different generations. While the world changes, the Word of God is steadfast. . . . I should not be discour-aged if some of my youth volunteers or parents are not communicating well or if students are not showing up. Relationships can't be rushed and must be cultivated. Awesome stuff in here!"

—**SHIN SUNG KANG**

Student Ministry Director, Journey Church, Huntersville, North Carolina

"If you are looking to actively build relationships in teen's lives in order to help them mature in *their* relationship with Jesus, then read on. If we want youth to experience God, it goes far beyond surface relationships. Students don't need to wait until heaven to experience God and His perfection, we can and should experience it now. Ron tackles this entire idea."

—**ERIC PELOQUIN**
Pastor of Emerging Generations, Bedford Community Church, Bedford, New Jersey

"When we continually join in with what God's doing rather than wishing He joins in with us, we'll see our programs become much more life-giving and transformational. Young people long to be invested into directly and intentionally. . . . Anything less and we do them an injustice. Within Ron's book, the nail has well and truly been hit on the head."

—**GRAEME WATSON**
The Climb Retreat, Newcastle, Northern Ireland

"Ron Belsterling takes another look at the topic of 'relationship building' that is both worthwhile and necessary. . . . His observations of past approaches to relational ministry, and his analysis of what is supposedly the 'current' and definitive approach to this topic, offer fresh insight into developing both a new and balanced perspective and, at the same time, a return to foundational—and frequently forgotten—principles not to be ignored."

—**DARRELL PEARSON**
author of *Can I Really Relate?*

A Defense of Youth Ministry

A DEFENSE OF YOUTH MINISTRY

Attachment Relationship Ministry (ARM)

RON BELSTERLING

Foreword by Leonard Kageler

Foreword by Alex Tufano

PICKWICK *Publications* · Eugene, Oregon

A DEFENSE OF YOUTH MINISTRY
Attachment Relationship Ministry (ARM)

Pickwick Publications
An Imprint of Wipf and Stock Publishers
199 W. 8th Ave., Suite 3
Eugene, OR 97401

www.wipfandstock.com

PAPERBACK ISBN: 978-1-5326-5155-7
HARDCOVER ISBN: 978-1-5326-5156-4
EBOOK ISBN: 978-1-5326-5157-1

Cataloguing-in-Publication data:

Names: Belsterling, Ronald, author. | Kageler, Leonard, foreword.

Title: A Defense of Youth Ministry : Attachment Relationship Ministry (ARM) / by Ronald Belsterling; foreword by Leonard Kageler.

Description: Eugene, OR: Pickwick Publications, 2019 | Includes bibliographical references and index.

Identifiers: ISBN 978-1-5326-5155-7 (paperback) | ISBN 978-1-5326-5156-4 (hardcover) | ISBN 978-1-5326-5157-1 (ebook)

Subjects: LCSH: Church work with youth. | Attachment behavior.

Classification: BV4447 B37 2019 (paperback) | BV4447 (ebook)

Manufactured in the U.S.A.   04/03/19

Dedication

To my God and my wife, both of whom I love with all my heart. You have loved me with gracious patience. This book is dedicated to you.

Lord, may this book bring glory to Your Great Name. Thank You for allowing me to partner with Jesus and His disciples. You are the One, True, Loving God and I love you.

Julie, you are the one through whom our Great God has loved me most. You have sacrificed so much time and energy on my behalf. I do need you. I love you.

Contents

PART 1: MODELS OF MINISTRY

Chapter 1

Chapter 2

Chapter 3

Chapter 4

PART 2: THE THEOLOGY & THEORY BEHIND ARM
These two chapters present the academic background behind ARM. The interaction of parental approaches and family systems create some clear and helpful-to-understand scenarios for youth leaders when using ARM.

Chapter 5

Chapter 6

PART 3: MEETING THE RELATIONAL NEEDS OF EVERY TEEN

These chapters focus on intentional relational approaches to differences in teen relational needs. Topics covered include student leadership potential, ministry to subcultures (LGBTQIA, etc.), spiritual formation approaches, and parents' needs. They also consider personal factors influencing ARM.

Foreword

EVERY AUGUST AND SEPTEMBER in the UK a very strange thing occurs in many farmlands around the country. Just after sunrise and a little before sunset *Roman towns appear*. Say what???

In some parts of the country there are Roman ruins just under the surface. When crops are planted every spring, their growth rate is partially determined by the water retention of the soil. Soil that has Roman ruins just 12 inches down absorbs and retains less water, so crops planted above do not grow as well. Late in the growing season, this growth difference is visible, not from the ground, but from the air and only when the sun is at a low angle. I have seen this once with my own eyes, flying north from London in early morning. . . . I looked down and boom! . . . there were the outlines of Roman buildings and roads in the shadows cast by the sun's low angle and clearly visible in the wheat, corn, or whatever had been planted months earlier.

Now that is a truly bizarre way to begin a foreword you say. Well, I agree but hear me out. In the UK, the low angle of the sun throws into sight something we didn't know was there. This is exactly what Ron Belsterling has given us in this book. He has come at the topic of youth ministry from a low angle, an angle never used before in this context, and he throws into clear view insights and implications many of us have never considered.

I have known Ron for more than two decades and have seen firsthand his application of attachment relationship ministry. When he first came to Nyack College to join me as a prof in what we now call Youth & Family Studies, he would sometimes be late to his next class because he was so deeply involved in conversation with students. As Department Chair, I had to (gently) point out that his heart to listen to and minister to students was admirable, yet the institution does expect professors to make it to class and actually be on time. Ron was committed to authentic relationships from day one here.

The gift Ron has given us in this book is a lavish combination of scholarship and practical real world application. Ron has years of paid and volunteer youth ministry in his background. He is open about his shortcomings, admitting some pretty spectacular ministry mistakes, but also open about the fruit that comes from ministry done faithfully in the Spirit of Jesus our Lord and Savior.

Most youth workers and youth ministry educators, myself included, have experienced well intentioned people who demean our calling, and advise us to abandon youth ministry. Ron is an encourager here, reminding us that our calling is legitimate and Kingdom worthy. And he has given us the gift of convincingly showing us how Attachment Theory has massive implications and applications to youth ministry. You see, he has come at our calling from a *unique low angle*, and, as a result, has thrown into sight and made accessible a whole host of insights and wisdom.

Have a yellow highlighter handy when you read this book, there will be MANY things here you will want to remember. I recommend you have your phone or tablet handy as well, with a doc titled: "Implications for my ministry." Thank you Ron!

Leonard Kageler
Emeritus Professor of Youth & Family Studies, Nyack College, Nyack, NY

Foreword

I STILL REMEMBER THE first class I had with Ron Belsterling. It was "American Youth Culture" in my second semester at Nyack College, and our first grade was a test on C. S. Lewis's *Mere Christianity*. I treated it like I had every test in my life up to that point—by not studying much at all. That's not to say that I wasn't a good student. I had simply been blessed with a good memory and had done well with little studying all through middle school, high school, and college up to that point. I got a C on that test. (*Mere Christianity* has actually become my favorite book, and I've gone back and reread it several times. I also did better academically in Ron's classes once I knew what I was in for!)

It was that moment that I knew that Ron Belsterling would challenge me and that I would grow to become a greater person as a result of knowing him. I spent the next three years studying youth ministry under him, growing in my love for teenagers and serving them, and desiring to do youth ministry with excellence. I came to know Ron's heart for Jesus and for teenagers even more when I served as his assistant, and that heart comes through in this book. This book is a culmination of his decades of experience in youth ministry, counseling, teaching, and research, and should challenge each youth worker who reads it to think more carefully about how they can best minister to the teenagers they serve.

We need more youth workers who understand the responsibility they have to serve God and teenagers with excellence. That means we have to take the academic side of our work seriously. We're called to love the Lord with all of our mind, and one concrete way we can do that is by understanding how psychology, neurology, social studies, and plenty of disciplines "outside" youth ministry can inform and improve our ministry.

This clearly is not a youth ministry book that is light, trendy, and devoid of theological and academic thought. Perhaps you're thinking, "Why do I need to consider these academic theories when I already love Jesus and have the Bible?" Let me pose it this way: do you see scientific study as unnecessary and unconnected to your worship of God? Or can the truth revealed in science complement God's word and cause you to stand in even greater awe of him when you see how intricate his creation is? In a similar way, the academic theories Ron presents in this book can give us a greater appreciation for how God created humans uniquely and designed us to be in relationship with him and with others. Not to mention they provide some practical steps for better ministry.

This book will be challenging at times, and Ron may step on your toes. One year at Nyack, a group of us created a meme with Ron's picture that said, "Grace? She isn't in this class." It was a humorous point about how tough Ron could be, and how grueling his assignments were at times. But it was only because of Ron's love and care for us that his classes were so hard. He knew that ministering to teenagers was a huge undertaking and responsibility, and that he would be doing us a disservice if he let us skate by. I am incredibly thankful for just how much Ron pushed me and my peers to excellence and to loving the Lord our God with all of our heart, soul, mind, and strength as we prepared for lives of ministry.

I trust that as you read through this book, you will be blessed in the same way. You will not be challenged to anything Ron has not committed himself to as well. He recognizes the depth of his sin and need for Jesus Christ and has been radically saved and transformed by his grace to where he now loves his Savior and treasures that relationship. So, when he challenges us to prioritize our time in prayer, the Word, and in not compromising our relationship with Christ, it's not at all hypocritical. Ron loves and cherishes his relationship with his wife and (now adult) children, putting them in the proper priority to making life changes for their sake. So, when he's challenging us to love our family well and to not sacrifice them for our ministry, it's because he is doing that himself (and you'll learn that he was failing at that once before). Take the challenges and pursue excellence in your ministry.

One of my prayers for you, the reader, is that you'll be able to see Ron's heart like I have, and that you'll be able to gain the wisdom as if you were his student. I know that as that happens, your ministry will benefit, because mine has. I've found it enormously helpful to have the Attachment Relationship Ministry model (ARM) to view teenagers through, and to cater various aspects of my ministry accordingly. When I've had large numbers of teens securely attached to their parents and to God, I can teach on much deeper topics of doctrine and challenge them in different ways. That includes offering local service and international missions opportunities that provide risk in their comfort. The ARM is also incredibly helpful in identifying those teenagers who seem apathetic to God while being in good families in the church—they have unique needs and opportunities for ministry. Even the way I interact with and minster to parents has been foundationally influenced by Ron and that comes through in this book.

If you're reading this far, let me say something to potentially different types of readers. If you are currently serving in a youth ministry position, especially in a church, I imagine you'll be immensely encouraged by Ron's exhortation for the value of and need for youth ministry. You have a ministry worth valuing—see the need for it to be taken seriously. You'll find the four most practical chapters to be the four attachment profiles and how to minister to them; there is a lot of gold in there. And if you skim over chapters 5 and 6 because of how heavy they are, where Ron lays the foundation and explains the theories and research behind the four profiles, go back and read them after you read the other chapters. As you learn about ARM consider where you fit and how that impacts your life and ministry.

And if you're a parent, elder, senior church leader, or someone else peering into the world of youth ministry, hear Ron's heart for excellent youth ministry and challenge the youth workers in your life to excellence. Support them too. And honor and reward appropriately.

Reader, I thank you for your love for Jesus and your desire to serve him and serve teenagers. I pray that as you read this book, you'll be blessed. I pray that you'll be made uncomfortable, encouraged, that you'll have a greater burden for serving teenagers, and that you'll be challenged to excellence in youth ministry. It is a blessing to be able to serve you in writing this preface. Now get to the actual work!

Ron, I love you and I am so thankful I had the opportunity to study under you, to learn and be challenged by you, and to now labor alongside you in serving our Lord and the teenagers he loves. This book has been a long time coming and the hard work has paid off. I pray that God uses it in powerful ways to bless youth workers, teenagers, parents, church leaders, and everyone else who will read it. And I pray that you see the light and become a Patriots fan. *(I, Ron, was tempted to edit that line out . . . it really hurts to include it.) (Really!)*

Alex Tufano, Minister of Students
Pascack Bible Church, Hillsdale, NJ

Acknowledgments

THANK YOU TO MY editing partners, Julie, Emily, Sam, and Alex. I can't imagine having tried to do this without your gracious, capable, patient, timely, and persevering assistance. Thank you to my colleagues and former students who took the time to read the book and share their thoughts.

Introduction

Youth ministry has proven successful throughout the ages of time. It succeeds because it's a smart approach directly reflecting the methods of Jesus Christ. The hard work required for its success has been misunderstood and misrepresented. With this book, I seek to defend youth ministry against false claims and short-sighted suggestions from those on the outside and inside of the church, including from within the field of youth ministry itself. I also desire to empower those doing the hard work by identifying and encouraging more strategic use of relational aspects that have made youth ministry successful. These aspects rise to the surface through the lens of Attachment Relationship Ministry (ARM). We can take what we've done well and make it better yet.

"The God of the universe . . . gives to His power, the name 'arm.'"[1] Jesus Christ, the arm of God, performs for God and as God, in tune with His will and thoughts.[2] Scripture portrays God's arm as outstretched, extending His reach towards His people.[3] He powerfully executes and lovingly embraces on God's behalf.[4] With His arm, God redeems.[5] His enemies fearfully regard the strength of His arm,[6] and His people seek God's shielding, assistance, and comfort through His arm.[7] "For My Arm they will wait expectantly . . . awake, awake, put on strength, O arm of the Lord. . . . I have put My words in your mouth, and have covered you with the shadow of My hand, to establish the heavens, to found the earth, and

1. Elliott, *Isaiah 40-66*, 153.
2. Isa 53:1; Job 40:9.
3. Deut 5:15; 1 Kgs 8:42; Ps 136:12.
4. Ps 136:12; Jer 32:17; Luk 1:51.
5. Exod 6:6; Deut 9:29; Ps 98:1; Isa 52:10.
6. Exod 15:16; Isa 30:30.
7. Isa 40:11; 51:5; 2 Chr 32:8; Job 35:9.

to say to Zion, 'You are My people.'"[8] In this passage the righteous and/or Isaiah call to God for His right arm, Jehovah, and God, hearing the call, invokes Jesus to respond. Yet, in this passage I also hear Jesus calling back to us with the same words and message, to be for Him as He is for God. "Then I heard the voice of the Lord, saying, 'Whom shall I send, and who will go for Us?'"[9]

Jesus stated His expectations for all of His disciples at the end of His earthly life, "As Thou did send Me into the world, I also have sent them into the world."[10] He equipped us with His vision and power to go, proclaim, and establish His plan.[11] Certainly we won't establish anything holy apart from Him; yet, we still must receive the commission that He desires to establish His kingdom through our work. We must believe His power runs through us to each other and to others not yet aware of God's greatness.[12] We have been commanded to work out our salvation, not by earning it, but by sharing it, and by watching God produce fruit from the abiding, multiplying seed of salvation within us.[13] "My words which I have put in your mouth, shall not depart from your mouth, nor from the mouth of your offspring, nor from the mouth of your offspring's offspring."[14] Through us, He says to the lost, "I've been looking for you."[15] Our flocks need His compassion, refuge, truth, and nurture from His love overflowing out of us.

God, in His unfathomable wisdom, assigned us to participate with Jesus in the privilege and responsibility to represent Him. He tells us countless times in Scripture, "I go before you."[16] Let us believe Him, receiving our call to be the right arm of Christ for His honor, willing to extend, suffer and serve as He sees fit.[17] We do youth ministry for this reason alone. We serve Christ as Christ served our God. For those who

---

8. Isa 51:5–16.

9. Isa 6:8.

10. John 17:18.

11. Ps 89:21; Jer 27:5; Matt 17:20.

12. John 1317.

13. Phil 2:9; John 15.

14. Isa 59:21.

15. Luke 15.

16. Isa 45:2.

17. Isa 53; Luke 9:23; John 13.

don't, we need to start. The only way to do this is to stay close to God in the Word, prayer, and fellowship of the saints.

After thirty plus years in the field of youth ministry, there is still an unquenchable ache in my soul to reach teenagers and young adults, and to help their leaders sense the fullness of a redeeming relationship with Jesus Christ in the here-and-now and for eternity, for the salvation of souls and redemption of every earthly relationship. I hope this book contributes to an increase in the efficacy of every youth worker, from the volunteer to the professional, from the novice to the tested expert, from the student to the professor. I'm aiming this book primarily at those who lead, study, and teach youth ministry. May it also help readers to grow more adept as spouses, parents and co-laborers. "Therefore, be careful how you walk, not as unwise men but as wise, making the most of your time."[18]

I write this book with the same goal that I teach every youth ministry class, trusting God that no ministry, of those who read it, will ever be the same again. I'm confident all will see personal and professional relationships from new angles. You'll see through teenagers' surface level and symptomatic needs, right down to their most basic need(s). Content focuses on informing and equipping youth workers as to how to proceed in meeting the two root level needs of each teenager. Rationale for why we specifically relate to certain teens the way we do should encourage readers and answer many questions.

Why do our best relational efforts in youth ministry sometimes fail and our worst sometimes succeed? How do we know how to minister to whom and when? How do I welcome LGBTQIA teens successfully without alienating anyone? What do we do with teens who suffocate us with their clinginess? Why does a teen who seems to like leaders and other kids in the church never attend youth group meetings? Why does a teen who complains about everything participate in almost everything?

What does one say to a mother who demands her child receive more attention? How does one advise a father who admits disconnect between he and his child? What does one say to an angry parent, wanting to know why we're talking about sex at youth group? We have personal questions too. Can I truly represent God to youth and aid them if I struggle with depression, pornographic temptation, or sexual identity issues? Some of these questions appear to have simple answers, but presumed answers

18. Eph 5:15–16.

only mask deeper level reasons. Knowing these reasons will help youth leaders to ask and answer the right questions, dismiss some questions, better address important questions and lead into others' questions with our own questions, like Jesus did.

Youth ministry's success depends on historic relational effort. And yet, most youth workers have not fully realized how people's two critical needs intertwine and dictate how we ought to meet those needs. We must offer more than un-contextualized, pop discipleship programs, technological worship wizardry, and fad emphases. For too many teens today, feeling insecure in crisis is a way of life. While ministry effort to these young people has always helped and should be applauded by the church instead of criticized by it, most of us can execute more accurately and thoroughly. In the words of Vince Lombardi, let's aim for perfection hoping that we might hit excellence along the way.

As a youth ministry lifer I trust that God will bless those reading this book with encouragement, confusions clarified, new insights and newfound passion due to those facts. Readers will likely notice the blend of my church and parachurch youth ministry experience, with study and experience in education, youth ministry research, clinical counseling of families and organizational leadership. While I've picked up some degrees in these areas and have been teaching over twenty years now, please know, I've stayed active in the field via a host of ways, directly working with adolescents and indirectly leading through various ministry organizations who assist teens. When challenged by a PhD professor to give up ministry for a season, I told him I'd rather give up the pursuit of the PhD

Secondary agendas for writing this book exist too. Any Christian who ministers to teens outside of the church or parachurch, such as teachers and coaches, should find the text helpful, with Parts 2 and 3 particularly explanatory and applicable in their fields. I hope many church leaders not associated with youth ministry or confused about the direction of youth ministry will read it and support or create a vision for youth ministry unparalleled in recent history. This would make a good text for all church leaders and those in Pastoral Ministry undergrad and seminary courses, particularly those who have been critical of the concept and accusatory of the failure of youth ministry. Hopefully some will repent. They should. The book explains why. Adolescents of today desperately need competent ministries targeting and designed for them.

The first part of the book defends the validity of the concept and success of youth ministry. It also analytically critiques the pros and cons of current, varying youth ministry philosophies and approaches. No matter one's philosophy or the types of relationships that youth workers have with youth, the case is made that we've all had successes by the grace of God. Ultimately, all contribute to defending the success and legitimacy of youth ministry.

The second part of the book advocates for an orientation called Attachment Relationship Ministry (ARM). ARM divides into approaches relative to adolescent relational styles. Each chapter includes profiles and illustrations, probably surprising most readers as to the uncanny similarity to members of their own flocks and their own personal experiences with them. Differing key needs associated with relational styles of youth become obvious the more one reads. Each chapter contains recommendations relative to spiritual formation, leadership selection, parental approach, and more.

Jesus' approach provides the fundamental rationale behind the model and the methodology suggested in ARM. I wish we in youth ministry leadership had Jesus' intuition and wise discernment. Since we don't, we must lean on His. If we wisely use a model based on what God has recorded and identified as the two critical needs for people and on Jesus' disciple making approach (which I've carefully researched), I trust God will bless those partnering with Him via the ARM model. Readers will experience more "Yeah, this makes sense" and "now I see why" moments than "Wow, this is an entirely new way of discipleship" ones. Respected former students and current youth leaders provide their thoughts and responses in every chapter.

ARM content will help to refine rather than redirect ministry efforts. God is an orderly and exacting God, and He blesses through prepared, diligent, and sometimes risky effort more than He does through determination alone. He also blesses through one's weakness. In my learned insecure modality of avoiding others, it's ironic that His greatest success through me has been through personal and professional relationships. "I will boast as to what pertains to my weakness," because it is there where I gratefully, humbly and most easily see God's light shine through me (2 Cor. 11:30). Recommendations through and within the chapters are not intended to handcuff anyone, but to simply offer a visual grid to see through. Outliers always exist, but do not negate the relevance of the suggestions.

Chapter 5 introduces the development of the ARM model, sharing critical theological and theoretical constructs. Chapter 6 presents ARM's explanation in a nutshell, acting as the foundation of the skyscraper built above it. Chapters 7–10 each specifically zone in on the four primary need centers of all youth and discuss how to approach evangelical and discipling ministry accordingly. These chapters take into consideration varying subgroups within the four quadrants of ARM. Chapters 7 and 8 address how best to work with adolescents in secure relationships with their parents. Chapters 9 and 10 guide work with youth from insecure family backgrounds. The remaining chapters discuss how intervening issues enhance or obstruct an ARM approach. It is hoped that readers will find this text not only time relevant, but also timeless in its Biblical, experiential and psychosocial awareness, sensitivity, emphasized principles and practical relational realities.

Our two primary relational needs will never change. The ways to meet those needs will also never change. The importance of community will never change. And God never changes. Youth ministry does not have to be like canoeing mountains.[19]

---

19. See Bolsinger, *Canoeing the Mountains*.

PART 1

Models of Ministry

CHAPTER 1

Youth Ministry in Crisis?

"The way we're doing things is already not working. We're failing at our calling. . . . We need an epochal shift in our assumptions, approaches, models and methods. . . . In many ways, youth ministry today is the horse drawn buggy." (Ostreicher, *Youth Ministry 3.0*, pp. 20, 25)

"All students leave church at 61%. Students in youth programs leave at 78–88%. Implication: Students attending a church with nothing for them attend church at a 50% higher rate in their 20's than if they went to a church with one of our youth programs!" (Marino, "Is the Way we are Doing Youth Ministry Emptying the Church?")

"Our models aren't working any more. The number of young people in the Church is halving every generation. . . . Finding ways to connect with teenagers in the community and grow the faith of those within the Church feels increasingly difficult. Ways of doing youth ministry that seemed so effective in the 90s and 2000s no longer fit our culture or the needs of young people. It's time to stop building the same old models and start building something new." (Curtis and Saunders, "Rethinking Youth Work")

THIS CHAPTER CAUTIONS THE youth leader to wisely hear the voices of those advocating for change in youth ministry. No matter one's approach and philosophy, surrendered souls committed to God and His service

3

have found and will find success. Other factors influence the degree of success. Therefore, relative to the above quotes, I feel like I did in 1999, when the doomsday crowd predicted global, catastrophic, crises. And nothing happened. I appreciate sober and alert cautions and God's ways always prevail. God doesn't change. Basic human needs do not change. Therefore, whether leaning more to historic emphases of strategy or recent emphases on relationship, God will bless. He gave people not only Himself, but He also gave us each other. The basic components of relationship within community have been intact forever. His Word shows the way in all fields, especially in youth ministry. Hearing these voices wisely might mean challenging them.

Clearly, some long time youth ministry field leaders are questioning the value and success of our field specifically.[1] Many renowned writers and speakers question the traditional (influence, strategic) ministry paradigm[2] and reactively are calling for an "epochal change" or "rethinking" or "re-imagining" of youth ministry. These realities are why some have reported the decline or called for the death of the "50 year failed experiment" of youth ministry.[3] They're why some have argued that ministry targeting youth specifically should be replaced by family ministry.[4]

I feel like today's youth workers have been asked to dig out the Grand Canyon of adolescence with spoons (volunteer or part time) because the church can't afford shovels (fulltime), with someone planted on each shoulder providing conflicting instructions and at least one heckler on the sidelines. Now they're being told they've failed because only a third of the job gets done in four years. In today's broken world, youth ministry is the ARM of Christ, the hand of God reaching down and out, the hand of Christ nailed to the cross. The twenty-first century adolescent journey makes yesteryear's journeys look like picnics, for both the saved and the lost. It pains me to see youth work organizations in the United States expanding due to need and established success of youth ministry,

---

1. Yaconelli, *Contemplative Youth Ministry*, 219; see Yaconelli, "Failure of Youth Ministry"; Clark, *Adoptive Youth Ministry*, 20.

2. Diaz, *Redefining*, 50; Kimball, *Emerging Church*, 915; Ostreicher, *Youth Ministry 3.0*, 20. I suggest reading a warranted ministry manifesto centering on encouraging a revolution under the authority of God's word by Francis Schaeffer, entitled *A Christian Manifesto*.

3. DeVries, "End of Paid Youth Ministry," 26–27.

4. Jones and Trentham, *Practical Family Ministry*; DeVries, *Family Based Youth Ministry*, 8.

while the church discredits youth ministry, blaming faulty programs for the masses of millennials avoiding church.[5] What pains me more is that field insiders seem to be capitulating to or capitalizing on the fervor of this movement, started by Mike Yaconelli's lament and exploited by Scott Brown, and others.[6] We don't need to yield to those second guessing their own value or criticizing youth ministry for their own profits.

We have to be willing to look in the mirror too, as there is usually some grain of truth in criticism. Some youth workers fail of their own accord; I'm not blind to that fact. More than a few see youth ministry as a stepping stone or practice ground for a future real ministry position. Some enter youth work only because they didn't know what else to do. Some entertain with no intent to teach because they have no intent to study. Others go into youth ministry more to become a local celebrity, to receive emotional ego boosts rather than to give emotional support. This minority of youth workers, however, jeopardizes the reputations of most solid youth leaders, working under difficult conditions, and many with less than proficient training.

Too many youth workers lack adequate time, training and/or support (spiritual, communal, financial) to capably meet all the growing adolescent needs. Too many churches and parachurch organizations hire people from within their ministries who have good hearts and knowledge of their organizations, but who lack necessary skills and education. They're hired either because many church and parachurch ministries treat the position and its' qualifications flippantly, or because some ministry education programs miss the mark, or because there simply aren't enough interested and qualified youth leaders to meet the need. Thus, for good or bad reasons, in-house training occurs. I address some of these issues later in the text.

Most church leaders wouldn't dream of using a doctor, lawyer, or accountant with in-house church training. How can elders be fine with such an approach for their youth ministry leaders, those charged with overseeing the development of impressionable and volatile adolescents' eternal destinies, amidst the chaos of a moral collapse in culture? Even the secular community recognizes the critical skill sets needed in

> Most church leaders wouldn't dream of using a doctor, lawyer, or accountant with in-house church training.

---

5. See Pozzoboni and Kirshner, *Changing Landscape of Youth Work*.

6. Brown, *Weed in the Church*, 110; Yaconelli, "Failure of Youth Ministry," lines 1–41.

working with teenagers![7] Loving Jesus and being a young adult doesn't automatically qualify one to effectively minister to today's teenager. Many who love Jesus and have yet to pass thirty-five know what I'm talking about.

OPENING CONCERNS AND CRITICISMS

Before proceeding I'd like to address the specific quotes at the beginning of this chapter. I don't do this with every chapter, but based on the speculation that youth ministry has had a negative impact, I feel obligated. And clearly, I am writing this whole book to address these accusations/assumptions. First, we're not failing at our calling. Can we improve? Yes. Failing? No. The only possible epochal shift I can imagine implementing would be to get rid of youth ministry. I believe many have cultivated this rhetoric of crisis for two reasons. First, to distract themselves from the hard work of youth ministry. Second, drama sells. But it also smells, especially when it's used to discredit hard and successful work on God's behalf and to sidetrack those who are doing it. I tire of those who care more about capitalizing from youth ministry than serving through it. "What then? Only that in every way, whether in pretense or in truth, Christ is proclaimed; and in this I rejoice" (Phil 1:18).

As for Marino's conjecture related to the merged statistics of two studies of young adults leaving the church, without knowing more information validating each study and their combined usage, Marino's inference illegitimately provokes God's servants. What and how many churches comprised both studies? How many participants in each research effort? How was the information gleaned? What if we're talking about a group of ten, led by an inconsistent volunteer in one situation and a two-hundred and fifty member youth group, led by a full time Youth Pastor in the other? What if the Youth Pastor had no training, but the volunteer did? What percentages of both groups consist of unchurched, unsaved, teenagers? How do the stats relate to outreach kids?

I could go on, but I'll stop here. These types of hit the panic button conclusions frustrate me. As we proceed, I'll choose to believe good motives lie behind the effort. While each quote raises fair issues, probably

---

7. Brion-Miesels indicates, "Prevention science research bolsters our assertion that youth workers should be trained in programs that are developed to suit contextual needs" (Brion-Meisels et al., "Not Anyone Can Do this Work," 73).

accurate relative to some youth ministries, we inside the field must stop jumping on the "blame youth ministry" band wagon. Every field has it's doers and it's imposters. We have to stop blaming the field of youth ministry and everyone serving in it for the problems created by posers. That's what the world does with the church and the church doesn't like it either.

All of those quoted seem to be concerned that while we've believed youth ministry to be relationally oriented, we haven't seen the fruit of abiding-relational success. Youth are leaving the church when they become adults![8] Alarming reactions include restructuring youth ministry more into a family ministry approach or just getting rid of such ministry all together. Some have concluded, in a less extremist response, that we need to redefine relational youth ministry to a *legitimate* incarnational-relational ministry. Of those, many believe we need to be *less influentially oriented*. Still others are presenting new approaches or strategies of influence.

This text encourages a merger of a strategic and a relational approach, which has essentially always existed in well run youth ministries. There appears to be encouragement and effort in a few other Christian youth ministry texts for such an idea.[9] I appreciate that others are thinking this way. Though I agree with small parts of the alarming concerns, I disagree with many assumptions and several, seemingly common, conclusions. If those waving the red flags are close to correct, we have no other option but to act more strategically (not react more emotionally). The Church[10] today desperately needs youth ministries that are *specifically focused* on building intentionally influential (strategic and loving) relationships between adults and teenagers. We need youth oriented ministry now more than ever. And we will for the next fifty years even more so.

For some, this new perspective will help to clarify what has always been slightly blurry; they just didn't know it. Others will see relational colors and details for the first time. By God's grace, this book will help youth leaders to more efficiently navigate old relational waters, swum through one-hundred times before and waters that seem new, though

---

8. Lipka indicates that 35 percent of adults ages 18–29 identify themselves as having no religious affiliation. Lipka, "Millennials Increasingly Are Driving Growth of 'Nones,'" lines 10–11.

9. See Kricher, *For a New Generation*; and Folmsbee, *Gladhearted Disciples*.

10. Meaning universal church, consisting of all church and parachurch youth ministry.

they've actually always been there. I pray for this to bring glory to God as He blesses you and through you.

STRATEGIC VERSUS RELATIONAL YOUTH MINISTRY

Sigmund Freud suggested people's personalities are set by the age of six and John Bowlby theorized that a person's lifelong attachment (secure or insecure) relationship style was formed by the age of three. But recent research indicates that attachment relationship styles and therefore perspectives of self-worth and others' reliability in relationships become open to revision during adolescence. This means huge opportunities exist for youth workers.

Youth leaders responding to relational cues can be used by the Holy Spirit to transform dysfunctional lives and, therefore, indefinable future relationships, including those with God. For youth already empowered by Jesus Christ and parents, youth leaders can meet often overlooked needs, invigorating life-style missional journeys. This book explores and analyzes current youth ministry philosophies, how the Holy Spirit transforms one through a precise love of another and about how the youth worker can minister specifically to different types of adolescents' core relational need.

God designed every human being to be in relationship with Himself and to want to feel the love of parents. These two life forces converge to drive every person completely in everything they do. The presence or lack of relationship with God and/or love of the parents either empowers or cripples people in multiple ways, some obvious, some concealed. Every relationship a person has reciprocally influences him or her by the combination effect of the presence or absence of each of these two powers (or power failures).[11] All of this culminates into four primary relational personalities, with insecure relationships typically showing as either avoidant or anxious (see Figure 1). Half of them need varying discipling approaches and the other half need dissimilar evangelistic approaches—some not necessarily desiring or needing an incarnational approach.

---

11. Siegel indicates that positive brain development depends on healthy relationships. Siegel, *Pocket Guide to Interpersonal Neurobiology*, 2, 15.

"I PLANTED, APOLLOS WATERED, BUT GOD WAS CAUSING THE GROWTH"[12]

It is necessary to acknowledge a reality that seems to get lost amidst much of the discussion. Truthfully, neither modern (traditional/strategic) nor postmodern (authentic/relational) orientations indicate impending relational doom or magical relational nirvana. If we are all honest, no matter how carefully relational intentionality is crafted or miserably ignored, God has had and will continue to have success through all and despite all of our worst and best efforts.

> Truthfully, neither modern (traditional/strategic) nor postmodern (authentic/relational) orientations indicate impending relational doom or magical relational nirvana.

He has had and will continue to have success through all and despite all of our best or worst traditions and reimaginations. Literally millions of Christ centered relationships exist today, essentially all generated through imperfect past and present ministries. At many points during every era, someone did something right. Let us be grateful for how God ministers to us through imperfect others and through us, despite ourselves.

Second, while we must be discerning,[13] we must not see people who emphasize one approach over another as being necessarily wrong; we must recognize that we disagree more over incomplete emphases. Disagreements and possibly even tensions occur because traditional (strategic) and authentic (relevant/connecting) approaches *both* show to be incomplete *and* valuable. We need to admit that some criticisms of our styles, no matter what they are, have validity.

It may be true that some in ministry seem to misunderstand and have an insatiable craving for relevance. It may also be true, however, that some ministries are so heavenly minded, they're no earthly good (quoting my old Seminary prof, Dr. Robert Kelly). The "new" incarnational emphasis presents just as incomplete as strategic or traditional approaches and less possible than imagined, or reimagined, or rereimagined, by some (see chapter 5). Most in ministry have tried to model Christ to those to whom they minister. Many have had success. What is true? We can make fewer relational mistakes, save valuable time and improve the

---

12. 1 Cor 3:6.

13. Matt 7:15; 10:16.

possibilities of reciprocal connections with teenagers in view of Attachment Relationship Ministry, ARM.

THE PRIMARY NEEDS OF HUMAN BEINGS DO NOT CHANGE

People in ministry in every era consistently believe their ideas are better than others'. While peoples' contexts do change, their primary needs,
those we've been called to meet, never change. We need to minister to
these critical needs first and foremost. Because we've become content by
convincing ourselves that our ideas are better than previous ones, we've
simply continued to pursue *good* incarnational or new/alternative ministry reflecting our own biases, instead of pursuing *excellent* ministry,
reflecting a total manifestation of Christ under the sober and alert inspiration of the Holy Spirit.

I agree with those today who believe that just because everyone in
youth ministry knows that fostering relationships is one of the most important things we do, it doesn't mean that we actually do it; or if we do,
that we do it well. Talking more about relational ministry, however, does
not mean that competent relational ministry occurs more today than it
did years ago. Just "being with" young people does not cultivate relational
growth or blessing. And our relationships with young people ought also
to never be our primary goal(s). Many folks echo Rayburn's ideas and
successfully reach young people; however, many echo Rayburn's ideas,
but fail to deliver—past and present.[14] They fail for several reasons—all of
which will be identified as this book unwinds.

ATTACHMENT RELATIONSHIP MINISTRY:
CONSIDERING CRITICAL CONTEXT OF YOUTH

We need to manifest Christ excellently, not adequately! We've been called
to manifest Christ entirely, not marginally! We should love as Christ by
both intention and by accident, through agenda, through influence and
through spontaneous conversations and interactions that occur when
pacing with, place sharing, or cohabitating with young people.[15]

14. Jim Rayburn ("relationship over religion") founded Young Life.

15. Youth ministry lingo terms. I empathize with those frustrated by *both*: the
dramatic and demanding penchant for "new" ideas *and* late twentieth century canned
discipleship/evangelism tactics.

God sends His people. God provides for His people. Those in ministry to youth are uniquely called and gifted in their time and place with the flock that God provides.[16] My prayer is that God will use us to love and communicate His love to young people as competently as God has with us.[17] This book advocates a relational approach to different kinds of teenagers, within potential spheres of influence, with an intention to meet their deepest relational needs. I encourage you to trust that God will make this happen with those willing to work intentionally outside of limited awareness, assumptions, patterns and comfort zones.

We all know that no matter the era, those not involved in youth ministry minimize the difficulties associated with leading life-changing ministries. Many churches and parachurches hire young college grads without a Youth Ministry degree simply because they're Christian, young and were involved in youth ministries. I brush regularly, floss occasionally and have gone to the dentist my whole life, but I doubt anyone would want me to be their new dentist! Many church leaders believe that anyone who loves the Lord can do youth ministry.

Yes they can, but *can they minister well to all youth*? Are they building life altering relationships in Christ? Possibly, by the grace of God. Maybe some churches should do away with Lead Pastors and just let lay people take turns preaching. Can they? Yes. But can we do ministry better? YES. Does God want anything we're willing to give Him or our first and best fruit? Readers will see (in the next two chapters specifically) where I agree and disagree with those on both sides of some of the issues identified in this chapter. But more importantly, as the text unwinds, I will offer a practical and simple lens to consider and minister to the deepest needs of teenagers. I hope you will experience many "aha" moments discovering why some teenagers behave the way they do and why some of what we've tried has or has not worked.

THE FOUNDATIONAL GIFT OF RELATIONSHIP

When God created humanity, He provided us with two gifts. God gave people life and life within relational context.[18] People enjoyed those gifts for a short time, but through and with Adam, humans rejected the gift of

16. John 17.
17. Eph 5:12.
18. Belsterling, "Scriptural Basis for Teaching," 25–33.

the relational context and walked away from relationship with God and the mediating influence of that relationship on all others. God sent Jesus to humanity to reestablish an opportunity for relationship. Those who gratefully acknowledge Christ as God's Son and the Savior of all find a reconnected relationship with God.

There are only three primary relational possibilities for Christians. First, there is relationship with

> There are only three primary relational possibilities for Christians.

God through Jesus Christ. Second, there is relationship with others within Jesus Christ. Third, there is relationship with others on behalf of Jesus Christ. The first vertical column of Figure 1 represents ministry within the body of Christ; a youth leader facilitates individual and communal growth of teens who know Christ so as to display the love of Christ. The second vertical column represents ministry on behalf of Jesus Christ; the youth leader and those in a youth group who know Christ reach out to those who don't, showing them the love of Christ, both verbally and non-verbally. Exceptional, competent, negligent or inappropriate relational effort (or lack thereof) on the part of a youth worker profoundly influences not just local teenagers, but whole communities and many future generations. The rest of the book explains this point more fully. Which groups do you relate to easiest? Hardest?

All human relationships, whether close and personal, or occasional and distant, are contained by the understanding of loving one another through Jesus Christ, or loving others representing the love of Jesus Christ. Romans 10, indicates that verbal acknowledgment of Christ as Savior holds weight as that which distinguishes Christians. In reality, we may be able to measure one's commitment through one's fruit, but we don't want to begin guessing games based on the degrees of production. Some may not accept this premise, having relational experiences which seem to disconfirm it, but this outline reflects God's ideal for the real as disclosed in Scripture (Matt 12; Luke 15; John 13).

Attachment Relationship Ministry model (ARM) (see chapter 4)		
Basic Relational Needs and Positions of All People;	Secure with God (SG) (Within Christ Relationships)	Insecure with God (IG) (On behalf of Christ Relationships)
Secure with Parents (SP)	Essentially Secure (SGSP)	Relationally Secure (IGSP) Spiritually Insecure
Insecure with Parents (IP)	Spiritually Secure (SGIP) Relationally Insecure	Essentially Insecure (IGIP)

Figure 1: SGSP (Secure relationship with Parents and with God); IGSP (Secure relationship with Parents and Insecure with God); SGIP (Secure relationship with God and Insecure with Parents); IGIP (Insecure relationship with God and with Parents).

Those in youth ministry need to carefully cultivate relationships in all three areas. Though the understanding of this reality may be commonly understood to most, the execution of it is not. Youth workers must passionately and wisely love Christ and thus, love youth who love Christ, *differently* from each other. Love must be sensitive to security or insecurity issues related to relationships, intact or broken, with those God intended to be His initial witnesses, parents. The rest of this book discusses the need for different expectations, approaches and methods, in these person-to-person horizontal relationships (dependent on this stated foundational relationship with Christ).

Attachment Relationship Ministry (ARM[19]): Two Basic Adolescent Needs

We need to proceed in ministry *centered on the two basic adolescent needs*, which break down into four clear types of initial youth worker adolescent relationships and emphases. The structure of the model and the ensuing suggestions stem from professional and volunteer church, parachurch and counseling experiences with youth and their families. The model presents critical components of successful relationships found in Scripture and through social-science research and study.

19. Ryken et al., "Right, Right Hand," 727–28; Elliott indicates, "For My Arm they will wait expectantly . . . awake, awake, put on strength, O arm of the Lord. . . . I have put My words in your mouth, and have covered you with the shadow of My hand, to establish the heavens, to found the earth, and to say to Zion, 'You are My people'" (Elliott, *Isaiah 40–66*, 141 (Isa 51:5–16)).

Ideas present in Attachment, Systems and Social-Cognitive Learning Theories complement scriptural principles to provide the framework of the model of ministry encouraged in this book. One does not need to have a working knowledge of any of these perspectives to understand the model or apply ministry suggestions related to it. Sometimes when we play games we read the rules before playing (chapters 5 and 6), sometimes we play first (chapters 7–12), then go back and read the rules and find we understand them better. I'd suggest reading in both ways.

The model frames ways to facilitate and advance relationships with teenagers, not restrict them. Practically, the model (the four types and additional sub-types) helps in identifying who, teens and parents, needs what type of ministry most. It helps in the process of considering and selecting leaders and assigning of responsibilities.

Readers will discover why some of one's best authentic-relational effort finds no response while occasional minimal effort finds great response. This model builds beyond simply acknowledging the reality that Christian youth leaders represent both God and parental—type figures in many adolescents' lives.

No, youth leaders are not Jesus and ought not to try to be the parents. They are often, however, many teenagers' best avenue to a representative relationship of God and/or parents. While parents will always remain the primary human-to-human relational influence on their children (good or bad), youth workers can be used by the Holy Spirit to stretch the brains, hearts and spirits of adolescents securely living in healthy homes. They can also be used to rewire the brains and hearts of those who have broken relationships with their parents. The security or insecurity that teens feel and develop in a relationship with a youth worker alters every relationship that teen has for the rest of life.

Ministry Leader Response

Jesus ministered to people as they were in their context. We imitate Jesus.

As my Youth & Young Adult Ministry Prof at Lancaster Bible College/Capital Seminary, Ron always brought fresh perspectives to youth ministry, grounded in meeting the deepest needs of youth as opposed to treating symptoms. ARM demonstrates Ron's commitment to seeing youth discipled well by anyone in contact with youth and young adults. In my own experience in youth ministry, I have highly valued Ron's wisdom.

This book will prove to be an appreciated resource for anyone beginning to work with youth and for those who have been at it for years.

Rachel Liddic, Director of Spiritual Formation and Student Life,
SCORE International, Costa Rica

God Desires Intentional Attachment Relationships

God provides for His people. He sends shepherds who know Him to them.[20] He also assures those who represent Him that He clearly accompanies them and will always "providentially guide, support and save" them.[21] Those in ministry to youth are uniquely called and gifted in their time and place with the flock that God provides (John 17).

For many, limitations and fears of leaving comfort zones probably relates more to lack of knowledge and awareness than lack of concern. While not abandoning age old wisdom, this text focuses on new ways of considering the knowledge and awareness needed to compliment the compassionate concerns of most youth workers. We can build successful relationships and know it and thank God for them.

CONCLUSION: WHY WE DO YOUTH MINISTRY

The critical question? How do we define *relationship*? In answering that question one must ponder several others. What do good relationships look like? Do they all look the same? Specifically, how does a youth worker optimally relate to teenagers? Are specific sub-cultures considered? Is it a priority to reach just some or all of the teens in one's community? Either way, this text can help. By the inspiration, grace and conviction of God, I guarantee that it can. We need to trust in the leading of God and in His ability and intent to influence all of us doing His work. While some may disagree with a few of the ministry approach suggestions, this text should at least make one consider more deeply particular contexts and primary needs of teens.

I'd like to end this section with a brief outline validating why we do youth ministry, why the church needs youth ministry, why our communities need youth ministry and why I believe that youth ministry can be understood to be the arm of Christ:

1. Jesus Himself modeled a youth ministry approach.[22] All but one of the 12 disciples were teenagers.

---

20. Jer 1, 2.

21. Lewis and Demarest, *Integrative Theology,* 85. Josh 1:9.

22. Matt 19:14: "Let the children alone and do not hinder them from coming to Me."

2. Most people are most responsive to the gospel and decide to accept an invitation into relationship with Christ prior to the age of eighteen. Half of the world's population is under the age of twenty.[23] If we're going to reach the lost and our days are limited, why not spend them where the odds of return are greatest?

3. Relative to developmental attributes and Systems Theory considerations, adolescents are the strongest age group of change agents in family, community and society (see ch. 5).

4. According to Steinberg and Monahan (2007),[24] susceptibility to peer influence peeks at the age of fourteen, at which point, teens become more adept at resisting peer pressure a little more every year thereafter until the age of eighteen. We need to serve as a resource for equipping and encouraging teens who love Christ as they counteract all of today's negative adolescent peer influences. We need to provide all teens with a socially unique and safe environment, structurally similar to school settings, but offering much more freedom, where expression of thoughts, feelings and values can be shared without punitive consequence (that is the goal).

5. The forging of one's identity[25] and the last developmental chance at major overhaul of one's internal perceptions of self (worth, esteem and efficacy) occur during adolescence (see ch. 5). Adolescents are the most likely to watch and imitate role models, literally, neurologically adjusting, with the intent to be like the role models (consider time, desire and proximity of potential role models).

6. The combination of not yet repressed spiritual inclinations, rebellious craving and emotional volatility and impulsiveness make adolescents susceptible to spiritual influences, good and bad.[26]

7. Political, academic and entertainment industries are increasing attention on and mimicking youth ministry approaches to adolescents

---

23. Stetzer, "Evangelism and Youth Ministry." Barna indicates that 64 percent of people make a decision to follow Christ by age 18 and 77 percent by age 21. Barna, "Evangelism," para 2.

24. Steinberg and Monahan, "Age Differences in Resistance to Peer Influence," 1531–43. This research was conducted on 3,600 ethnically and socioeconomically diverse people, ages 10–30.

25. See Eric Erikson's Psychosocial Stages (Erikson, *Childhood and Society*).

26. Davis, *Teen TV,* 165–85; Alupoaicei and Burroughs, *Generation Hex,* 13.

specifically.[27] Right now, some in the secular world are desperately open to the church: Several years after starting a Young Life program in our community, the School Superintendent of a neighboring public school system contacted us and asked if we could bring Youth Life's ministry into his High School.

No wonder Jesus was a Youth Pastor. If the church thinks things are bad now, let's see what getting rid of ministry targeting teenagers does in the next fifty years. Need I really say more?

PERSONAL CHALLENGE AND DISCUSSION QUESTIONS FOR LEADERSHIP TEAMS

1. Relative to time, training and support (communal, financial, familial), where do you lack the least? The most? What can be done to try to address the lack? When?

2. How are you more oriented—to cultivate within the body of Christ relationships or on behalf of Christ relationships?

3. How does your personal perspective fit in with or assist the perspectives of the rest of your team? The larger organization?

27. Haddock and Falkner, *Who Am I*, 177–93; Turner, *Popcultured*, 158–234.

CHAPTER 2

Traditional Model

"For decades so much of youth ministry has been program driven—serving teenagers with the assumption that its primary function is to use activities and events that attract young people to church and to keep them occupied until they're ready to be adult members in the faith. However, in recent years, it's become increasingly obvious that this paradigm has failed." (Kirk and Thorne, *Missional Youth Ministry*, p. 13)

"By programming youth ministry on one night of the week, we inhibit the growth of the youth ministry because we immediately eliminate the teens who are not available on that day of the week and adult volunteers who cannot volunteer on that particular day. . . . A small group provides the opportunity for discipleship and relationships to grow deeply. No silly youth group games, no gimmicks—just straight up mentoring and ministering." (Fritz, "The Problem With the Youth Group Mentality")

"To fully assess the quality of youth mentoring relationships, we must understand the characteristics and processes of individual relationships and the components of programs that support their development. In other words, we must consider mentoring as being made up of two interrelated settings, the mentoring relationship and the mentoring program." (Deutsch and Spencer, "Capturing the Magic," p. 47)

WHETHER SMALL OR LARGE, rural or urban, focusing on Gen Z, Gen Alpha, or Gen Beta, we in youth ministry all use programs. Programs aren't solely the property of traditional youth ministry. It's just a matter of what type of planning and schedule one uses. This chapter suggests, despite the hype, traditional approaches ought not to be abandoned. Chapters in Part 2 explain why not more specifically. If we're interested in meeting core needs of people, then we need to emphasize community. If we foster community to meet personal needs, we need to make sure that community influences broader communities to have lasting impact. To do this we need traditional approaches.

PROGRAMS

"Program" has literally become a *bad word*. Some youth leaders avoid using it more than curse words. Having the word "program" associated with one's ministry gives it the kiss of death as a traditional, program-centered, legalistic, inside-the-box thinking, influence oriented, restrictive, manifestation *not of the name of God, but instead* of religious, fundamentalist institutionalism! Unfortunately, it seems that along with the advocacy of *authentic relational* ministry, many seem to blame "program centered" ministries and their lack of cultivating and prioritizing true relationships for the exodus of young adults leaving the church.[1] I understand why they do this (though I disagree with that conclusion) as I've had my own concerns and battles with "program."[2]

Burn Out—I Was Not a Victim

One of my ministries started to grow beyond my capacity, time, energy, and provided resources to oversee it, while also maintaining *relational* contact. Every young person I met with represented another one hundred that I didn't meet. Volunteer adults already gave as much time as they could. The more competently relational we became, the more administrative oversight was demanded. Every task that was delegated only freed me up to take on other tasks that had been neglected. Relational misadventures from adult volunteer-mentors and other issues on my

---

1. See Fritz, *Art of Making Disciples;* Keuss, *Blur.*
2. Belsterling, "Youth Work," 31–47.

leadership teams exhausted me more than most of my "troubled" youth.[3] I looked like and became more of a manager than a Pastor. Loving others on behalf of Christ had become—*a job.*

Just Doing the Job

I read the Bible *(typically for the sole purpose of turning it around in a lesson).* I prayed for Staff, Elder, Governing Board, C.E. Committee, Youth Cabinet, Youth Council, and Small Group Leaders *(to survive them and for many to go away).* I obeyed my Lead Pastor *(and the whimsical edicts not related to Youth Ministry whatsoever).* I connected with young people *(mostly to check them off of a list so I could move onto the next teen).* I ministered to parents *(scanning abilities and availabilities to see who could do what for me tomorrow, next week, next month, and next year).* I led other leaders *(connected to, of course, sensibly crafted, bi-annually reviewed, goals, purpose, missions, and value statements).* Much of my time was all about *the job.*

I had packaged an attractive ministry, encouraging others to respond to God's love, but I had lost my own intimacy with Christ. The key relationship on which all of my other relationships depended was being squeezed out by ministry. Irony fills life. I was losing my joy and my compassion for others was often more show than real. I was leading a team that was running our program machine—and doing it (essentially) well. But I was burning out, noticed by reflecting on having made some decisions that I typically would not make. By the grace of God, some less than careful decisions did not result in greater consequences.[4]

> The key relationship on which all of my other relationships depended was being squeezed out by ministry. Irony fills life.

After having discovered my program managing, relational vacuum, I started giving God my first two hours of every Monday morning. I read the Bible and prayed, with no project or without anyone else in mind. My Senior Pastor occasionally wasn't too happy when I refused to give up this time to do a "critical" task. Every three months I also took one

---

3. In one setting, my Lead Pastor required that I put certain people on my leadership teams. Inappropriate relational dynamics (dating youth members, instigation of other adult leaders, etc.) destructively ensued.

4. Belsterling, "Screwed Up," 313. The related near-disastrous consequence? Two of my teen girls boarding an Argentinian naval ship, which I couldn't get on.

full day to hike alone with the Lord (no family/no youth). Increasing the amount of prayer partners and the extent of what they prayed for also helped. Gradually, I also eliminated, seriously reduced, or delegated less important, time killing tasks. Calendaring and budgeting weekly, monthly, and annual time and ministry took administrative priority. Those intentional steps helped restore unto me the joy of my salvation (Ps 51). Those steps helped me to offer relationship to others that was actually, for them, worth having.

RUNNING MINISTRY MACHINES

I once interviewed with a church who told me flat out that they did not want me to bring any vision, just the ability to run an already well-oiled program. Most interview questions had little to do with my relationship with Christ. Overemphasizing commitment to program not tied to God given vision and philosophy isn't ministry. It felt so cold.

We can get caught up managing programs—no doubt. Whether large or small, just running on the weekly program treadmill, saps one of time and energy. Vision gives way to check lists. To better reach young people, personal contact time with them must be sacrificed. This doesn't seem to make sense. Often we do all kinds of nonsensical things in keeping our machines chugging along.

Canned Salvation and Meeting Leadership Expectations

"Where are your white roses?!" the Pastor asked me in a staff meeting one day, clearly implying that the lack of white roses meant there was a problem. More than a few in the congregation doubted the impact of a ministry if there were never any white roses displayed on the altar of the church on a Sunday morning. Each rose represented the salvation of another lost person and a slew of potential "likes" from the congregation for whatever ministry they represented. Other ministries were putting white roses up at the front semi-regularly. The intent was to give God thanks, to encourage the congregation, and to demonstrate accountability. Most of those involved were sincerely counting each rose as a victory for Christ. Healthy motive, however, fostered unhealthy pressure.

Up to the point of about two years into my time at the church, I had never put any white roses on the altar for a Sunday service. There were several reasons. First, how did I know for sure? Second, the practice seemed gimmickry to me. Many roses represented our church's *Evangelism Explosion* ministry—which put too much emphasis on a person accepting Christ so he or she could get to heaven. "Jesus is your ticket and if you don't accept Him, you'll just be going to hell." Most folks who were associated with EE and other ministries clearly owned Godly intent, but it seemed "decisions" were based more on fear of hell and selfish motives than on gratitude and a desire to become a partner in God's mission. There were other reasons for not worrying about placing roses too.

Teens, like everyone else but more so, are fickle. Some who said they accepted Christ didn't seem like they had. Others who stated having no interest in Christ were attending Bible studies. The whole idea of identifying people with or without roses felt somewhat less than genuine and definitely more fuzzy than clear. I didn't condemn (at least not consciously) the others for identifying their "white roses," it just wasn't a priority for me. Honestly, though, I started to feel the pressure.

Even though the attendance of youth not affiliated with the church had grown from about 10 percent when I came, to close to 50 percent, at this point, I had already begun to feel some pressure before the Pastor's comment. Now, called out in front of the other staff, I started to crack in my own mind. Perhaps I should show others that my youth ministry was valid—that young people were being saved. I didn't want others to think that having young people accept Christ was not a priority for me! Not to mention, we were seeing signs of success, so why not prove it?

I designed an "Outreach" evening, like many times in the past, but on this particular evening there was going to be some intentional and carefully orchestrated, heavy "reaping" effort. (*Reaping* conversations occur far less today than they should, but this effort was based more on manipulation than concern.) Right after some effective Gospel presentations by some teen leaders, and the night's talk, a call for response was made, while soft music played in the background. Student leaders and I prayed aloud, encouraging those who were confused, lonely or curious to pray with me to receive Christ as Savior. And then I insisted that the only way to follow through on those decisions was to make public proclamation immediately. This whole process took some time, with some judiciously executed encouragements and pauses. The result?

I was able to put six white roses on the altar on the next Sunday in church! Woot. Woot. Most members of the congregation seemed excited, like something new and wonderful was happening in the Youth Ministry!

Hallelujah! Of course, who wouldn't be grateful for others finding new life in Christ, however . . .

Meeting with those "new brothers and sisters" was not easy. Most of the six had very little interest in follow-up chats. Most did not come back to future youth group meetings. Only one of the six continued to participate indicating curiosity in growing in a relationship with Jesus. And those signs were evident in that person before that night.

Though I gained a new sense of importance on making "reaping" efforts in relational ministry, it didn't take me long to realize that I never wanted to manipulate a response to the Gospel again. I didn't need for a person to first meet Christ and be ready to accept Him as Savior all in the same evening. I didn't want to put pressure on Christian kids to help me manipulate others. I'd share and challenge and trust God to convict.

God sent us here to share His love with each other and those who don't know him. But just like God didn't force anyone to accept His love, and Jesus certainly didn't either, neither do we have to sacrifice loving integrity out of fear of missed opportunity. We can trust God's design: everyone has to make his or her own choice. Having fear inspired agenda interferes with relational integrity. We need to operate out of faith based agenda assertively, not aggressively.

THE BUILDING OF POPULAR EMPIRES: BIGGER IS BETTER

Kirk and Thorne (quote at the beginning) accurately describe pressures on youth pastors from LeadPastors and lay leadership. Even if they state numerical growth should not be an emphasis, church leaders want to see it. And we know it. Root astutely points out that we're enamored by the idea and that motivates much of what we do and who we emulate. As an example, ask, "Who are the exemplary youth leaders identified today"? Who is asked to speak and write? Youth ministry leaders who've created or oversee large youth ministries. It's the same phenomena across the whole church. The publishers, conference leaders, and we ourselves make celebrities. They're the ones we tell our friends we chatted with one-on-one at the last conference. Pressure to be *fresh* and to create a popular empire often leads us to feeling competitive with other local youth ministries, halting potential camaraderie. We need to resist and change the way we think about these issues.

When Katie, one of my popular female youth members, told me we were attracting too many nerds and she might have to go to another youth group, I gently rebuked her attitude and quickly suggested two other excellent youth ministries in our city that I thought would help her to mature in Christ. That was not the reply she expected. Too often we cater to our own insecurities and the whims of adults and youth alike so as to keep or build numbers—often at the expense of doing what is right and by sacrificing long term vision. We should be willing to grow and offer compelling ministry, and able to grow, but we should never be governed by the need to grow numerically.

Much to the chagrin of those who hired me, several of my ministries decreased in size in my first year or two. In one church, some of the action steps we took alienated a large contingency of those who actually worshipped Satan—and were simply present to destroy focus on Christ. In an urban situation I was accused of not ministering in love and lacking in contextual awareness when continually escorting youth out of group gatherings for inappropriate behavior. These ministries needed to refocus—numerical loss was inevitable. Growth occurred later in both cases, but only in response to Christ-centered ministry with robust goals and clear relational objectives. Note, some ministries will do everything right *and not grow*. Others will do many things wrong and will grow *exponentially*. Spiritual growth in as many as possible, not numerical growth, is the essential litmus test.

Keeping Up with the Latest Youth Ministry Trends

We all get caught up in the trends that come and go. And, we find ourselves playing tiring catch up with the details of constant revision. Conferences, magazines, blogs, and books all help many youth workers, but confuse and distract countless others. Well intentioned leaders juggle all of the good ideas, feeling subtle pressures to make sure their youth ministries meet every fashionable criteria. They never craft solid foundations or long term plans; they so desperately want to do it well and right they are afraid of being stuck (or labeled as) "inside the box." Imagining not to emphasize program,

> We all get caught up in the trends that come and go. And, we find ourselves playing tiring catch up with the details of constant revision.

they replace one method with another, over and over again. Because one approach never takes shape, their work has no appearance of a program. Some perceive that as success. Not me.

WHAT TO DO WITH "PROGRAM"?

Programs and those who demand we automatically run them can drive a youth worker crazy, but we must not discard or overreact to programs. Yes, sadly, some involved in ministry today operate like detached spiritual physicians, memorizing manuals and only offering prescriptions. But this does not necessarily mean they're not trying to love others from the heart. This does not mean that they have not experienced God's guided and intervening successes as well—just like we have. They might just be folks with good intentions, but overwhelmed by the plethora of drama laced expert opinions. Some may not have enough time, education, or resources, especially volunteer led ministries, to stay current on new approaches. God blesses faithful service in many programs.

Do receive exhortations to be involved in young peoples' lives personally, but don't believe we have to sacrifice programs and agendas to legitimately craft deeper level relationships. In fact, most programs offer the large group, safe space, opportunity to build the needed rapport with varying personality types to build deeper one on one, teen to adult and peer-to-peer relationships. Most who dismiss using programs have actually not scrapped them, but have just created alternative action plans. No matter one's approach as a youth worker (paid, volunteer, full time, part time), everyone utilizes programs. Large fellowship gatherings, small group meetings, triads, and one on one relational emphasis in ministry all represent programmatic ideology and method.

Jesus used one on one, small group, and large group time for good reasons. Eliminating any to focus on one is like eliminating proteins and vitamins from a diet to focus on mineral intake. Each enhances the effectiveness of the others. The same goes for different types of people called into youth ministry, some who rely heavily on program.

Every person involved in youth ministry is uniquely gifted. Each of us has a place. Youth workers use programs to steer ministries by vision and toward goals. Well-crafted methods often facilitate relational successes.

Len Kageler and I worked together for almost twenty years. We are naturally very different from one another. He would be the first to say that he is more administratively oriented than relationally oriented.[5] As I've observed the effect of Len's imprint on our field in multiple settings, many have clearly been assisted personally, though indirectly. He hired me to complement his work at Nyack because he needed a relationally oriented partner for his program to run more capably. Vision, not habit or trend, led his program. We taught future youth leaders (by God's grace) quite successfully together, like peanut butter and jelly combine to make one great sandwich. One may be the leader who competently relates, or the one who creates programs which assist others in relating. Some do both well. Not everyone needs to be a deep relational person to contribute to Kingdom work in guiding teens. Deep with God spills over one way or another.

"Program" Is Not an Enemy

Eliminating program is not only unadvisable, it's impossible. Programs are not merely cold, non-relational, "inside the box" strategies. Traditional churches, trend conscious ministries, and very successful relational ministries work through carelessly or carefully crafted action plans. It is impossible for a group of people to minister together without strategies to organize focused priorities, boundaries, flexibility, and supervision, to name just a few criteria. Ministries not utilizing any type of program have no relational agendas and no action plans for carrying out relationship or training others to lead relationally. Even if one wants to reduce or eliminate much program, say, due to the busy schedules of young people, that which remains still equates to program, it's just philosophically and operationally different.

5. The students loved Len and very much enjoyed his company, please don't misinterpret the emphasis on his ministry orientation. Len and I no longer work together at the same institution.

Ministry Leader Response

We make decisions, build programs, have relational models, and lead the church more rooted in fear over faith. This is why I believe we read books that give us false permission to take the easy way out. We don't listen to the voice of the Holy Spirit because we don't want to release control to God. We don't want to leave the outcomes of our job and calling in God's hands. We idolize efficiency over effectiveness.

So many Christian authors easily point out problems, but very seldom do these people offer solutions without favoring one side of the relational or program spectrum.

When we stop listening to or seeking God's Word, ministry will not be fruitful. After 10 years of full time ministry I have learned if something is not popular, makes me uncomfortable, or has 100 reasons why I can't do it, then I can almost guarantee God is telling me I need to do it and trust him. Not that we should seek to fail but we must not get caught up in avoiding possible failure, otherwise we will never experience the beauty of God reaching down with his "ARM" and lifting us back up.

The world is obsessed with youthfulness and increasingly so is the church. Parents no longer determine kid's schedules it is the other way around. We as the church are overreacting to the supposed "youth" exodus, when in reality the church has had an "exodus" from the world. We are no longer "in" the world which creates us to be more "of" the world than we like to admit. If we are not different nor encountering God, or following his Word then why would anyone stay?

Rev. Arnie Buehler, Director of the Bridge Community Center, Johnson City, New York

---

Why does doing one (deep personal relations) necessitate not doing the other (programs)? Is cultivating personal relationships really antithetical to a desire to help groom others to be able to do the same? Doesn't the one actually qualify and enable the other? Did God use a program? Did Jesus? Did Paul? It appears to me as though they did. While some volunteer leaders might build relationships with young people unrelated to church and/or para-church agencies, most end up coming alongside of young people as a result of participating in local youth ministry programs run by pastors and professionals. Constructing opportunities for relationship building meets God's desires. Programs contribute to authentic ministry in several ways.

PROGRAMS CONTRIBUTE TO AUTHENTIC MINISTRY

Young People Mature into Christlikeness

Young people and adult leaders discipled correctly, grow compassionate and concerned for the salvation of others; they learn why sharing compassion and concern for the salvation of others matters; they also learn how to best communicate their compassion and concerns. As do the adults we train to help us in the discipling endeavor. We hope to influence. God trusted that we would, otherwise Christ would not have been sent. Discipled youth find and provide accountability through planned meetings and annual calendars as they learn how to intentionally be truly authentically available. When I was young I avoided wearing a watch because I thought governance by time was restricting, then I learned it was actually freeing, allowing me to use it more wisely to God's glory rather than my human affinity for a care free life. Ministries focused on discipleship give teens access to wiser mentors who have the time and energy for them specifically. Participating teens discuss with likeminded friends their relational efforts and experiences. They find and share encouragement, example, correction, and forgiveness when needed. They find safe places to express their doubts and explore their thoughts. And this frequently occurs in group contexts more than it does in one to one connections. Intentional conversations and efforts help encourage youth to share the gospel as teammates.

CONCLUSION: CREATING AND LEADING PROGRAMS FORCES ONE TO IDENTIFY PRIORITIES

When my ministry became *a job*, I realized I needed to reacquaint myself with the Lord, spend time with Him on His terms, as indicated earlier. I needed to spend more time reading the Bible simply to understand God's mind more deeply. His word is more important than this word or any word in any other "how to" ministry book. The time we take to be with Him covers whatever other "to do" list sacrifices occur. And this time together must be personal, not with family members, and not for teaching purposes. Whatever one learns and applies about building relationships in this text will be nothing more than mechanical if there is not intent or ability to cultivate relationships out of the overflowing love of Christ.

> Whatever one learns and applies about building relationships in this text will be nothing more than mechanical if there is not intent or ability to cultivate relationships out of the overflowing love of Christ.

By the way, it may not just be the Sr. Pastor, parents, elders, etc. who interferes in relational time with the Lord. Those who most need us to relate His love to them interfere. Everyone in the church or parachurch family will tell us they want us to have a good relationship with God first and our family second. Most of them forget, however, to acknowledge out loud, "as long as that time you spend with the Lord or your family conflicts with others' needs, not mine!" If we're not prioritizing God, we begin relating to everyone from a joyless position, not as a joy filled person. They'll notice the lack of passion and compassion and begin to buzz that perhaps we're not the right person for *the job*.

Sometimes we try to manifest Christ, wanting to feel in love with Christ more than we actually do, therefore, desperately trying to manufacture *in love* feelings. Bible discussions replace rather than enhance Bible studies. Worship services gear up more to express ourselves than to hear God's voice. People pray in any way they want (because "God can take it"), rather than praying honestly *and* reverently. Too many, rightfully intrigued by the power of the Holy Spirit, try to conjure up the sense of His presence, without fully understanding His mission.

In the words of F.B. Meyers, "He is like a ray of light that falls on the beloved face of Jesus, so that as in the photograph you do not think about the light or the origin of the light, but you think about the face that it reveals."[6] Ideas of Christ are based more on pet topics and select preferred passages creating more of an imagined Christ than the Christ of His holy Word. Transformed minds (Rom 12) are spurred on by the heart, but also reciprocally stimulate the heart for the longer season.

We cannot bring others into relationship with Christ more through crazes than through His teachings. If we're not reading God's word on a regular basis, he won't be able to convey His thoughts clearly. If we try to love others on behalf of Christ based more on our own ideas of what His love looks like rather than what it is, we will struggle to compel most to Him, even if we're popular.

6. Hartley, *Holy Spirit Fill Me*, 1.

PERSONAL CHALLENGE AND DISCUSSION QUESTIONS
FOR LEADERSHIP TEAMS

1. Where do you retreat? To the Lord? Sports? Your family? The Outlets? Where should we find comfort, peace, and restorative energy? What needs to change?

2. What parts of your ministry are not essential? Golden calves?

3. What you do reflects your vision, or lack thereof. How much time do you carve out every year and/or month to reflect on and craft ministry vision?

CHAPTER 3

Authentic Model

"Relational youth ministry cannot be about influence because it would use relationships as a means to another end." (Root, *Relationships Unfiltered*, p. 33)

"I'm convinced that the relationships we make with students have to be seen as more than the vehicle for accomplishing our agenda . . . ministries where "no strings attached relationships" aren't valued don't have long term impact." (Blanks, "Five Fatal Youth Ministry Flaws")

"We can say with confidence, that a significant part of Christianity in the U.S. . . . . has morphed into Christian Moralistic Therapeutic Deism. . . . The language, and therefore experience, of Trinity, holiness, sin, grace . . . heaven and hell appear among most Christian teenagers in the U.S. to be supplanted by the language of happiness, niceness and an earned heavenly reward. . . . Therapeutic individualism defines the self as the source and standard of authentic moral knowledge and authority, and individual self-fulfillment as the preoccupying purpose of life. Subjective, personal experience is the touchstone of all that is authentic, right, and true." (Smith and Denton, *Soul Searching*, pp. 171–73)

ANDY DE FEU, DIRECTOR of Youth and Community Work at Moorlands College, in Christchurch, England, believes this chapter is the heart of the book. The conversation about this topic can't help but to be philosophical.

I try making it practical. I'm hoping that though I include thought provoking questions at the back of each chapter, readers will pause as they
go, thinking deeply about the conversation we're having. Dialogue related to incarnational ministry and Practical Theology actually expands
in chapter 5.

AUTHENTIC (RELEVANT, PRACTICAL, INCARNATIONAL) MINISTRY

While grateful for emphases on re-thinking stale approaches and wanting to emphasize relationship, I empathize with those weary of trying
to understand frequent emerging and vague ideas, new meanings to old
words, and the many language/concept tweaks, twists and turns. Every
few years we get a few new bandwagon words that, if we desire to be
relevantly relational, we better incorporate! Really, most ideas being advocated in this vein are fine in our contemporary use of them—though
not as fresh, distinct, or profound as a concept as some suggest.

As asked previously, relative to the ideas within incarnational ministry, what youth worker would protest being authentic, listening carefully, or manifesting the love of Christ[1] in relationships with youth? Yet, it
is upon us as God's teachers to show extra diligence in the ministries we
execute, and care for the weapons He provides.[2] Words we use to describe
our ministry must be soberly considered; God showed the way (*The Way)*
in emphasis of His chosen words.[3] Words and meaning matter to God.
They should to us too.

Thus, I truly struggled with what to name this chapter. It's been
named "incarnational," "authentic," and "relevant" ministry at various
points in the process of writing. All terms actually work to describe *the*
current youth ministry cultural climate. Each also has historic roots
which shade the validity of its placement as the concept of choice for
Christians. Perhaps, I could or should have used all of them. I've been
told I overthink things. True. But I'd rather not under-think them. "Incarnational" could have worked as the chapter title, but it seemed most
inappropriate.

---

1. In 2 Cor 4:11, Paul talks about manifesting the presence of Christ in such a
way that some, depending on their hermeneutic, find as supportive of the concept of
incarnational ministry.

2. Jas 3:1; Heb 4:12.

3. John 1:1; Matt 5:18; Prov 30:5–6; Eph 4:14.

While joyfully receiving the commission of Christ and trusting for the empowerment of the Holy Spirit (John 20:21–22; Matt 28:19), I am not convinced that we as humans are called or able to offer a "uniquely divine act of the Word becoming flesh."[4] This incarnating idea, essentially illustrating a god complex, shifted the church from sharing the good news of Jesus to telling others they can just be themselves, and has already been "identified and confronted by the church of the fourth century" and done much damage.[5] It may be semantics to some, but since I would rather err on the side of not being nonchalantly irreverent (a common casualty in the quest of being relevant) to our divine Lord, I opted for another common term. *Authentic*[6] was chosen as the title as it seems to be the best other prolific word option and a way to encompass and represent the intent of those using today's varied terms.

Related to the concept more than the word, several critical questions must be asked. Has, does, or will an *authentic* approach help youth workers to be more *competently relational* with young people than those of days gone by? Has it in the last fifteen years? Also, in this approach, are the deeper level needs of *all* teens being carefully weighed? Or are some minimized or ignored? My answer to all but the last question is "no." I'm not alone. Those who agree with me in answering these questions are from within and outside of the body of Christ.[7]

No Agenda, No Strings Attached?

A key ingredient of today's incarnational emphasis is that successful relationships between youth workers and youth are devoid of agenda.[8] We're told, "Just be present. If you love young people incarnationally, young people will receive more of Jesus and less of you." Though I understand

---

4. Svboda, "Re-thinking Incarnational Ministry," lines 1–50.

5. Svboda, "Re-thinking Incarnational Ministry," lines 1–50.

6. Please read footnotes for my concerns regarding authentic. I'd prefer to think those using these words today use them with little idea as to their historic origins and emphases. Some don't care.

7. DeVries, *Sustainable Youth Ministry*, 1718. Harris, *End of Faith*, 15. A common theme in the popular atheist Sam Harris' stated and written frustrations with Christians, is his observation of the ambiguous, emotionally based, and fluid terminology/thinking of today's Christian. Whereas I agree with DeVries and Harris relative to their concerns, I disagree with both of them as to their suggested solutions.

8. See Blank's comment at beginning of this chapter.

the point (see reflection box) trying to be made, I strongly disagree with the premise that the best way to represent Christ is to proceed in relationships with no agenda to influence. First, that approach is antithetical to Christ's approach. Second, it's not even possible.

No agendas? No desire to influence? Is that a valid mission?[9] Didn't Jesus say, "As You sent Me into the world, I also have sent them into the world" (John 17:18; 20:21)? How can one fulfill such a mission or reconcile such a perspective with Jesus' call? To be blunt, if one truly has no agenda, why get involved in youth ministry in the first place? Did Jesus come to us with an agenda? Did He minister to anyone in such a way that showed a lack of desire to influence? Did He ever advocate for us to love others—agenda free? Did Paul or any of the other New Testament writers? What is the point of suffering with or on behalf of another? Since overt goals are unacceptable and no relationship exists without goals, what are the covert goals for relationships? Agendas in relationships facilitate good things, usually for both parties. Relationships devoid of agenda indicate acquaintanceship, not relationship.

> Relationships devoid of agenda indicate acquaintanceship, not relationship.

To minister to another with "no agenda" is only to pretend to have no agenda. When someone encourages others to proceed into ministry relationships with no agendas, that person has just articulated a type of relational agenda with us and for us to use with others. If I'm aware that my presence is "shaping" another, isn't it more authentic to acknowledge my intentions in relationship? Shouldn't a teenager legitimately wonder about an adult who wants to connect but who has no stated intentions for the relationship? Those who write that we ought not worry about influencing today's youth are writing ministry books trying to influence others to not try to influence others. Am I the only one that sees that and finds it odd?

---

9. John 4:34, 38; 17:18; Acts 13:4. Folmsbe: "Gladhearted Disciples know it is their purpose to bring the redemptive reign of God in Christ into every dimension of life" (Folmsbee, *Gladhearted Disciples*, 5).

> *Personal Reflection: Helping a Homeless Man (?)*
>
> *One day I was in a city park in Philadelphia reading during lunch time. A homeless man sat across from me. He wore a suit that fit him well and recently polished black shoes. In addition to the absence of socks, his behavior indicated the presence of some psychological issues and the likelihood of his being homeless.*
>
> *Wanting to help him feel more complete and comfortable in his delusion, I quickly left to purchase some black socks and brought them to him. Mistake. I offended him. I realized I took from him the little he thought he had—the idea that he fit in with everyone else. It hurt to know that in a moment of what felt like Spirit-led-compassion, I actually robbed someone of his dignity. Or did I?*
>
> *Or, would I simply have enabled a dysfunctional motif keeping the man from having true dignity—and comfort? Helping others is never easy. Your thoughts?*

In *Revisiting Relational Youth Ministry (2007)*, Andy Root suggests that incarnational ministry goes beyond sharing laughs and becomes more transformative when unsolicited conversations allow a youth worker to incarnationally enter deeply into another's life (place sharing), actively addressing the poverty issues (emotional, spiritual, cultural, financial, or physical) in that life, and standing as an advocate for that life. True relationship is about being "completely other than the other while being completely for the other" (p. 127). To some extent, my experience with the homeless man illustrates the validity of this point—being completely for the other. But Root's ideas of what this means within the realm of youth ministry go *too far*, doing the reverse of what those in ministry are called to do, making the simple complex.[10]

According to Root, relational ministry is not about influential leverage, holding up moral principles, emphasizing "shoulds" and "oughts," or holding up an ethic of right and wrong. To Root relationships *should* not be used as a means to a Youth Pastor-determined (I-It, un-I-Thou) end goal.[11] Jones advocates for authenticity in relationship over absolutes.[12] Keuss concurs with both, encouraging youth workers to love via "a new

10. John 4:38; 1 Cor 1–2; 4:6 (v.2, "I determined to know nothing among you except Jesus Christ, and Him crucified"). See Root, *Relationships Unfiltered*; *Taking Theology to Youth Ministry*; *Revisiting Relational Youth Ministry*. Paradoxically Root seems in various places to bemoan current teenagers' moral therapeutic deism; see Smith quote at beginning of chapter.

11. Martin Buber, existentialist philosopher, distinguished an I-Thou relationship as one in which a person interacts with another so that the other is known, not cast as a simple generic human. I-It relationships objectify another to manipulate. In I-It relationships one denies personhood of self and other.

12. Jones, *Post-Modern Youth Ministry*, 24, 200–209.

level of transcendence."[13] Too many today give the impression that relationships themselves are the end goals. If there is no agenda beyond the relationship itself, then the relationship is the goal. My presence may encourage another, but I can't save anyone, and I cannot be available nonstop for the rest of life to every sheep in my flock, even with all the various forms of social media at my fingertips.

Living for another or suffering for another does not support the notion that Youth Pastors should abandon relational agendas or teaching about right and wrong. Youth leaders should not sacrifice the commission or desire to influence. Loving someone in an I-Thou relationship means that a Youth Pastor might need to frequently determine how love will best be communicated (particularly in crisis situations). After all, sadly, some who desperately need true love have only an imagined idea as to what it looks or feels like (see Part 2).

Relationship between a young person and oneself must never be one's end goal. Many leaders in youth ministry have turned the idea of relationship into a false god and a new religion. Our end goal must always

> Relationship between a young person and oneself must never be one's end goal. Many leaders in youth ministry have turned the idea of relationship into a false god and a new religion.

be to help young people mature in relationship with Jesus Christ. Straying from that goal leaves us believing that teaching youth about right and wrong is of only secondary importance. The command for people to learn and obey the statutes of God fills every book in the Bible. Jesus made it very clear that living rightly is of primary importance, "If you keep my commandments, you will abide in my love, just as I have kept my Father's commandments" (John 15:10). One cannot live rightly without knowing rightly.

13. Keuss indicates, we ought to reach "a new level of transcendence" (Keuss, *Blur*, 185). Really? Words like "authenticity," "transcendence," "choice," "authorship," "courage to be"/"being," and "phenomenology" show up more and particularly in spiritual formation writing and speaking. The roots of these terms are found in existentialistic-humanistic philosophy and existential nihilism (main tenets: life has no purpose and devalues rationality of faith), of which many philosophers who espouse such were depressed, alcoholics, and advocated for suicide. See the works of Heidegger and Nietzsche (death of God), Sartre and Barth (Christian), Camus (denied being existentialist), and Hume.

Some youth, Christian and non-Christian, desperately need teaching about right and wrong far more than they need someone to "place share." In fact Root's *inconsistency* shows in his encouragement to abandon the "shoulds" and "oughts" and an ethic of teaching about "right and wrong." First, though he doesn't state the word "should," he tells us what we should do—as the "right" way to minister. We clearly should not use should. Second, this way of thinking has its roots in humanistic psychology, which Root says he abhors, and contradicts Scriptural teaching (see ch. 5, Bandura). Are implied "shoulds" more legitimate than stated ones? Do some relationships need them and others not? Everyone has an agenda whether stated or not. What matters most is surrendering our agendas to God so that we meet His agenda.

Self-determined agendas must be abandoned. Agendas must not be motivated by self-gain (feeling good about oneself with the idea of helping another), and sensitive to the nudging of God's Holy Spirit. Only time with God in His word, in prayer, and in fellowship helps to transform agendas. I'm sure that we as Youth Pastors do not need a new way of thinking, unless we've abandoned Jesus' way of thinking.

Realistically, it seems to me that for those who steadfastly advocate loving young people agenda free, they're either deluded that they are able to do that or they're constructing practical theologies and revisiting philosophies relying too much on feelings and not enough on discernment.[14] The main criteria considered as essential to the deconstructed and reconstructed modalities of ministry seems to be that it has to be "new." As with an earlier issue, is that even possible? We may have new verbiage, but so much of what I've read lately simply recycles many ideas of the last twenty years.

---

14. A major irony here is that while Practical Theology arose as a reaction against Barthian theological paradox (dialectical thinking—accepting contradictions in one's theology as fine, pure, and more complete) and hyperbole (think: hyper-bull), this approach has been advocated by those who also appeal to existential thinkers and thinking to justify practical ministry work. As a professor in an applied discipline, Youth Ministry, I appreciate those defending the legitimacy of our work as educationally worthy, yet lament that to some that means we must dismantle doctrinal comprehension, socially constructing new doctrine—as if God isn't able to consistently communicate and be understood across eras and cultures; see Heffelfinger and McGlinchey, *Atonement as Gift*. Some seem to neglect the OT in their theology. Their justifying defenses are built on personal assumptions indicative of new self-constructed hermeneutic ideology (eisegesis—I see Jesus any way I want, many interpretations), not the historical-grammatical method of hermeneutic effort (exegesis: finding God's intent and author's intent to original audience, with one interpretation, many applications).

Scriptural teaching has been replaced with trendy concepts. Some would disagree by saying that a new way of understanding Scripture is different than discarding Scripture. It seems clear to me, that the teaching of doctrine is being replaced with indoctrinating teaching. Too many prefer "new" ways to old ways, almost no matter what the new ways advocate.

No Absolutes?

A colleague recently told me that emphasizing "absolutes" in ministry no longer applies today—people have no interest in absolutes (he didn't say "absolutely" out loud, but he was absolutely conclusive in his insistence no one cares about absolutes); they only need authentic relationships. Authentic relationships without emphasized absolutes are impossible. Relationships need definitive boundaries, stated expectations, clear commitments, and unbending accountability to qualify as relationships. The more important the relationship, the more absolutes involved. Many teach youth workers to help others not with the mirror of God (Jas 1:23) but with reimagined theological concoctions of man. Sadly, it seems that "reimagining" applies more to the hermeneutic of Scripture than anything else. Additionally there are several ironies within this movement of the last couple decades.

Paradoxically, those who wanted to emerge to avoid division within the body, divided rather quickly (into emerging and emergent). Many who participated in the emerging movement, and still remain influential today, call for authenticity and sell "messy" so as to be able to remain in perpetual spiritual limbo, benefitting from slippery accountability. "You don't say anything to me, I won't say anything to you." Many encouraging the discarding of agenda do so with

> Those of the "reimagination" ilk simply mimic trendy counter cultural group think, jumping on trendy band wagons of those they perceive to be today's youth ministry celebrities.

an obvious agenda. It's somewhat comical. Those of the "reimagination" ilk simply mimic trendy counter cultural group think, jumping on trendy band wagons of those they perceive to be today's youth ministry celebrities. Because many work hard with little recognition, it's tempting to be connected to "big names," I get it. Someone, however, has to tell one or two of our emperors, they have no clothes on.

As just alluded to, what seems most perplexing in this new wave of authentic emphasis, is the watering down of biblical truth, doctrinal teaching, and particularly a lack of communication regarding obedient living. Type "authentic" into Google and the dictionary definition immediately surfacing states, "of undisputed origin, genuine," "the letter is now accepted as an authentic document"; "synonyms: genuine, real, true, veritable." Can we get any greater affirmation of the importance of authenticity being linked to the veritable, authentic document of undisputed origin than that? I appreciate an emphasis on authentic and relevant ministry, if it legitimately represents authenticity and relevance according to God and His Word. If it's of Christ, it's authentic, if it doesn't square with His word (and we are able to figure that out) it's not applicable, no matter what anyone says. It certainly isn't relevant towards eternal ends.

No Program?

Are the new "relational" youth ministries of today really less programmatically oriented than yesteryear's traditional ministries? Are relational ministries and strategically oriented program ministries truly on opposite ends of a program ministry continuum? As hinted at in the first chapter, the answer is "no." These ministries merely offer different types of program. A program gives shape to philosophy like words give shape to thoughts. The problem with traditional ministries wasn't program itself, it's that the tail (program) wagged the dog (the youth worker). This still occurs with many who embrace relevant authentic ministry.

We need authentic ministry. We need strategic relational ministry which intentionally ministers to all teenagers' core needs—Attachment Relational Ministry (ARM). This statement describes how I think relational ministry ought to be considered, defined, and applied. No apologies. Agendas are stated and not hidden in implications made. Agree or disagree, at least one knows what is being advocated. I hope. More specifically, leading via a traditional youth ministry program does not mean exclusion of an important authentic approach. There are points of common intersect.

As we explore the issue of expressing Christ accurately, I want to ask several questions. Please pause and reflect over them before continuing reading. Think honorably. Do we really understand what it means to emphasize relationships in youth ministry? Do we want to understand? Or do we just want to have a handy buzz word ready so we can justify almost any time we spend with a young person as "ministry"? After a few paragraphs of contextual pondering, I'll give what I think are the best and truest answers to those questions.

TRULY RELEVANT AUTHENTIC RELATIONSHIPS

My son says of me that when it comes to work, my motto is to work harder not smarter. While I accuse him of exaggerating, practically speaking, as he has observed me with multiple home projects, he is more right than I prefer to admit. I regret that I have often wasted time and energy in hard work due to lazy or impatient preparation. I regret necessary work being delayed or interfered with by unnecessary problems and frustrations. This applies to home projects and to relationships.

Reciprocally influential (towards transformation in the image of Christ and manifestation of God—John 17:6) relationships depend on work, a lot of smart and hard work. The better the relationship, the more work involved. When it comes to all work, smarter preventative measures often make more draining remedial efforts less necessary. In youth ministry, remedial needs and realities often so overwhelm us that we forget we could be available early enough to assist many preventatively. Many of my frustrations with youth ministry resources or popular waves stems from those who so gravitate to preventative or remedial efforts they downplay or discredit the necessary other.

Devoid of agenda, one cannot help others preventatively or remedially. Humbly representing Christ, means compassionately considering everyone's varying needs. When someone was blind, Jesus healed their eyes. When they couldn't walk, He healed their legs. He also knew that everyone needed Him, not just the ones who looked like they needed Him. I'm pretty confident Peter and Andrew looked and smelled less than stellar. Though Matthew was detested by the Jews, he probably dressed well. Judas seems to have been quite popular among the disciples. Though Jesus was not received by everyone, He made Himself available to everyone, not just the noticeable downcast and not just to the popular.

Some youth workers are so anxious to imitate Christ by healing sick gentiles that they ignore teaching opportunities in the synagogue.

Others are so comfortable with the disciples in the boat they don't notice the crowds on the shore or the loner languishing on the periphery of one's ministry circles, desperate to be noticed, but too ashamed to make it obvious. Many have not ever imagined what it means to walk on water today and certainly wouldn't dare to exhort others to walk with them or to stop sinning. None of these approaches exemplify missional or transformational ministry. While Jesus noticed socio-economic injustice, and encouraged addressing it, His priority of ministry was to the eternal state of a person, commending the widow's mite.[15] Jesus offered compassion to all, primarily in relationship. He expected accountability from all. Jesus never wasted His time superficially accompanying or indulging anyone. Never.

RELATIONAL MINISTRY RIGHTLY UNDERSTOOD

First, most understand somewhat, but many do not fully understand. Second, I think most do want to understand, but are afraid to take real steps towards understanding. The best relationships are those in which both (or all participants) become unified or "better off" for having known one another. There is a unity of spirit that helps each in the relationship more powerfully experience living in God's Spirit. This is what Paul means in Ephesians 4 when he encourages Christians to preserve the unity of the Spirit and to build the body of Christ. People in a good, Godly, relationship mutually better understand and more joyfully and peacefully live by their purpose for living—fruitfully surviving and serving others that they too might enjoy a similar life journey.

The most successful relationship has positive results for people inside—and outside—of the relationship. This kind of relationship "provokes one another's graces"[16]. Because of the relationship, God's grace emanates more clearly through each of the individuals in the relationship and through the relationship as well. The good relationship attracts others to desires for similar relationship and, thus, increases others' willingness to risk trusting another. There is a multiplied effect of witness as to the grace of God. Communal experience of grace always grows from true personal experience of grace. They always reciprocally influence each

15. I realize some believe that Jesus was not commending the woman. I disagree.
16. Heb 10:24; 3:13.

other. I agree with Wright and Kinser, who state, "communities of faith more authentically incarnate the Gospel than individuals do."[17]

People in deeper relationships provide for one another what they know the other person truly needs, personally and communally. These relationships are truly the "I-Thou" relationships that Martin Buber described. In true relationships people speak into each other's lives because at least one of them is not content to merely watch the other. Basically, what makes relationships relevant and authentic (good, great, what they're supposed to be) are when they actually help people to mature and grow in Christ like awareness, and thus, into desire for and manifestation of Christlikeness. Christlikeness is the goal, not Christian-clichéness (by using all of the right buzz words and phrases).

Practical Theology that Trusts Jesus Christ

We need to know God and know how He desires us to love His people to effectively minister in life changing ways to them. If we just want to practically "be with" young folks, leaving strategy and agenda behind, waiting for them to first consciously identify, and then actually, successfully communicate what they need, we may be waiting for most way beyond the time we realistically will have together. Many young people will in their immaturity, fear, or confusion remain socially content to live parallel to a youth worker, as they do with almost everyone else in their lives in pseudo-relationship. Teens have way too many surface level relationships already (hooking up, Instagram, Snapchat, Facebook, absent parents).

> Many young people will in their immaturity, fear, or confusion remain socially content to live parallel to a youth worker, as they do with almost everyone else in their lives in pseudo-relationship.

God didn't send youth workers to be another "friend"; He sent us to minister to young people's needs—whether we feel capable of meeting them or not. Most of us don't, but if God used Jonah, He can use me. He can use us. We can spend a lot of time with young people and make very little long term difference in their lives. Many know exactly what I'm talking about. Some of us feel this way occasionally, others frequently. Recent

---

17. Wright and Kinser, "Post-Relational Youth Ministry," para 32.

research, sadly, confirms it's true.[18] And some are using the poor ministry of a few to disparage the field of youth ministry and the multitude of steadfast youth ministry soldiers. By the grace of God, for those to whom it is a problem, may it change. For true soldiers, stand your ground. Meeting Christ makes change inevitable, mandatory, and life giving. Let's share life by forging healthy relationships with healthy desires for teens.

Healthy relationships are those where at least one person in a relationship wants the best kind of appropriate relationship with the other person, whether or not there are signs of success. How fantastic it would be if most youth workers had the best kind of relationships with most of their young people, even those who don't look like us. Thankfully, it seems like the majority of youth workers have good relationships with lots of their youth. But, do we have the best possible relationships with most of our youth? Don't forget about the ones who could be involved in the ministry but aren't [yet]. Also, don't settle for less than the impossible by getting too pragmatic. Jesus expressed gratitude to God that He "lost not one" of His flock (John 18:9). We sometimes seem content when we reach one. Let's reach for the stars! Forget that, let's reach for galaxies![19] Let's not let one grain of sand sift through our fingers.

If we want the best relationships possible, we can't lose God's agenda for His workers. We must love young people the way Christ does—striving to know each sheep in our flock, personally . . . the way God knows each of us (John 10; Luke 15:4–7). To do this well we must recognize several key realities.

Relevant Ministry Means Something Different to Each Teenager

First, young people have critical relational needs. Second, because of these needs, different young people need different kinds of relationship with adult youth workers. Third, if we are not intentional in pursuing young people relationally, according to their differing relational needs, we may become a friend, but we will not help them in lifelong ways. All teenagers have two primary relational needs and four basic possible

---

18. Clark, *Hurt, 2.0*, 192–93. See Smith, "National Study of Youth and Religion"; Lifeway Research, "American Millennials Prefer Experience Over Expertise," 2007 and 2010.

19. Eph 3:20.

relational profiles. God can and wants to use all of us to meet all of them in their most basic places.

Ministry Leader Response
I have always approached youth ministry with the mindset that if God says, "Let my will be done on earth as in heaven," and if heaven is perfect, why aren't we striving for perfection? It is what God wants. Youth don't need to wait until heaven to experience God and His perfection.
One thing that really resonated with me through reading this chapter is as youth workers we have to have an agenda! Jesus makes it clear to us as Christian go "go therefore and make disciples of all nations" (Matt 28:19). He doesn't say go therefore and make friends.
As I was reading this chapter it was taking everything inside of me not to post quotes. I'm glad this book doesn't share the same ideas as the majority of youth ministry books. One thing abundantly clear in this chapter is that the end goal of youth ministry should not be about relationships with teens, but should be about their maturity in relationship with Jesus. Ron nails this entire idea in this chapter.
Eric (Pelly) Peloquin, Pastor of Emerging Generations, Bedford Community Church, Bedford, NJ

As conveyed more fully in the last chapter, some youth leaders try to manifest Christ, wanting to feel in love with Christ, but not knowing Him. They manufacture ideas of Christ based more on select preferred passages of the Bible and a reimagined Christ. They're intrigued by the power of the Holy Spirit, but fail to understand the Holy Spirit's mission.

HOW MUCH ONE KNOWS HAS EVERYTHING TO DO WITH HOW MUCH ONE CARES

"People don't care how much you know until they know how much you care." "People over program." "Relationship over religion." While I get the point of these mantras, they provide an ongoing perplexity for me; I think repetitive use of these clichés hurt the cause of Christ more than they help. Of course all contain grains of validity. Some in ministry have invested intellect but no heart. Some have smooth ministry machines, but only produce cross wearing Christians, not cross bearing Christians. And knowing Christ and others intimately is important. But somehow, we've minimized the importance of what gets scrapped on the other end of these phrases. We no longer need to know anything, can't use the word program, and treat the importance of regular church attendance pretty apathetically.[20] Ministry definitely starts with caring about people, no doubt. Receptivity to one's ministry also probably starts with an awareness that the youth worker truly cares. This makes sense for some, perhaps many, but not for all.

These phrases imply that all we need to do to be relationally successful is to be personally present, after all, true ministry is "messy," and that's all we can really do for people.[21] Advocates of these ideas represent an equal reactionary problem to the problems of ministries which have been sterile. How can one argue that appreciation for knowledge of the Bible hasn't eroded? How can one argue that push back against the high priority of evangelism hasn't occurred? In the ad nauseam repetition of Christian phrases, Christians find ways to avoid the hard work of God's anticipated relational ministries. Satisfaction with messy doesn't cut it.

CONCLUSION: REMEDIAL MINISTRY

Let's face it, remedial ministry feels more like ministry than preventative efforts do. It can be so messy, so personal, and non-programmatic. At the end of the day, in our exhaustion with curative ministry, we can at least fall asleep knowing that we're trying. (And perhaps feel better about judging those who—unlike us—are running traditional programs.)

I don't want to fall asleep at night content knowing that I tried. I want to fall asleep trusting that He is succeeding through me, yes even me, even if I can't see it or feel it. If I can try some preventative ministry before after-the-fact ministry then perhaps I'll help more folks with no one ever knowing it, and others won't have to try as hard with as many people later. I can make the most use of my time.[22] My ministry will be relevant and authentic in God's eyes. Remedial ministry is no more authentic than preventative ministry.

> Remedial ministry is no more authentic than preventative ministry.

---

20. Rainer, *I Am a Church Member*, 18. How many youth workers dismiss the importance of a developed eschatology, creation perspective?

21. See Yaconelli, *Messy Spirituality*; Parsley, *Messy Church*; Moore and Leadbetter, *Messy Church*; Zemple, *Community Is Messy*. Messy is another vogue buzz word.

22. 2 Cor 6:2; Eph 5:16.

In fact, if preventative efforts (through program or not) have been neglected, helpful efforts may be closer to those of an enabling accomplice rather than those of a true servant. Let us be more motivated by doing good than by looking good or feeling good. Let's bear the fruit that Christ seeks.[23]

No one really may ever notice the deep impact on the five youth not having premarital sex mostly because of a Spirit led, diligently prepared, effective youth group Bible study, led by someone who truly cares. Others definitely notice a youth worker spending lots of effort and time helping a teen mom. Personally, I'd rather help ten teenagers avoid the consequences of premarital sex than one experiencing them.

Please don't misinterpret this out of the context of this whole chapter and the whole book—I wholeheartedly believe we need to be there for troubled teens too! My wife was a Mentor Mom for *Young Lives—Young Life's* ministry to teen moms and because our teen mom's baby daddy is still in the picture, I've also been quite involved. We've also had youth living with us at different times, one for almost a year. Hear the point. Help in both ways, to prevent problems and amidst them.

If we abandon programs for the sake of relational ministry, we're stepping further away from mutual accountability of each other and our supporting partners (churches, networks, committees, boards). Due to varying reasons, those in parachurch ministry have seen abject failures connected mostly to the lack of body accountability, and thus, diluted supervision. Even for those for whom this statement is true, just because those youth may not care how much we know, it doesn't negate the reality that how much we know actually influences how much we care. And how diligently and competently we communicate our care. "Caring begins with knowing; it requires listening, understanding, and accepting" and following this will ultimately lead to loving one another."[24]

---

23. John 15.

24. Bolman and Deal, *Reframing Organizations*, 401, not a Christian text.

PERSONAL CHALLENGE AND DISCUSSION QUESTIONS
FOR LEADERSHIP TEAMS

1. Is God able to communicate the message of His word consistently through varying eras and cultures so that His intended meaning is understood by all?

2. Does it matter what words we use to describe relational ministry? What might the ramifications be relative to an answer of either "yes" or "no"?

3. How do you know when a youth ministry book or speaker conveys poor theological study and understanding? How can you know?

CHAPTER 4

Family Based Model

"What if this separation between students and adults, something that I was trained to see as a solution, has actually been a part of the problem? What if God never intended youth ministry staff members to be the primary sustainers of students' spiritual lives? What if something is profoundly wrong with the entire way the church has structured ministries to youth and children?" (Renfro et al., *Perspectives on Family Ministry*, p. 10)

"Family ministry in all its complexity has found itself primarily the responsibility of the children's and youth departments at most churches around the U.S. . . . Today's family ministry needs a mission that says the entire faith community will feel the responsibility of raising a spiritually transformed generation of children and (adolescents)." (Anthony and Marshman, *7 Family Ministry Essentials*, pp. 26, 40, 52)

"It seems as though once churches make the switch from youth ministry to family ministry the temptation is to turn inward, to spend their time equipping believing parents to engage their teenagers spiritually. Evangelism becomes something moms and dads lecture on, instead of actually do and equip their teenagers to do. There's no longer a full court press to reach unbelieving teenagers as much as there is a push to train Christian teenagers in the faith." (Stier, "The Hidden Danger in Dropping Youth Ministry for a Family Ministry Approach")

The family desperately needs attention and guidance from the church today. Many thus advocate for a ministry paradigm shift which either eliminates youth ministry programs, or at least reshapes them into more holistically oriented family ministry programs. Such an approach will not only hurt millions of current families, it will hurt millions of future families. This notion reflects a historical disregard for a proven ministry approach which most reflects the ministry that Jesus Christ modeled. Churches who offer youth ministry programs actually assist families more than family based ministry approaches.

HISTORY OF YOUTH MINISTRY: FOLLOWING THE PRECEDENT SET BY JESUS CHRIST

The Jewish practice of Rabbi Mentors, Torah teachers, guiding children has been occurring for literally thousands of years. Teenagers and young adults who proved more interested and capable in the memorization and grasping of Scripture would study more seriously under the mentoring guidance of rabbis. For those who proved more advanced yet,[1] in ability and passion, these "talmidim" (disciples), typically starting at the age of fifteen, followed closely, imitated persistently, and essentially lived with s'mikhah rabbis, the most highly regarded rabbis of Jesus' day.[2] Disciples of such leader teachers were not what we think of today when we think of typical students. "There is much more to a talmid than what we call a student. A student wants to know what the teacher knows . . . a talmid wants to be like the teacher . . . the rabbi-talmid relationship was very intense and personal."[3] Jesus Christ, a s'mikhah rabbi, led his closest disciples, his youth group of teenagers and one young adult (Peter) into changing the world.[4] The Western Christian church of today left behind many of the ways and practices of the early church and our Jewish forefathers. Some Jewish practices still continue today through contextualized application of key rabbi to disciple relationship principles. We call this youth ministry.

1. These youth would have memorized the *Thanach*, what Christians call the Old Testament.

2. Vander Laan, "Follow the Rabbi Lectures," lesson 2.

3. Vander Laan, "Follow the Rabbi Lectures," lesson 2. 1 Cor 4:16; 1 Cor 11:1. Paul tells his disciples to imitate him as he imitates Christ. Paul studied under a s'mikhah rabbi, Gamaliel, see Acts 22:3.

4. See Keener, "Jesus's Disciples were Teenagers."

Some Jewish practices still continue today through contextualized application of key rabbi to disciple relationship principles. We call this youth ministry. Consider twentieth to twenty-first century church and parachurch youth ministry in the U.S. In what

Some Jewish practices still continue today through contextualized application of key rabbi to disciple relationship principles. We call this youth ministry.

other context do disciples very often express a desire to be like their Pastor (while at the same time, developmentally fixated on the forging of one's identity)? In what church (people of God) context do we find similar dramatic amounts of time being spent together between a church leader (Youth Pastor) and church member (teenager)? More than any other church ministry of today, youth ministry most resembles Jesus' specific ministry approach and potentially fosters authentic rabbi and talmid relationships.

Youth ministry is the ARM of Christ in today's church. Even considering dismembering youth ministry hurts the ministry of the church and the future people of God dramatically. The enemy has distracted us from the inside, on a topic that ought not even to be discussed. Two thousand years ago God's people provided opportunity for their most mature, intelligent, and gifted ministry leaders to spend most of their time specifically focusing on leading and developing teenagers and young adults. That approach has blessed Israel throughout its history and led to the expansion of Christianity around the world.

For about a fifty-year period in the late 1900s and into the early 2000s, the American church tried to do the same (albeit, in the eyes of some, with those not yet ready to be "real Pastors," see the next section). At this same time, however, the faults of traditional legalism started to give way to the faults of reactive, culturally influenced, postmodern superficiality. The fruit of these two plagues disturbs today's church (the Christian academy, the church, the parachurch) quite profoundly. But now, the answer to this problematic reality and all of the church's many associated problems, is to eliminate the one key focus of the church most resembling the ministry of Christ specifically? What sense does that make?

HISTORY OF DISRESPECT FOR VALUE OF YOUTH MINISTRY
WITHIN THE CHURCH IN GENERAL

All systems have scapegoat members, businesses, families, basketball teams, and churches alike. In one church I used to have a flowchart on my door presenting a series of yes or no questions. No matter what the problem in a church was, all troubles easily traced to the Youth Pastor. If the body of Christ does away with "Youth Pastors" specifically, I wonder who will be the source of tomorrow's church's problems. Did that flowchart illustrate my own bias? Perhaps. But someone else created it and it seemed like most who read it couldn't help but laughingly agree with the streams to the conclusion. At

> At some point soon the church needs to realize it has not overvalued youth ministry; it has undervalued it.

some point soon the church needs to realize it has not overvalued youth ministry; it has undervalued it.

How many congregants and parents have told youth workers to, "Have a nice vacation," when taking groups of youth on a Mission's trip? Many adults saying similar comments have a difficult time taking their own few children on a true vacation. How many times do members in a church assume it's the youth ministry's fault when a church van is left dirty or something in the church is broken? Relative to Senior and Associate Pastors, how many Youth Pastors have retirement accounts set aside for them? Sit on Elder Boards? Get sabbaticals or five weeks of vacation? Youth Pastors often get to live in parsonages, true, typically for one (or both) of two reasons: other Pastors on staff would rather build assets and/ or the church can now pay the Youth Pastor minimal salary by offering a place to live, which they already have, want to keep, and pay for anyway. These arrangements might benefit a Youth Pastor. They might not. I doubt anyone has evil motive. But I can't say that about selfish or lazy motives.

The problem with a backlash against youth ministry today, in favor of advocating for family ministry, reflects and displays uninformed bias, evangelical immaturity, and a lack of awareness and compassion for the breadth and depth of missiological, sociological, theological, and psychological understanding and skills required by today's youth worker. It also unfairly pins the burden of parents not being equipped well or the lack of youth participation in the greater life of the church on the shoulders of a Youth Pastor. How does that not reflect more of a problem with the leadership of lead pastors and elders? If ministry targeting youth specifically has failed, why? How many churches have totally set up their own youth ministries to fail?

Many view youth ministry as a "stepping stone," a training ground for those not yet ready to do *real* ministry (ministry focused on helping adults). After several years in one ministry a lay person approached me with the intent to encourage me. He stated something like, "You're doing an amazing job in youth ministry here. We've been blessed. I imagine we'll lose you soon when you decide you want to be a *real* Pastor." Thank you for the encouragement. Clearly many youth workers relate to this story. I recently spoke about relational youth ministry for a podcast called, *notarealpastor.com*. One church I know of determined to hire a Youth Pastor who desired and studied to be a Senior Pastor. Apparently former Pastoral Ministry students received more valid training and represented the more mature of those desiring to go into ministry. The young man hired because he did not want to do youth ministry proved his honesty and that his education did not equip him for youth ministry. The church, getting exactly what it wanted, was surprised at his lack of success.

Pastoral Ministry professors target gifted Youth Ministry Majors telling them they're too talented for youth ministry. Many church leaders believe that almost any young adult who loves God possesses all that is needed to run a fine youth ministry. Thus, they hire young adults who agree with them (and who were not hired by anyone in the fields for which they trained). I've received plenty of phone calls over the years from such youth workers, recent graduates with (insert preference: _____) degrees. They ask if we can sit down so they can pick my brain for an hour on how to lead a youth ministry. Why so long? Surely we could cover everything in 30 minutes. Somehow or another many of these youth ministries flounder.

Some say a key indication of the failure of youth ministry are the amounts of young adults who never developed into mature Christians. Which youth ministries? Those run by carefully selected and trained leaders or those discussed above? Now, I'm not blind, truly some well-trained, yet immature Youth Pastors share some blame here. But let's consider a few other possible reasons why this might be true. And before we do that, let's be clear, most adults (Pastors, Elders, parents, lay people) in the Church do not see most Youth Pastors as a potentially authoritative influence in their lives. This seriously undermines the possibility of the

Youth Pastor effectively carrying the brunt of responsibility for equipping parents to be the primary spiritual leaders of their families.

How many Youth Pastors have experienced blatant disrespect? When they try to disciple church teens, evangelizing and receiving lost teens, how many parents fight those efforts? Some parents suggested I be fired when I brought my youth group to a Jewish synagogue and a Catholic church to dialogue with a rabbi and priest regarding belief similarities and differences. A father reamed me out for wanting to discuss sex with early adolescents (calendared and well communicated months ahead of time and scheduled because a young teen girl asked me if oral sex was okay). That young lady happened to be the daughter of the father who chastised me. "You know, you're not worth what you get paid," said one Deacon. My income was below the poverty line and I dealt weekly with his son's insecure hostilities. Many capable youth workers leave youth ministry because of the ignorance of parents and church leaders.

How many parents have made sports and other activities a higher priority for their own children than ownership of ministry? I know parents and teenagers have it very difficult here. All three of my now grown children played high school sports. I'm simply suggesting Youth Pastors are not to blame for parents' decisions. While the parents (strong Christians and dependable supporters of the youth ministry) blessed their daughter's decision, when one of my seniors, the captain of the girls' soccer team, quit to oversee the start of a monthly youth led worship service, the parents asked if I would help their daughter reconsider her decision. I explained to them that it was not my youth ministry, it was the teenagers' youth ministry and that God allowed me to be a guiding steward of it. She owned the ministry.[5] They received that, but how many wouldn't?

On many levels the church universal has communicated loud and clear they only desire Youth Pastors to keep church raised teens busy, entertained, and in the Bible enough to keep them from getting into trouble (but not so much that they expose spiritual weaknesses in the home or the church). Why have so many youth ministries operated in silos? Is it possible the church leadership quarantined youth (and the Youth Pastor) into youth ministry silos by not considering their desires, tolerating their voices, or incorporating their abilities to contribute on a larger scale

---

5. When Sarah approached me, I did challenge her not to quit the soccer team. I was glad she was a leader in her school and wasn't sure she should give that up. She prayed and heard from God to start this ministry. She felt that the commitment to soccer would interfere in her ability to focus. Who was I to question?

(e.g., worship, committees, collecting the offering)? Tell teens they're not welcome, then blame them for not coming back. Hey, and we might as well blame the Youth Pastor for not leading them well. Sadly, influenced by the naysayers, many churches keeping youth specific ministry today hire part time help or use only volunteers (while still retaining fulltime expectations). The defense for such moves, often being a need to focus on family ministry.

HISTORY OF THE DEMAND FOR A PARADIGM SHIFT AND/OR MANIFESTO OF INTEGRATION

DeVries and others propose that ministry to youth might not only be unproductive, but that it might be counterproductive. Near the end of the 1950s, Oscar Feucht encouraged the church to focus ministry toward families rather than to children, believing that without support at home, children's ministry would not have lasting impact.[6] Based on research with Christian Educators and Youth Directors in the 1970s, Wright concluded that they were not helping families.[7] In the 1980s Charles Sell, echoing both, suggested that targeting ministry to youth was proving unproductive and that more energy should be made toward "family based Christian Education."[8] Mark DeVries, 1990s, advanced Sell's position one step further, "Could it be that the majority of our efforts in programming and publicity may, in fact, be moving teens away from rather than toward mature Christian adulthood"?[9]

DeVries continued lamenting youth ministry during the 2000s, suggesting that despite being popular, they've failed to make lasting differences in nurturing healthier families or youth ministry participants' long term commitments to the church. To support his notion, he referred to his own struggles, one friend's despair, anecdotal stories, and two pieces of research.[10] The first study referenced, in *Youth Ministry that Transforms*, found that self-evaluating youth workers believed they were least successful in building connections between parents and teenagers. This study, however, identified an operational challenge, not a verdict that

6. See Feucht, *Helping Families through the Church*.

7. See Wright, *Marriage and Family Enrichment Resource Manual*.

8. Sell, *Family Ministry*, 151.

9. DeVries, *Family Based Youth Ministry*, 28.

10. Strommen et al., *Youth Ministry that Transforms*, 217–19.

youth ministries interfere with household discipleship. DeVries also cited research indicating lack of increase in church attendance for young adults in the 1990s relative to previous eras as an indication of failure. He didn't consider the possibility that many youth ministries might be responsible for attendance figures not being worse, especially in the light of the parallel cultural moral decline.

In DeVries' inability to guide his own youth ministry successfully he concluded the problem had nothing to do with his own leadership and everything to do with the concept of youth ministry, "youth ministry is in crisis. . . . We need an entirely new way of looking at youth ministry."[11] Wow. What a conclusion. I always believed when I'm doing something and it's not working, don't blame anyone else or the tools I'm using, "get er done." His claim and book brought him into prominence as a youth ministry writer and speaker. I don't get it. Sadly, his voice, directly or indirectly, lingers in the words of many today.

WOULD THE FAMILY AND FAMILY MINISTRY FARE BETTER WITH NO YOUTH MINISTRY?

If all of the churches today totally shut down all youth ministries, if they either fired or re-job-described all now "former" Youth Pastors, the church still won't prepare parents to be the spiritual caretakers of the souls of their children. Churches will not magically transform into bastions of family care and guidance. The churches that might do that, already are, as well as families will let them.

Youth ministry and ministry to the family are related, but separate issues. Youth and family ministry do not have to be either or options. And, as alluded to in the above discussion, we have to stop blaming Youth Ministries for operating as a "One Eared Mickey Mouse."[12] We have to stop perpetuating Christian clichés that have no merit! It's a creative illustration that paints a biased picture of the truth.

Have youth ministries often operated as silos, distinct from the whole church? Yes. See the above for some reasons why. Let's consider other aspects of this conversation. First, the way they operate is not very different than any/every other ministry of the church. The Nifty Fifties? Woman's Bible Study? The church pushes most of the ministry that takes

11. DeVries, *Family Based Youth Ministry*, 22, 30, 32.
12. DeVries, *Family Based Youth Ministry*, 42.

place within it into distinct silos across the board. I'm not advocating for or arguing against. I see potential problems and benefits. But I do wonder why "Youth Ministry" has been singled out as the family annihilating culprit. (Actually, no I don't. See the opening paragraphs.) Is it really always an immature, family negligent, Youth Pastor's fault? Is the concept of youth ministry really at fault?

Many today listen to and agree with those calling for transition, and have begun to reimagine youth ministry, reflexively blaming traditional youth ministry for, seemingly, all of the current church's problems. Relative to youth ministry some believe, "Rather than healing ruptured connections between the generations, significant numbers of churches unintentionally welcomed and perhaps even widened the chasm between children and parents."[13]

Key tenets of this movement include several criticisms of youth ministry. God never intended a Youth Pastor to be *the primary spiritual influence* of teenagers. Youth ministry has been more about entertaining youth than maturing them. Most youth workers spend more time managing programs than in walking with people.[14] The Family Integrated Church Ministry model fully represent the culminating power of this trend.

THE FAMILY INTEGRATED CHURCH MOVEMENT (FICM)

In their 2009 book, *Perspectives on Family Ministry*, Renfro, Shields, and Strother identified three specific types of family centered church ministries: Family Based, Family Equipping, and Family Integrated. Two forms seemingly present more of a healthy family sensitive approach. Family Based Churches retain age segmented ministry but emphasize intergenerational and family focused events in each ministry. Family Equipping Churches also retain age segmented ministry, but "restructure the congregation to partner with parents at every level of ministry" (p. 144). Growing in popularity, Family Integrated Churches reject the fragmentation of ministry.

In a synopsis of the FICM movement, considered by many within it to be an undertaking comparable to a second reformation, Douglas Brown indicates there are over 800 affiliated churches from a variety of

---

13. Renfro et al., *Perspectives on Family Ministry*, 34.
14. Diaz, *Redefining the Role of the Youth Pastor*, 29–51.

denominational backgrounds who believe churches have usurped the authority and responsibility of the parents in the home.[15] Family Integrated Churches affirm the sole authority of Scripture and entirely reject the worldliness and fragmentation of ministry through age segregated ministry; they, thus, have no youth, children's, or nursery ministries. "At every level, adults and children engage in service and fellowship together."[16] Structure and calendars are very simple, centering on the weekly worship service.

Brown points out several problems associated with this separatist perspective.

Hermeneutically, the FICM misinterprets the lack of clear Biblical directives for age distinctive ministry as a mandate to not provide age segregated ministry. Theologically, the leaders of the FICM misunderstand the churches authority to make disciples, which "both includes families and transcends families."[17] Practically, this movement alienates those without families or those from broken families and has failed to prove that age distinct ministries are the reason for all of the current problems associated with church and culture. Though very sad, one also can't help but wonder relative to recent moral failures or perplexities of key leaders associated with this movement, how this could happen to people who are supposedly leading a truly righteous revolution within the church.[18] Could it actually be a revolution against the church?

15. See Brown, "United Families Dividing Churches."

16. Renfro et al., *Perspectives on Family Ministry*, 57.

17. Brown, "United Families Dividing Churches," line 114.

18. Dean, "What Went Wrong," line 12.

Ministry Leader Response

As I was the youth pastor here for ten years and now the Family Ministry Pastor for almost six years, I agree with much of what is talked about in the chapter.

—Our church has more of a Family Equipping approach.

—I really don't believe this is an either/or issue but rather a both/and opportunity.

—Parents should see the value of other trusted adults speaking into the life of their kids.

One challenge the church has to address is trying not to create a "drop off" culture that in subtle and even unintentional ways dismisses the parent's role in the faith development of their kids. The question we should be asking is how children and youth ministries can work alongside parents and family ministries to help give age specific instruction and community for kids and adolescents while also promoting faith development at home.

Mike Thompson, Family Ministry Pastor, Alliance Church, Sarasota, Florida

---

Brown's key criticism echoes the whole of the pushback emphasized in this chapter, most children's and youth ministries provide helpful and God ordained right ministry. Youth Ministries cannot be held responsible for the negligence of those parents who abdicate their responsibility and/or by those churches who have failed to disciple adults appropriately. Age distinct ministry enhances rather than interferes with a church's ministry to families.

In *God, Marriage, and Family,* Andreas Kostenberger expresses concerns that an FICM approach/mentality emphasizes focus on family ministry at a status that is not scripturally warranted, and states, "using a peer group structure does not necessarily mean that the natural family structure is subverted but may helpfully complement and supplement it."[19] The key criticism against traditional notions of youth ministry seems to reflect the idea that the church has misconstrued the role of a youth worker and miscommunicated to youth workers and teenagers that youth workers are to be the primary spiritual leaders of those in the adolescent population.

YOUTH PASTORS SHOULD NOT BE
THE PRIMARY INFLUENCE ON CHILDREN

The idea that God never intended for the Youth Pastor to be the primary spiritual influence is 100 percent correct. This admittedly is not a

---

19. Kostenberger, *God, Marriage, and Family,* 258.

supportive argument against the traditional format of youth ministry. It is an observation of a truth with which almost everyone who has done youth ministry would agree. And while that is true, those of us who've done youth ministry also know, that unfortunately, in many cases, if we're unwilling to assume responsibility for that role, then no one will be the primary spiritual influence. We minister to the family through the teenager. Is it really the Youth Pastor's role to minister to the family through the adults? Or does that sound like the Lead or Associate Pastor's responsibility? To fill a parent's empty shoes here suggests surrender to what God wants, not what any reasonable Youth Pastor would prefer.

I know of no well-intentioned youth leader who has ever desired or intended to literally try to replace a parent.[20] I know of no church or parachurch leader who has verbally encouraged a youth worker to operate in such a manner. While there is no doubt that some, and possibly many, parents and ministries became guilty of subtly placing expectations on youth workers to be the primary spiritual influence, most youth workers did not and do not do this to themselves. And admitting that many parents/churches made this mistake still does not affirm the notion that churches need to move away from youth ministry and toward family ministry.

LOST PARENTS NEED HOPE

We cannot talk about this subject while avoiding the reality of the moral decline in our country today and the parallel disruption in the family. Many children live in homes where God's values are clearly not valued. What about all of today's children growing up in homes with very little notion of what God's ideal of a family looks like? How a family operates? With no option of a father and mother led household able or interested to guide one's spiritual growth? Note, essentially one-third of today's children grow up in non-Christian homes.

In this era of declining morality, fractured families, sociopolitical plethora of believed lies, non-church families desperately need and even desire ministry assistance. While most of the parents of these homes may not opt for church, many children will. And typically, it will be the local

---

20. Caution here relates to the phrase "well intentioned," which I believe most youth workers are. I'm not talking about the wolves in sheep's clothing, those who pretend to love youth so as to prey upon them.

Christian youth worker, the ARM of the church, extending out to the lost most often. The change agent of the family, the teen, may be the only bridge between a family and the church of Jesus Christ.

Adolescent Developmental Realities

Do we really want to help the family? Challenge and equip parents? Then note key developmental realities. Teens crave change! Adults crave status quo. Healthy teens crave exploring and individuation. They want to pick the brains of adults, even parents, just not always their own parents. Adults know what they believe, even if they don't. Teens crave novelty. Adults crave predictable safety and assurance. Teens feel invincible. Adults avoid aspects of life reminding them they're not. Teens desire to be difference makers. Adults desire to comfortably read a book or watch television. Most teens love their parents, no matter how good or bad they've been. (Some teens' love shows as hate because they're dreadfully aware of the love they always desired but never felt.) Most familial change depends on motives of love and the nature of the teen.

If there is hope for a family (Christian or non-Christian) to grow, to mature, to be more than it has been, the impetus for maturing change will probably most likely occur through the curiosity, rebellious spirit, or prodding insistence of a maturing teen. Mature adults become convicted out of the ruts of existing to pay bills, cut the grass, go to work, etc. Immature adults become attracted to Christ in hope for ability to change as they observe the faith and life changes within their teenagers.

I was a Youth Pastor from the '80s through the '90s. By the grace of God, many families benefitted as lost parents became attracted to God's church (the body of Christ) because of the visible maturation they saw in their own children. One parent stated, "We're attending this church, which is forty-five minutes away from where we live because my daughter loves engaging with and learning from youth who pray with passion and focus. She wants that in her life." Another parent, after dragging/guiding me into the boiler room, in the basement of the church, for a conversation (literally), said, "I'm watching the growth of my son, and the attraction of other kids to this ministry, and I've figured it out . . . you're one of those 'born again' guys, aren't you? My son challenged us to sell our home, buy one at half the cost, and give the other half of the proceeds to the poor. When we told him we want to see him do it first, he put white medical tape down the middle of his room, sold one half of it to his friends and gave the money to a ministry for the homeless."

One mom came to me and offered to help in the ministry, "I've watched my delinquent son change in so many ways, I can't believe it. Whatever is going on here, I want to be a part of it." Another father once shared, "Our family reads C. S. Lewis books together now. We started doing that after our daughter came home from youth group with one and was enthralled with it. Thank you." Adults who I'd never met approached me in grocery stores and told me they couldn't wait for their children to

> All ministries succeed, fail, and can improve relative to family sensitivity. What needs to occur, is what has already occurred in many ministries, a perspective from the whole church that all ministries are family ministry partners.

participate in our ministry when they were old enough. And there are more stories, more of my own and more from many others. Youth Pastors change families through the teens.

ALL PARENTS NEED ALLIES

I loved asking parents at parent meetings how they might handle some of the more common problem situations that show up in youth ministry. I would mention mundane issues (talking through a meeting or not getting $ in for a trip) to extreme ones (someone groping someone at a youth event or a teen who "disappears" on a trip). Typically, this led to much discussion with varying answers and ensuing disagreements and sometimes an escalation in emotion. Though I never let it go on for too long, this exercise made obvious the disparity in their own attitudes, perspectives, frustrations, and solutions. It usually felt rewarding when they saw the impossibility of satisfying everyone, but the more important victories occurred in their receptivity to my solicitation for prayer and their need to vulnerably trust my decisions and motives in making the decisions.

I also would inform them that their children would often confide in me things that were personal and sometimes familial. And in that confiding would sometimes complain about a parent. This afforded me the opportunity to share with them my awareness that they weren't perfect and that I wasn't either. I knew that on occasion the youth might complain about me (or a leader in the ministry) to them. I assured them that when I was with the youth, I had the parents' back and would defend them as appropriately as possible. And if I had a true concern, I would always approach the parent first. I asked for the same from them. I made it clear to the parents that we were allies in the raising of their children. With this approach, and commitment to it, most parents grew to appreciate that we were allies. Many found some sense of relief. Others felt some hope. Others enjoyed knowing a trustworthy and caring adult was working alongside of them.

Parents need allies who they trust, who on occasion, may teach or interact with their children in a way slightly different from their own. Arguments with teenagers can be intense. In some moments many parents beg God for wisdom,

> Parents need allies who they trust, who on occasion, may teach or interact with their children in a way slightly different from their own.

even parents who otherwise don't seem to care about God. Some find small amounts of relief in knowing that at least their children have access to another adult who loves their children rightly. They have access to an adult who desires to see their children mature in Christ.

While such an adult could be a coach or a teacher, it really doesn't matter what role that person fills. What matters is that the other adult cares and makes himself or herself appropriately available. The Church should be providing this other adult to families because there are no guarantees relative to teachers and coaches. And often, while their children may regard those other adults, many of them do not know Christ and therefore, cannot offer His true love from the context of His wisdom. There has never been a parent of a teenager who cannot relate to what I'm writing here.

As a parent who has assumed the primary responsibility of nurturing my own teenagers in Christ, I also know however, how desperate a parent can be for a young adult to come along side one's teenagers to affirm the teachings of Christ. Sometimes my children would say, "Paul said so and so and he's right . . . etc." Paul said what I'd said 10 times before (how many parents relate to this experience?), but my children *only heard it when Paul said it*.[21] Thank God he was with them and that

21. Their youth leader, not the biblical writer.

he did. My church's and community's parachurch's youth leaders were not the primary spiritual influences of my teenage children, but their focused ministries to them were significantly influential and significantly missed by spiritually mature parents when they were unavailable.

CONCLUSION: FOCUSING OF FAILURE AND EXCLUDING A CONSIDERATION OF SUCCESS

Youth ministries can sensitively enhance family life potential or they can blindly disrupt family schedules and home-life. They can do either, just like Elder meetings, Worship Teams, and other ministries. As a C.E. Director I spear-headed a move to make all church committees meet on the same one Monday night a month, while limiting all regular church ministries taking place to the same one night every week. After masses of initial resistance, everyone loved the changes. All ministries succeed, fail, and can improve relative to family sensitivity. What needs to occur, is what has already occurred in many ministries, a perspective from the whole church that all ministries are family ministry partners.[22]

I will never support the notion that churches wanting to equip families successfully should ever abandon a sold-out youth ministry focus. It's possible we're already beginning to see the fall out of such mistaken family-ministry fixation. I've noticed recently that a prominent church, proudly vocal about not providing ministry specifically focused on teens in recent past (2012) seems to have most recently subtly recanted; they currently offer youth specific ministry.[23] If the tide doesn't turn, as this church was willing to do, the church in general seems to be moving in a disastrous direction. Instead of young adult church attendance figures imitating past era percentages in 2030, we will see *significant declines*. Significant. Guaranteed.

How many youth ministries, within the context of churches with appropriate expectations, have thrived in ministry to adolescents? How many families have benefitted and grown together because of effective youth ministries? Many mature Christian parents, fed through their own devotion and the preaching and teaching of the church have realized that their Youth Pastors and their ministries were helpful allies. Many parents

22. Vandergriff, "Family Ministry," 119–32; Anthony and Marshman, *7 Family Ministry Essentials*, 25–30.

23. Gray, *Transformation Church*.

and Youth Pastors have reciprocally influenced each other to bring many children to Christian maturity. Youth leaders must never simply entertain young people, but when they do so strategically, such efforts typically, purposively, enhance one's effort to train adolescents in the way of Christ. Pragmatically speaking, the accusation that youth ministry has to go due to troubles in the church today or because we need to equip parents to be the primary spiritual leaders of their children, simply has little to no merit.

While God has always intended parents to be the primary spiritual influence on their children's lives, He has also always intended that parents train their children from within an extensive spiritual support network.[24] This is where many of these advocates for change and I agree whole heartedly. We diverge in that some just totally overemphasize that young adult church participation has not increased. It does not seem to dawn on critics that perhaps, rather than fragmenting families and cultivating immature "disciples," many (many, many) youth ministries discipled teens who held families together and/or provoked mature changes within families.

It is true that many youth workers have not intentionally assisted parents. Some have not developed one direct ministry to or for parents. But even if Youth Pastors may not function well in nurturing families directly, they do indirectly. Not all familial support and impact can be measured via direct efforts. The most effective systems demonstrate universal commitment and partnership relative to common articulated purposes by individual members. Members fill different interdependent roles. Youth ministries typically guide teens toward maturity in these types of youth ministry systems. Teens learn how to partner with adults to accomplish God's work. Any change in one teen system, typically initiates change by that teen in other systems, depending on system health relative to communication, boundaries, flexibility, and cohesion (see ch. 5). Family systems benefit.

The teen who doesn't talk to her parents, doesn't tell her parents about the two hour coffee shop chat in which the youth worker totally advocated for the parents relative to some fight at home. But it makes huge differences. The teen who experimented with smoking or alcohol or drugs or . . . doesn't run home to his parents to inform them. But he might (and often does) talk about it with his youth worker. And while

24. Deut 6; Eph 4–6. See the example of Paul with Timothy throughout the NT.

the youth worker may not approach the conversation the way the parent would, that might be a good thing. And the experiment, might actually end as one experiment because of points made (and heard) by someone the teens knows cares for him. Not being the parent frees youth workers from being the rebel-against figure. All of those people talking about the emerging generation leaving the church will never know about these successes.

Are Youth Pastors getting all of the credit for the Millennials who are coming to church? Gen Xers? Gen Zers? They shouldn't get the blame or the credit. But they should be acknowledged as instrumental team mates, as the ARM representative of Christ.

PERSONAL CHALLENGE AND DISCUSSION QUESTIONS FOR LEADERSHIP TEAMS

1. Respond to Renfro's quote at the beginning of the chapter.

2. How can you begin to address with the larger church some of the criticisms I levy against it? Who will you address? How? When?

3. How do parents of your teenagers see you as an ally? How do you see them or treat them as allies? What changes can be made to accommodate and minister to families better? When will you implement them?

PART 2

The Theology & Theory Behind ARM

These two chapters present the academic background behind ARM. The interaction of parental approaches and family systems create some clear and helpful-to-understand scenarios for youth leaders when using ARM.

CHAPTER 5

Theological and Theoretical Support for ARM

"Identity formation in the Christian faith is ultimately grounded in what theologian James McClendon stated as 'biography as theology'. Our identity is formed by those we surround ourselves with and who shape us." (Keuss, *Blur*, p. 61)

"Is Practical Theology the most helpful way to frame the task of doing youth ministry? It may be. But if it is, I would argue that our approach be one of simplicity, rather than of sophistication. . . . We are unwise then to take our cues from the latest and splashiest biblical scholar, theologian, social critic or social scientist whose starting point often happens to be one of suspicion and skepticism." (Parrett, "Toward What End?" p. 63)

"Factor analytic studies of how people view God consistently reflect relational items and dimensions that can be understood through attachment terms (Zahl and Gibson, "God Representations, Attachment to God, and Satisfaction with Life," p. 218)

DISREGARD FOR LOVING GOD with all one's mind prevails in the church. I remember being made fun of by the other Youth Pastors in my District for pursuing a PhD. (We all made fun of each other for as many things as we could.) Most of them laughed at the idea of reading a book cover to cover. So many of them, like so many current youth workers just want to do God's work, not making it more "complicated" than it needs to be. About two years ago, I heard from one Youth Pastor that another Youth Pastor in the area saw no need to attend a seminar led by someone from the world of academia—after all, "those who can, do, and those who can't, teach." Clichés exist because people believe them. And there are plenty of youth-workers out there who believe this one. I also remember concerns being brought up in a job interview because I had been a Psychology major in college and I had a Master's degree in Counseling. The church elders were concerned that I would be too psychologically oriented. As far as the elders were concerned a good Pastor doesn't need anything more than a thorough understanding of God's word.

God's youth workers minister in the trenches. We work with a difficult people group, one which most adults avoid. We all need as much training and ammunition as is possible. If any of us, no matter whether in the role of boot-camp Sargent or field Sargent, think we're done learning, particularly from each other, we're wrong. Studying God's word makes the critical difference in a youth worker's ministry. Learning broadly would assist more youth workers than they and their church leaders realize. Hopefully, this chapter, though academically packed, will make this argument convincingly.

Heads up folks, this is a thick chapter, pretty academic. Material critically supports ARM, but it's not necessary to understand everything to capably see and serve through an ARM lens. So, those who like discussing theology and theory, have fun. Those who don't? Read quickly, not stressing about grasping everything. Slow back down a little for chapter 6, where we start the glide back down the academic mountain into the most practical chapters 7–10. When there, dance back and forth a little between those chapters and 5 and 6. Some "ohhh, ok, now I get it" moments will probably occur.

Ministry and Theology

In today's climate, we take pictures of a beautiful landscape to post online, without actually ever pausing in stillness to admire the beauty, notice every aspect of it, and notice the context that surrounds it. In youth ministry we often wolf down a meal that God provides (via His word, a message, wise counsel, or time in meditation) less concerned with digesting it than with regurgitating it in a blog, podcast, or Youth Group meeting. Thankfully, when we acknowledge struggles, God graciously helps us regain our focus on our first love.

Biblical Perspective

Our First Love, God Himself, has to be loved with all our hearts, all our souls, and all our minds. We start by spending time with God in His word, getting to know His heart and mind so we can closely resemble Him. We grow in His likeness as we follow Christ, going where He would go and doing what He would do. As Christ did, we will learn how to manifest the name of God (John 17:6). We love God and others as God loves us. Jesus made sure to teach us this truth that all God fearing Israelites understood intellectually and emotionally. Not all Christians do. If we love others apart from this love, our love will soon run out. Many of those who know Him only marginally base their receptivity to Him on how much they feel He has cared for them.

"No one cares how much you know until they know how much you care." While this pithy cliché may accurately summarize people's perspectives, many do not realize that what we know often (not always) facilitates how much we care. It also facilitates our competency in communicating that care. There is also an aspect of this saying that is simply not true for many, but we'll wait until chapter 7 to deal with that reality.

"You shall be careful to present My offering, My food for My offerings by fire, of a soothing aroma to me, at their appointed time" (Num 28:2). I've always taught my students those who do without thinking just do—do. They do—do. Those who just think, justink, just stink. Doing one thing without the other does not present the aroma of Christ, an aroma soothing to God (Lev 4; 2 Cor 2:15). I know, this is hurting humor, but it does introduce the point I want to emphasize here. "You are presenting defiled food upon My altar. But you say, 'How have we defiled You?' In that you say, 'The table of the LORD is to be despised' (Mal 1:7)."

Ministry leaders who pretend to worship God, but make evident their lack of honoring Him in their good enough, but not excellent offerings, actually profane the name of God. Those

> Those whose hearts are "so on fire" and are so busy that they have little time to pray, study God's word, or develop theologically, personally dictate to God the parameters of their sacrifices and ministry.

whose hearts are "so on fire" and are so busy that they have little time to pray, study God's word, or develop theologically, personally dictate to God the parameters of their sacrifices and ministry. The primary sin of the priests? Their utter ignorance of the essence of God's desires and/or refusal to pay attention to the ones they clearly understood. Many youth workers love God with all their hearts. How many with all their minds?

Some try to manifest Christ, feeling in love with Christ, but not knowing Him. They're intrigued by the power of the Holy Spirit, but fail to understand the Holy Spirit's mission to glorify Christ in us and through us. Whimsical awareness of and response to His presence and use/ignorance of select passages of the Bible limit ability to know Christ as He desires to be known, therefore limiting capacity to represent Him. Craving God's presence, many manufacture it. For some, His "presence" often has more to do with arrested psychological development (emotionally stuck relative to an unresolved issue of the past) than to conscious conviction to proclaim His name.

Many see and express Christ as more of a Picasso painting than a rock. Their creative work attracts attention and applause, though more often to themselves or trophy ministries than to Christ. Their followers end up looking more like them than Christ. When their youth end up leaving the church it's often because God "let them down" or they stopped believing in the reliability of the Bible—even though they may have never really studied it. They may all have good hearts but they have not been (or are not being) transformed by the renewing of their minds (Rom 12).

God gave us Special Revelation by the way of Jesus Christ and His word. He gave us General Revelation by His visible, stunning, and profound creation. Both communicate the laws of God. Both, with deeper level effort, can be studied so as to reveal the stunning truth, beauty, and consistencies behind His unimaginable imagination realized. For those who dissect His word, His sky, His oceans, His lands, His history, His people groups, His human beings, His plant life, and His animal life, seeking to discover more of Him, they will be blessed much by what they get, but more in how much more understanding of His love they're able to give.

Practical Theology and Ministry

Practical theology means "relating to others with openness, attentiveness, and prayerfulness . . . opening up the possibilities of the I-Thou relationship in which others are known and encountered in all their uniqueness and otherness, a quality of relationship that ultimately depends on the communion-creating presence of the Holy Spirit" leaders give to people.[1] Such ministry requires that youth workers reconcile careful psychosocial study of the context of the youth with careful theological study of Scripture.[2] In other words, to make disciples of adolescents, we'll need to follow the example of missionaries, learning difficult languages and consuming foods we're not real excited to eat. True ministry never has been and never will be easy; youth workers must not only be psycho-socially and theologically astute, they must also offer presence in ministry, the availability of one's heart and mind being the key ingredients.

Incarnational Ministry

"Isn't this what we've been doing"? Les Christie and I were talking at an *AYME (Association of Youth Ministry Educators)* conference and that was his quietly stated reaction to this "new" emphasis by the speaker. Many innovative advocates of incarnational ministry methods lament that youth ministry from 1980s to early 2000s had become too socially and psychologically strategic and too programmatically oriented to building bigger ministries. Some offer alternative ideas, focusing on what they present as truly practical, relational, authentic or incarnational.

Most suggest we need to represent Jesus personally, as we enter deeply into another's life.[3] In practicing incarnational ministry we invest ourselves into others so as to try to manifest the presence and love of Christ in their lives. Countless writing efforts over the last twenty years emphasize such an approach under varied names: "incarnational" (Gerali, 2001; Wells, 2017); "pacing with" (Dunn, 2001); "presence-centered" (King, 2006); "be with" (Boshers and Poling, 2006; Wells, 2017); "place sharing" (Root, 2007); "Jesus Centered" (Lawrence, 2007); "a spirituality of presence" (Osmer, 2008); "one on one/connect" (McKee, 2009);

---

1. Osmer, *Practical Theology*, 33–34.

2. Jacober, *Adolescent Journey*, 15–47.

3. John 15; Gerali, "Seeing Clearly," 295.

"integration" (Diaz, 2013); "cohabitation/cantus firmus" (Keuss, 2014); "authentic" (Moore, 2016); "warmth" (Powell et al., 2016), and "movement" (Woodward and White, Jr. 2016).[4] Based on personal experiences in ministry, some authors and speakers seem to believe that still today, youth ministries stray from this ministry maxim.

TRADITIONAL RELATIONSHIPS OR RELEVANT AUTHENTIC RELATIONSHIPS?

Relative to our life callings and the shape of the world today, some of the trendy concerns for youth ministry are entirely valid. Some are not. It is true that many have approached reaching young people *too* strategically. It is also true that our sociologies, psychologies, and organizational leadership models have influenced many ministries too strongly. And it is also true that some people in the church far too confidently revere traditional theology and religious practice more than the written word and influence of the Holy Spirit. "But if our children reject the core truths of Christianity because we have expected and assumed that they would accept our preferred approach to church (ministry), may God have mercy on us."[5]

Relative to the ways in which recent literature describes "authentic," however, there are several issues of concern. First, not all people have the same depth of need for the emotional side of such ministry. It seems that in zealous oversight, critical relational need differences in many teenagers are minimized or ignored. Some "authentic" ministry also seems to deemphasize Christ's teachings and stated expectations in relationships.

> It seems that in zealous oversight, critical relational need differences in many teenagers are minimized or ignored. Some "authentic" ministry also seems to deemphasize Christ's teachings and stated expectations in relationships.

---

4. Gerali, "Seeing Clearly," 295; Dunn, *Shaping*, 16; King, *Presence-Centered*, 112; Root, *Revisiting Relational Youth Ministry*, 77–94; Lawrence, *Jesus Centered*; Osmer, *Practical Theology*, 33; Boshers and Poling, *Be-With Factor*, 19; Moore, *Authentic Youth Ministry*; Keuss, *Blur*, 33; McKee, *Connect*, 46–61; Diaz, *Redefining the Role of the Youth Pastor*, 50; Woodward and White, *Church as Movement*, 18–27; Wells, *Incarnational Ministry*, 723.

5. Kricher, *For a New Generation*, 19.

In addition to hanging out with sinners (Luke 15:2) and assisting the poor (Matt 19:21), Jesus also teaches doctrinal position (Matt 16:11–12; 17:15–20; John 6:59; 7:17; 2 John 1:9) and expects life change response and obedience to His teaching (John 3:36; 8:11; Matt 5:48; Gal 6:1–2). "The study of the doctrine of Christ is central to the Christian faith."[6] Relationships grounded in doctrinal truth empower them. Paul sternly warns that relationships disregarding Jesus' doctrinal teaching destroy them.[7] "In vain do they worship Me, teaching as doctrines the precepts of man."[8]

Second, we have major youth ministry thought leaders today turning God's passion for substance over appearance literally upside down, advocating, up front on stage, to select leaders using what amounts to be Hollister's physical appearance based model over God's heart based model.[9] Incredibly popular conference gatherings offer lots of style, but some unabashed teaching at them distresses God. According to one speaker, the "New Model of Youth Ministry" more practically reduces youth ministry meetings down to one monthly rally, and one weekly "Interest Affinity" small group (in homes). This approach steadfastly allows for only 15 minutes per week of either Bible "Study" *or* prayer *or* chilling together listening to Christian music. I'm saddened, but not surprised that some seriously growing churches and leaders hold these perspectives ("for the time will come when they will not endure sound doctrine."[10]) Popular teaching doesn't necessarily negate or equate to right teaching, but keep in mind this thought, "Son, rats don't like poison, but they love peanut butter. If you put just enough poison with something they love, they'll be fooled into eating the deadly poison every time."[11] Five hearts in mode of surrender to God indicate more fruit than five-thousand amused tour or rally attendees. Be discerning.

Some "Practical" theologies and philosophies harm and inhibit youth ministry more than some psychological and sociological insights. As the megachurch model grows in admiration, note that church size and commitment to doctrine almost always inversely relate, the larger the church, the thinner the commitment to Jesus' doctrinal standards.

6. Geisler and Potter, *Doctrine of Christ*, 7.

7. 1 Tim 6:3–5.

8. Matt 15:9.

9. Kaplan, *Rise and Fall*, line 2; there are two youth-ministry-conference-leading-organizations today, that I know of, whose speakers advocate for such. Be discerning.

10. 2 Tim 4:3.

11. Quintana, *Momentum*, 180.

So, when a conference speaker from a megachurch starts to speak, hear through scriptural filters. Those who limit the authority and trust of Scripture, emphasizing differences in human interpretation over clear Godly inspiration (neo-orthodoxy), sabotage ministry credibility. Those who create new perspectives on Scripture desperately trying to be dramatically "relevant" (heterodoxy) actually nullify their relevance. Additionally, there are several ironies relative to the criticisms of traditional youth ministry being too reliant on the social sciences.

Some who criticize the psychological influences on traditional youth ministry cloak their new approaches in theological language, yet reflect more psychological orientation than those they criticize. Also, relative to *fundamentalist* churches (those seemingly most associated with traditional programs), these churches typically vet out potential youth leaders with psychological leanings during their interview processes. I know this personally as one church where I worked almost did not hire me because of their concern for my education in Psychology. Additionally, a main cog in current emphases of a few today rightfully advocates *for more sociologically aware ministry*. Paying attention to cultural context and community appears as a valuable hot theme in evolving ministry literature.[12]

Third, I disagree that what is identified today as incarnational or relational ministry has been mostly neglected by the church in any time period or by those who have ministered via "traditional" or "strategic" models. Many assumptions based on one's own flawed experiences accompany disparaging beliefs, comments, and deconstructions of traditional approaches.[13]

Jim Rayburn's "we're not into religion; we're all about relationship"[14] has been the primary mantra of most parachurch and church youth min-

12. See Clark, *Adoptive Youth Ministry*; Folmsbee, *Gladhearted Disciples*; Arzola, *Towards a Prophetic Youth Ministry*.

13. If one carefully reads some recent literature criticizing traditional approaches, it seems possible that the problems experienced were more with the abilities and theologies of those dismissing their effectiveness.

14. I realize that Root contends that Rayburn's (and Young Life's) motto really is not incarnational in that relationships were/are used to build programs more than to care for the souls of the youth. While he makes fair points relative to many ministries and a common problem within Young Life that too many ministries focus on numbers, I disagree that most traditional church and parachurch ministry leaders simply cultivate relationships for the purpose of growing a ministry numerically. Most often, the pressure for numerical growth, stated or implied, starts higher up the authority ladder than the Youth Pastor.

istries for a long time. One would have to be half brain dead not to be able to at least *say* the right thing. "It's all about relationships"! And I have a hunch that someone *was doing relational* (incarnational) youth ministry before that too. Agreeing with Christie, I'm not so sure this "new" emphasis on building deep relationships in youth ministry is so new. While most going into ministry leadership typically proceed with intent to bring glory to God, those in ministry of every generation have proven distractible and fallible. Ministry relationships have always reflected that.

We all get too busy. So busy, that sometimes even the people who we care most about, become background figures in the daily motion of life. Family members, neighbors, and yes even young people in youth group occasionally blur into and out of the world of constant movement. Then someone shares that Tom's grandparent just died. Or that Ann is pregnant. We might think, "Wow, I just saw him/her at youth group yesterday and he/she didn't say anything, but now, come to think of it, he/she really did seem awful down." To a hurting young person, it really doesn't matter what we know, didn't know, or don't know. Remember, developmentally and paradoxically, teens often operate as if they're the center of the universe. What matters to Tom and Ann, is if I truly cared, I should have seen something was wrong. Even though I do care, the perception is that I didn't or don't. And, he or she is right, on one level. And wrong on another level. I know I do care. The paradoxes of life.

If I were truly concerned, I would have checked. While ultimately I care, in that needed moment, I didn't care, at least not enough. When I don't care enough, it means in the moment, I don't care. This is why true reconciliation with others requires frequent repentance. While a teen doesn't "care how much you know," her perception of your care, and therefore your relationship, *might hinge entirely on how much you know.* One's compassionate, theologically sober, and psychosocially trained empathy to competently hear and sit with her in her pain, and then to help her move on from that pain or adapt to it, impacts ministry successes.

MINISTRY EXPERIENCE AND PSYCHOSOCIAL EDUCATION

Education and experience have taught me that not all youth want and/ or need the same kind of relationships. All youth benefit from practical ministry in some way, but not all need it in the same ways. For many teens, their conscious considerations of God hover far more in the intellectual realm than in the emotional arena. Some youth may actually far prefer to see how much one knows (sociologically, theologically, philosophically, etc.) with little concern as to how much one cares before they're willing to even consider giving a youth worker a chance at providing an incarnational relationship.

Society and schools evangelistically advance atheistic perspectives today, and many of today's young, coming from loving and unloving homes, consider themselves to be atheists. As representatives of God, no matter how competent or careful we may be, many students have already formulated opinions that we're not worth their time investment. Christians represent *the ignorant.*[15] Therefore, the offer of capable intellectual dialogue may stand more chance of eliciting interest from some teenagers than does an offer of friendship.

Lastly, lack of knowing tolerates lack of caring. Often we don't want to know something because we know that if we know more, we'll have to care more and thus, either be stimulated to do something, or suffer the guilt because we won't, or the pain because we can't. Thus, if we're not striving

> Therefore, the offer of capable intellectual dialogue may stand more chance of eliciting interest from some teenagers than does an offer of friendship.

to know more about God, His Word, His children, and how we can intentionally minister to them, specifically relative to their greatest needs, we must be careful about saying that we care and that we believe in relational ministry. What we know, influences how diligently and successfully we may communicate our care, where impact equals intent. We need to know the Bible and how to understand people.

The merging of Biblical teaching, Attachment Theory, Social Learning/ Cognitive Theory and Systems Theory creates a holistic framework for

> What we know influences how diligently and successfully we may communicate our care, where impact equals intent.

understanding the basic needs, personalities, and spiritual and behavioral responses of most people (see Figure 2). Since I believe most youth leaders know Biblical principles about relationships well, this chapter focuses on a thorough review of Social Science theory which complements

15. Chamorro-Premuzic, "Why Are Religious People Generally Less Intelligent," lines 10–38; Harris, *End of Faith*, 13.

Scripture. After the review, in the next chapter I'll present ARM, the Attachment Relationship Ministry model.

FOUNDATIONAL SOCIAL SCIENCE THEORIES UNCOVERING GOD'S TRUTH

Systems Theories

In this section we're going to consider two systems oriented theories, Bronfenbrenner's *Ecological Systems Theory* and Bowen's *Family Systems Theory*. Bronfenbrenner suggested that people can be understood relative to interactive influences of common cultural systems surrounding them.[16] Key systems impacting a child include peers, family, school, church (microsystems), media and technology (mesosystems), and government (macrosystem). Murray Bowen adapted aspects of General Systems Theory to explain how the family in particular influences a child more than any other system.[17]

Ministries which abandon programs and/or trade youth ministries for family based approaches may demonstrate awareness of the importance of system influences, but they show a lack of understanding regarding critical nuances of systems. Systems seek equilibrium, they *resist* change, particularly those within a system who hold the power. Systems with staunchly closed boundaries foster unhealthy environments as much as entirely open systems (see Figure 1—rigidly enmeshed v chaotically disengaged). Change in one member of a system (a teen) *necessitates change* in all other members (and subsystems[18]) of a system. Change within a subsystem (siblings) applies more pressure than one unit (person). Practically speaking, any youth ministry initiated change in a teen unsettles many parents and whole families.

---

16. See Erwin, *Critical Approach to Youth Culture*.

17. See Olson, *Circumplex Model*. David Olson developed the circumplex model, on which figure 1 is entirely based upon. Ludwig Von Bertalanffy originated the idea of General Systems Theory in his work in the field of biology.

18. Subsystems are comprised of smaller groupings within a family. A dad and his sons. A mom and her daughters. Siblings. The married couple.

Youth Leaders Already Do Family Ministry

When my relationship with Christ became real, I encouraged my parents to take our stated Christian faith more seriously. My mother told me that while she was happy for me, not to expect anything in our (dysfunctional, culturally Christian) home to change. But over the next few years, my brothers and mother began to consider God and her faith in Christ way more seriously. My father always had, but hardly discussed, his very simple faith in Christ. Through a *System's Theory* perspective, the following explains how these dominos fell.

Because I no longer behaved as I did previously, that dramatically effected the ways I interacted with my family members. My twin brother, Don, and I had grown up doing almost everything together, a strong twin brother subsystem. He resented the changes in me because it changed how we were able to socially interact with our friends, and thus his lifestyle. He also grew curious. After an evangelical fist fight between us and a couple of years contemplating Christ, Don acknowledged his self-centered lifestyle and re-committed to following Christ.[19] Soon after, he quit a high paying job to join a parachurch youth ministry organization, having to raise his support.

The Circumplex Model of Family Systems					
		Low	*Levels of Cohesion*		*High*
Levels of Flexibility		*Disengaged*	*Separated*	*Connected*	*Enmeshed*
High	*Chaotic*	*Chaotically Disengaged*	*Chaotically Separated*	*Chaotically Connected*	*Chaotically Enmeshed*
	Flexible	*Flexibly Disengaged*	*Flexibly Separated*	*Flexibly Connected*	*Flexibly Enmeshed*
	Structured	*Structurally Disengaged*	*Structurally Separated*	*Structurally Connected*	*Structurally Enmeshed*
Low	*Rigid*	*Rigidly Disengaged*	*Rigidly Separated*	*Rigidly Connected*	*Rigidly Enmeshed*

Figure 1: Adapted from: Olson et al., Families, 1989 (Circumplex Model, p. 50). The more central the square, the more balanced and healthier the family dynamics relative to cohesion and adaptability (flexibility). The four corners indicate unhealthy family dynamics.

19. My ministry at home was fairly raw in its approach. I decided one day that I was going to interfere with Don in his doing something he wanted to do, no matter what it took. The Lord blessed the intent more than the approach. I don't recommend this style of evangelism.

My parents and older brother were disappointedly stunned. But soon, my mother, who admitted noticing some positive changes in her sons, started worshipping Christ in a more robust church and then acknowledged her need of Christ as her Savior. Over the following few years Don had as many conversations with Bob about God, Scripture, marriage, and heaven and hell as I did, strengthening a previously passable three brother subsystem. Bob, my mother's clear favorite (an unhealthy codependent subsystem) and in an uneasy marriage, skeptically participated in these conversations with baffled interest.[20] When he divorced, he realized his attempts to love his wife and children more than Christ, failed them all. He started reading the Bible regularly and after a year or two found in Christ the love he desired to have and to give.

Despite clear "imperfections" in all of us, we seem to be working well together to reach other family members who would benefit by more of Christ's love and leading. This personal example illustrates how dominoes ideally fall within a family when a teen brings spiritual changes home. Those who do youth ministry do family ministry.

Dealing with parents in youth ministry (see Figure 2) frequently proves the most difficult aspect of one's responsibilities. Healthy parents articulate desires and expectations for the ministry that conflict with each other (see middle four squares of Figures 1 and 2). Unhealthy parents exert pressure to succumb to their unhealthy tendencies (see outside four corner squares of Figures 1 and 2). When teenagers mess up, *deficient* youth ministries become everyone's easy scapegoat.

Appropriate youth ministry, ARM, actually assists families more than many family-focused ministries. Those who lead via other ministry titles (Lead, Associate, Children, etc.) also do family ministry. We all do family ministry indirectly through those with whom we work with directly. I choose to continue to work in youth ministry because teenagers are the most likely effective change agents in a family system. Developmentally teens are wired to resist conformity and behave correspondingly. Parents try hard to maintain rules and roles (written and unwritten), even when they know they're not healthy or working. Typically, children hold the least power in a family.

Most people thrive more in a healthy system than outside of one. Look at different NFL QBs who credit their own and their teammates' successes to their "systems." Unhealthy systems resist individuals wanting

---

20. Being the favorite had privileges, but not enough to outweigh the costs.

to be healthy. We need accountability and complementarity in the context of the church system's unified representation of Jesus Christ. Utilizing insights from System's Theory enhances the way I build community within the spheres of my personal and ministry influence. Similarly, they enhance the ministries of those who apply what they've learned as part of those communities.

Attachment Theory

Attachment theory originated with God since the beginning of time, but it was identified and shaped as a concept by John Bowlby from the 1960s through the 1980s.[21] *Attachment* describes the style of relationship an infant forms with his or her parent(s). This style shapes the way a person perceives one's own worth and interacts in every other relationship (including relationship with God) for the rest of life. Mary Ainsworth helped Bowlby to propose two potential types of infant-parent attachment relationships: Secure and Insecure.[22]

Insecure attachments break down further into three more descriptive and specific alternatives: Avoidant (one mistrusts and thus avoids an attachment figure); Anxious or Ambivalent (one mistrusts and thus clings to, agitates, or forces relationship with an attachment figure); and Disorganized (one both trusts AND distrusts the attachment figure, leading to random and unpredictable ways of behaving in relationship). Glasser suggests that rejection by attachment figures provokes people's core anxieties and consequentially, they develop desires to either destroy or abandon attachment figures.[23] Siegel suggests approximations of the percentage of the population that comprise each of these types: Secure (50–66 percent), Avoidant (20 percent), Anxious (15 percent), and Disorganized (5–15 percent).[24] One-half of today's population prove insecure in distance from God, crooked personal relationships, and askew psychosocial functioning.

Early attachment styles seriously impact how teenagers feel about themselves ("internal-working models") in terms of worth and potential in this world. They influence how adolescents behave in every potential

21. See Bowlby, *Attachment*.

22. See Ainsworth, *Patterns of Attachment*.

23. Nathanson, "Embracing Darkness," 272–84.

24. Siegel, *Brainstorm*, 149–54.

new relationship. The secure demonstrate balance between proximity seeking (relational contact) and exploratory (seeking to discover new parts of the world) behaviors.[25] These children grow into autonomous adults. Insecure-avoidant teens become dismissive adults. Insecure-anxious teens become adults preoccupied with real and desired relationships. Disorganized children become unsettled adults.[26] While youth leaders may find the adult descriptions more suitable for how they see their teens interacting with them and others, I use the child descriptors throughout this text because it's one way for me to emphasize that teen attachment patterns are not yet fixed! Because adolescent years are so critical in reshaping self-perceptions, our interaction with teens seriously impacts every future relationship (including the one with God) they'll ever have.

Securely attached people tend to trust others and have more reciprocally healthy psychosocial relationships. Due to unresolved intra-and inter-personal pains, insecurely attached people frequently struggle in all relationships, but more so with healthy people. *Anxiously* insecure people tend to become more easily jealous, co-dependent, and thus, demanding in relationships. *Avoidant* personalities guard emotions, dodge vulnerability, and therefore struggle with an ability to grow intimate with others. Disorganized people display a variety both in breadth and intensity of these issues. Bowlby believed that a person's attachment type would remain with a person for the rest of one's life.

Adolescent Attachment Potential

Recent research supports that people's internal working models remain intact up to adolescence, but that starting in adolescence, self-perceptions (and therefore, interpersonal patterns) become *open to revision.* As adolescents re-experience rapid physiological upheavals similar to those of two-year olds, crises spread across the spectrum of a person spiritually, intellectually, and emotionally. Who a person is physically makes a difference in who he or she is spiritually, emotionally and intellectually, and thus socially. As the adolescent begins to developmentally seek and experience autonomy, he or she begins to re-evaluate previous attachment relationships and to seek to form new ones, particularly not with parents.

25. Underwood and Dailey, *Counseling Adolescents Competently*, 54.

26. See Hughes, *8 Keys to Building Your Best Relationships.*

Circumplex Model Immersed with Attachment Concepts and Parenting Styles					
		Low	Levels of Cohesion		High
Levels of Flexibility		Disengaged	Separated	Connected	Enmeshed
High	Chaotic	Chaotically Disengaged Unpredictably Insecure Fearful Teen Independent Detached or Uninvolved Parents	Chaotically Separated	Chaotically Connected	Chaotically Enmeshed Insecure Fearful Teen Co-dependent Passive or Permissive Parents
	Flexible	Flexibly Disengaged	Flexibly Separated, Secure Teen Parents lean Authoritative	Flexibly Connected, Secure Teen Parents lean Authoritative	Flexibly Enmeshed
	Structured	Structurally Disengaged	Structurally Separated Secure Teen Authoritative Parents	Structurally Connected Secure Teen Authoritative Parents	Structurally Enmeshed
Low	Rigid	Rigidly Disengaged Frustrated Insecure Angry Teen Authoritarian Rejecting Parents	Rigidly Separated	Rigidly Connected	Rigidly Enmeshed Frustrated Insecure Angry Teen Authoritarian Parents

Figure 2: Attachment Concepts and Parenting Styles (adapted from Huggins, Parenting Adolescents, 1992) immersed into Olson et al.'s Circumplex Model. This is a theoretical model supporting recommendations for ministry in chapters 7–10. Parents in the different quadrants emphasize authority, rules, roles, duty, trust, demonstration of loyalty, and willingness to adjust differently from one another. Teens respond accordingly. Olson has recently updated the Circumplex Model relative to an updated measure (FACES IV).

Today a critical misunderstood assumption about teenagers exists; teens prefer peers to adults. Though teens share similar interests with each other and may prefer spending the majority of their social time with peers, most adolescents yearn for and/or enjoy interaction with non-parental adults, especially the teens one least suspects.[27] For example, on the surface, it might appear that a teen girl has a great relationship with her mother and doesn't need another female adult role model in her life. But, insecure anxious females, in overprotective, enmeshed relationships with their mothers (see bottom right corner in Figure 2), actually develop internalizing struggles (e.g., fearful, somatic complaints) and desperately need chats with objective leaders.[28] Having a non-parental adult leader available to listen helps this young lady to share her fears, actually addressing the source problem of those fears. Individuating (rebelling) requires reevaluating personal and family development dynamics. Teens depend on input from and interaction with respected adults to individuate successfully. (So do parents.)

While adolescents may subconsciously feel motivated to change unhealthy attachment styles, they also subconsciously resist such changes. Paradoxically, they'll look for ways to convince themselves that their dysfunctional relational ways are actually valid. Because most teens are not aware of their own internal battles, it is so important for youth workers to be aware. Awareness helps intentional youth workers to relationally fight on behalf of a youth to facilitate right relationship with that same youth.

Research suggests insecure teens preoccupied with attachment desires most likely suffer from maladaptive external (e.g., delinquency) and internal (e.g., cutting, depression, anorexia) behaviors.[29] Antisocial behaviors represent teens' misguided attempts to find someone who cares. Rather than addressing the needs and behaviors of troubled youth, however, adult society generally responds punitively, ambivalently, or superficially—reinforcing already poor self-perceptions.

Whereas life change presents as possible for anyone with the help of the Holy Spirit, we can fairly easily help those most predisposed to be receptive to the direct and indirect influence of the Holy Spirit. Again, ministry experience and research indicate that adolescent intra-personal awareness and inter-personal styles turn vulnerable.[30]

While those most inclined to utilize the insights of attachment theory with adolescents do so through professional therapy, youth leaders are those by proximity and responsibility who seem most capable in helping

27. See Larson, *At Risk*.

28. Pauletti et al., "Sex Differences," 390–404.

29. Belsterling, "Adolescent Attachment," 236.

30. Belsterling, "Adolescent Attachment," 236.

teens to reimagine themselves and their own worth to society. Research affirms the youth leader as a viable attachment figure.[31]

Social Cognitive Learning Theory

The key goals of Bandura's theory, which started in the 1960's with his research on imitation, are to help people anticipate positive outcomes, correct self-deficiencies, and find ways to succeed no matter the environment. These emphases seem quite complicit with Scriptural teaching.

Bandura's research has always highlighted the prominent role of models in peoples' lives. People learn best by watching models. They watch how mentors adjust, assimilate, express their thoughts and feelings, and how aware they are of their own and others' behaviors (failures and successes).[32] Essential learning takes place through "mirror neurons,"

> Essential learning takes place through "mirror neurons," neurons which enable people to soak up the feelings of those around them.

neurons which enable people to soak up the feelings of those around them. According to one of Bandura's fundamental tenets, youth leaders can generate "triadic-reciprocal causation" for young people. First, they help adolescents to learn how to self-regulate through discussions, prayer, and journaling, which in turn helps them to learn how to anticipate positive outcomes, desire to correct self-deficiencies, and manage an environment. Second, teens gain a sense of positive mastery via learning and leading opportunities, such as playing guitar or cleaning a neighborhood. Third, teens learn vicariously as they observe those who model trustworthiness and innovative spirit. According to Bandura, each of these social-learning experiences reciprocally influences each so as to cognitively restructure teen's brains as to how they feel about how they fit into this world.

Current research on human brains affirms Bowlby's, Bandura's and God's beliefs that social interaction with attachment-models literally stimulates individual neural change.[33] Social experiences revamp

---

31. Belsterling, "Youth Work," 31–47.

32. Siegel, *Brainstorm*, 153.

33. Belnap, "Current Trends in the Diagnosis and Treatment," 179–86: Belnap discovered that babies who are held more often develop enhanced dendrite formation in

adolescents' brains, how they think and develop patterns of thinking. Interacting in youth ministries with Godly, positive, adult role models helps develop potential for present and future discerning decisions. In Scripture an inspired Paul encourages adults to pour into youth and the church to foster the unity of the body for reasons God knows—and now we do too.[34] With God's insights, Paul encourages Christians "imitate God" and "imitate me."[35] The writer of Hebrews advocates imitating the faith of leaders. John warns against imitating those who do evil.

Relative to differing relational needs, different teens need different ministry emphases. To varying extents, some youth may need to experience mastery of something in life and to anticipate positive outcomes more than anything else. Others may need to learn how to self-regulate emotionally. Typically, young people who are secure with God and parents look more similar to youth not secure with God in their needs than to other youth who are secure with God. How do we know which youth need what?

Ministry Leader Response
I may come across abrasively in presenting these theological beliefs, so forgive me. I'm not trying to. Paul describes mankind apart from God as "dead in sins" (Eph 2:1–2). Man is part of the kingdom of darkness, immersed and blinded, and complete enemies of God. How can a dead person unknowingly know something about God? The fall of man is a turning from God. Because of this, everything man develops is futile.
I'm not convinced that an engineer can communicate an equation to me that clues me in to who God is. Besides, I don't need an equation for knowing God's vastness. I can simply stand at the summit of any local mountain here in Seattle and marvel at the vastness of God. I believe I Cor. 1:20–25 confirms this root idea: "Where is the wise man? Where is the scholar? Where is the philosopher of this age"? The wisdom of man is foolishness to God. Additionally, Job 28:1–23 indicates that true wisdom and understanding are NOT found in the realm of man. It lies only with God.
Therefore I am not convinced secular psychology (engineering or whatever field) has an avenue for understanding God.
Matt Elser, Pastor of Student Ministries, Mountain View Community Church, Snohomish, WA

The ARM model identifies the most basic needs of young people, helping youth leaders to more accurately attempt to meet them. To

---

the brain, making these children more intellectually capable in later years; Escobar et al., "Brain Signatures of Moral Sensitivity in Adolescents." Arain et al., "Maturation of the Adolescent Brain," 449–61.

34. Eph 4; Titus 2.

35. Eph 5:1; 1 Cor 11:1; Matt 5:16; John 17:6.

remove the "shoulds" out of one's life, unfortunately as Bandura also suggests, shows spiritual irresponsibility, no matter how genuinely motivated. As a Youth Pastor, offering potential "should" suggestions (*only after listening*) might help teens to visualize themselves in new ways, potentially escaping not only society's labels, but also self labels. We cannot live socially responsibly, or communally/personally competently with no "shoulds" or "oughts."

Theology, Psychology, and Sociology

Youth leaders must present as trustworthy as God is trustworthy. Whether youth hunger emotionally (Ps 56:3), psychologically (Judg 6:12), physically (Exod 16:13), socially (Gen 2:18), and/or spiritually (Ps 73:25), we must feed them with God's provision. People have varying relational needs. When we meet others relative to these needs we manifest Christ as completely as possible, and essentially cultivate attachment relationships as we succeed. And in the context of those attachments, we can motivate spiritual curiosity and growth by highlighting the many awe inspiring activities of God in and through the lives of Christians and non-Christians alike.

There are engineers who based on their understanding of God's physical universe and its laws, astound me with the beautiful and functional bridges and buildings they design. There are non-Christian navigators, and meteorologists, and oceanographers, who understand aspects of the creation of God that I wish I knew. Many of their discoveries affirm "Intelligent Design" and biblical reliability. There are social scientists who have committed their lives to understanding the workings of the human mind and human relationships; Freud's theoretical dissection of the conscious, subconscious, and preconscious, fascinates and appears affirmed by much of today's neurological research. While none may be Christians, all have been created in the image of God and may have an avenue of understanding God (even if they don't know it) that can benefit our own understanding of God, if we consider their thoughts.

My relationship with my wife has been blessed for having read "thick"[36] books on love and marriage, like Gary Thomas' *Sacred Marriage*. My relationship with God has benefitted greatly from studying

---

36. Moreland, *Kingdom Triangle*, 269; "thicker" refers more to deep thought than literal pages.

Scripture and reading works written by C. S. Lewis, Francis Schaeffer, Charles Spurgeon, J.I. Packer, and Ravi Zacharias. Many of these writers have helped to translate Scripture in ways that have very much clarified it. Both of these relationships have been enhanced by my study of God's word, Christian writing, and the social sciences.[37] Both of these relationships enable me to effectively minister in all other relationships.

Nothing in the social sciences is revelatory; they only offer insights related to natural exploratory yearnings and valuable discovery of that which God revealed. They find it not of their own accord, whether acknowledging Him as Savior or not, but of God's unfolding, benevolence. If any social science teaching conflicts with scriptural teaching, it's wrong.

CONCLUSION

When utilized together the combination of the theories presented in this chapter filter out lots of social, political, and even religious noise that keeps youth workers from knowing how to engage youth, parents and multiple communities. Right now, some of this may feel overwhelming in terms of trying to either remember it all or apply what is being discussed. But, remember, chapters 7–10 show how to apply these concepts in very simple and practical ways. Filtering all thoughts and creating all plans through study of His word, prayer, and team discussions, will clarify directions to be taken.

"Deep calls to deep, the Lord will command His loving kindness in the daytime; and His song will be with me in the night." (Ps 42:78) Those who ponder God's ways carefully possess more possibility of demonstrating God's ways clearly. "All truth is God's truth." Pondering God's ways means allowing His word to transform our minds through both special and general revelation and through the insights of those who have studied both areas. Although the truth of Special Revelation provides the context and filter for interpreting general revelation (making the truth of

---

37. There is nothing I wish to do more than affirm the historicity and validity of Scripture, Sola Scriptura, as God's sole (by the illumination of His Spirit), authoritative revelation and filter, by which any and all allusions to, presentations of, or claims made about "truth" should be sifted. Clearly what Freud or any others postulate in one idea or a whole ideology, which conflicts with Scripture, should be entirely rejected. I reject much of Freud's teaching, as I reject some of C. S. Lewis' perspectives. I don't entirely trust any man's thoughts as purely God's thoughts. And, the Holy Spirit can speak to any human being.

Special Revelation authoritative over general revelation), Christian leaders benefit greatly from the intellectual ponderings and studied findings of those in the worlds of theology and the social sciences.

One last caveat, no doubt that many youth leaders today exemplify some of the points made or discussed in this chapter. Any finding this to be personally true, don't panic. No one is perfect. Most don't have perfect pasts. We can all be used by God powerfully. Simply pray for healing, and since awareness is the first step of healing, that restorative process has probably already begun, praise God. Seek accountable assistance, either professional or from a potentially dependable companion. I'm sure God has provided one to you, whether or not, you've allowed yourself to acknowledge it. Deny unhealthy relational instincts and steps one at a time. Prepare for a lifelong journey of struggle, our thorn in the flesh, so that should victory occur in this life, it's more appreciated than expected. Pray as Christ, in compassion for those who hurt you, as they probably also had their own difficult life experiences. Lastly, pray in gratitude for weaknesses, for despite them, God works. Praise Him.

PERSONAL CHALLENGE AND DISCUSSION QUESTIONS
FOR LEADERSHIP TEAMS

1. How are you inclined to see and express Christ? How do others on team diverge?

2. Respond to the idea that perhaps we can help another more by what we know than by how much we care.

3. How do you see the social sciences impeding or enhancing ministry?

CHAPTER 6

Attachment Relationship Ministry: The ARM of Christ

"Styles of attachment to God are more potent and consistent predictors of distress than are images of God." (Bradshaw et al., "Attachment to God, Images of God, and Psychological Distress," p. 143)

"We argue that attachment theory can help to deepen our understanding of the need for redemption and restoration, or a return to the "circle of attachment," culminating with a restored attachment bond between God and God's creation through the work and teachings of Jesus Christ." (Knabb and Emerson, "Attachment Theory and the Grand Metanarrative of Scripture," p. 829)

"If you can make sense of your childhood experiences, you can transform your attachment models toward security . . . your relationships with friends, romantic partners, with present or possible future offspring—will be profoundly enhanced." (Siegel, *Brainstorm*, p. 161)

THE YOUTH WORKER—ADOLESCENT RELATIONSHIP

WHY DO SOME YOUTH seem to withstand our worst efforts and others show no interest in our best? Why does the kid who complains so much keep coming back or connecting? Why do some friends of youth group members show sincere interest in us and our ministries, then fade away fairly quickly? How do we connect with some but not others? Why the differences? Is it personality? Chemistry? Busyness? Comfort or anger or apathy? Is there something wrong with us? Our programs? The church? A little bit of everything? Is there any way to healthfully connect with or get through to potentially every teen? Can we find the patience needed to be with youth who drive us crazy? How do we minister to those we have no idea exist?

We can increase the odds of healthy interaction and ministry with young people whom we currently are not reaching. If God can reach anyone, then we can too. In fact, we've been sent to find the ones we don't know exist—as we follow God's leading. Life-giving relationships hardly ever prove easy. The more clearly-relationally-intentional we are, however, the better shot we'll have with all of the teens identified above. Since young people have two basic relational needs and styles, we need to initiate and cultivate relationships with teens in generally four different critical ways (see Figures 1 and 4). For those with insecure relationships with parents, those two ways (quadrants) further divide one more time, relative to anxious/ambivalent or avoidant insecurity.

Attachment Relationship Ministry (ARM)		
Basic Relational Needs and Positions of All People:	*Secure Attachment with God (SG)*	*Insecure Attachment with God (IG)*
Secure Attachment with Parents(SP)	SGSP-Essentially Secure	IGSP-Socially Secure Spiritually Insecure
Insecure Attachment with Parents (IP)	SGIP-Spiritually Secure Socially Insecure	IGIP-Essentially Insecure

Figure 1. Basic Adolescent Relational Needs. [SGSP (Secure relationship with Parents and with God); IGSP (Secure relationship with Parents and Insecure with God); SGIP (Insecure with Parents and Secure with God); IGIP (Insecure relationship with God and with Parents)].

A PERSON'S GREATEST NEED?

What is the worst punishment in a prison? Of those who have been in prison, most will tell you—solitary confinement. In the United States, prisoners have shelter, food, and clothing. All basic needs met, except one: intimate relationship.

We were designed by God not just to be individuals, but to be persons within a people group. We were designed to be in community, fellowship, and relationship. Without relationship we die inside. If we in youth ministry want to help others, we must offer and build relationship(s), both vertically with God and horizontally with people.[1] We must work with God to connect people back to our God. If that is not our agenda, we may be in youth work, but we are not in youth ministry. "Getting people back to church is pointless unless God comes back first."[2] Getting kids to connect with other teens is pointless if those connections are not through Jesus Christ. Girlfriends and boyfriends provide fun and drama, but they're not critical relationships. Peer relationships prove more important yet, and while they're necessary for healthy social development, they're still not as critical as some others.

The paramount relationship a young person can have is with God through Jesus Christ. The second most important relationship that a young person has is with his or her parents (good or bad). As pointed out in chapter four, parents are the primary relationships God provides to people through whom He desires to communicate and bless. Unfortunately, many parents fail to introduce their children to God. Though the youth leader is important on the relational landscape, most of us know we can never replace a parent or perfectly represent God. We can, however, love adolescents in the way God does and a parent should. People's horizontal relationships with others, parents or peers, will never make as much sense or serve to fully facilitate community without the influence of the most important vertical relationship. Some teens wade through a world of broken relationships on all fronts.

We are called to bring redemption to individuals and communities. For teens who do not know God, we must verbally and non-verbally introduce them to God. Young people need to see, hear, feel, and share the love of the Gospel message. Value transmission occurs most successfully in that context.[3] Value

> We are called to bring redemption to individuals and communities.

---

1. Matt 22:37–39.

2. MacDonald, *Vertical Church*, 21.

3. Whitbeck and Gecas, "Value Attributions and Value Transmission," 829.

transmission is needed, as without proper values or with erroneous values, one will never feel worthwhile in a world filled with shifting meaning, morals, *and* social norms.

For teens in broken familial relationships, we must try to assist teens and parents to reconcile (though not right away). As an ally of both God and parent, we should make strong differences for teens who have either one or both of those relationships intact. Despite familial contexts, good or bad, we need to create a youth ministry context available to embrace every teen within reach and assure each one that he or she is a person of extreme worth.

GAME OF CLONES

In reality several groups of teens look more like one-another and more distinct from others than we may realize. The following games and characters, example teens, by no means represents an exhaustive list, but, they do help to demonstrate the profiles represented in ARM. The subheadings for these example teens are described via games that may make recall easier. The choice of games obviously represent my biases regarding them, but I imagine the titles and content will resonate for most. These profiles (see Figure 2) represent the teaser trailers to the rest of this chapter and the next four.

Monopoly[4]

We all have someone who seems to always want all of our attention. He might be the one who unfortunately *"has to"* sit in the front passenger seat of the Church van on almost every youth group trip. He might be the one who always seems to have a reason why he has no ride home after an all-day event. It may feel as though there is no limit, no end in sight, as to this person's craving and capacity to message, call, show up, text, pin, Snapchat, or Instagram. With social media platforms expanding, connections should grow even more! *(The exclamation mark represents sarcastic excitement.)*

Even the best youth leader will be tempted to ignore this teen. In true face to face interaction, the youth worker might find herself avoiding the Velcro-teen or being rude with her if avoidance proves impossible—the

4. My daughter Emily provided this game analogy. Thanks, Emily.

youth leader, perhaps subconsciously, hoping that he'll take the hint for the need for some space. But, no! He just keeps coming back, no matter how ill treated. Hints seem to have the reverse effect. The end never seems near in a *Monopoly* game and usually occurs when someone gives up. What started out as a planned fun endeavor becomes laborious. (Apologies to Monopoly fans.)

Twister

Has anyone ever made a hobby of complaining about the youth ministry? If it's a teen, an obvious oddity is that she regularly commits to group meetings, studies, and events. Why does someone who doesn't like the ministry, continue to willingly participate? These types of experiences confuse youth workers and compromise their sense of self-confidence in being able to (or sometimes even wanting to) navigate ministry to the adolescent population. This is why so many adults avoid teenagers, especially angry ones. These relationships, like *Twister*, require so many awkward maneuvers, the likelihood of a relationship collapsing before succeeding seems imminent, but it shouldn't. In these types of encounters, a youth leader takes one for the team. "Blessed are you when people insult and persecute you, and say all kinds of evil against you because of Me." (Jesus, Matt 5:11) Rather than causing one to question one's calling or competency, these experiences gift a youth leader with confirmation of calling and that he safely, represents God.

Life

Bored teens raised in the church comprise the majority audience in many youth groups, by the preference of the parents and the deference of the youth workers. Most of them feel like they've heard the same Bible stories, dictums, and principles, over and over (and over and over . . .) Many represent conscientious homes, where parents cautiously shield children from the morally downward spiraling culture. While these parents must be supported as to their desire to protect, they must also be challenged as to their desire to avoid any risk. Offering ministry experiences akin to *Exploding Kittens* (which I do like) seems out of the question. Some of these teens simply seem impossible to motivate. I dread the idea of playing *Life* even before we start. No one can get me excited to play that game, not even my daughter, though she tries. That's how some young people feel (inside) about God, church, and ministry.

Attachment Based Profiles of Teenagers		
Personality Profiles	*Secure-Attachment with God*	*Insecure-Attachment with God*
Secure Attachment with Parents	*(SGSP) As stable as a teen can be. Naïve-generous with trust. Many living on the extreme of either "on fire" or "bored/going through the motions."*	*(IGSP) Interest in God is likely complacent (agnostic-just doesn't care) or skeptical; Physically, Socially and Emotionally-essentially content.*
Insecure-Attachment with Parents	*(SGIP) Trust in God is intellectu-ally volitional more than emo-tionally stable. With ambivalent youth, this manifests in relation-ship with YW as extremely clingy and/or critical. With avoidant youth, this manifests in relation-ship with YW as unavailable or distant.*	*(IGIP) Extreme Internalization (quiet/avoiding-the potential cutter/SI) or Externalization (potentially agitating, rude, bitter, or loud/attention seek-ing). Primary difference from SGIP is no spiritual assent to God. Those raised in the church are typically more dif-ficult to work with.*
Figure 2: Adolescent Profiles		

Scotland Yard

There were times I felt a *no doubt about it* connection between a young person and myself and/or others in the youth ministry. Some of these kids seemed so sincerely interested in and happy when interacting with the group. I enjoyed their company and was excited for the potential new friendships. But then, bam, many of these young people disappeared for another month or longer. Later in the year I might see the likable guy at a game. We'd catch up, talk, joke, and laugh together; and then, out of the blue, he'd ask if anything was coming up. I'm thinking, "Ok, my instincts were right"! At the next event, I'd look for him, but he doesn't show up. After all of my strategic deducing, this teen often acts just like the thief in *Scotland Yard*, shows up then goes back in hiding. Like *Chutes & Ladders*, we need to go back to the start after every failed guess and/or move forward.

ADOLESCENT ATTACHMENT AND YOUTH WORKER REPRESENTATION OF GOD AND PARENT

As discussed in the last chapter, attachment describes the amount of security or insecurity a child senses in the trustworthiness of early interpersonal relationships. The more trustworthy and competent a child's caregiver, the more secure an attachment relationship becomes. Those with untrustworthy or unpredictable care develop insecure attachments and self-worth. For the last twenty-five years research demonstrates that because of similar rates of physiological change as that which occurs during infancy, attachment orientations become open to revision during adolescence. Noffke and Hall suggest that for a teenager, the building of a relationship with someone like a youth worker actually may trigger a person's development of neural networks, establishing a new neuronal basis for different ways of understanding and forging relationship with God.[5]

Young people learn self-worth by being loved and acknowledged by adults they discover they wish to be like. Young people prefer to "be with" people they want to "be like."[6] Not "be like" in terms of personality, career, etc. necessarily, but more in terms of being like the one who cares, who intentionally connects, who manifests a sense of life purpose, who makes a difference, who walks in integrity, etc. Teens need relationships with those who live truly and, therefore, truly live.[7] They also need those significant others to pass on how to truly live.[8] Concerned adults invest energy and time to figure out how to best communicate such a message, considering the personal life context of those they wish to love, reach, and guide.

While youth workers need to cultivate relationships with teenagers, some teenagers, based on attachment styles, need strategic intentional influence as much, if not more, than relationship. "Youth Pastors who view their youth ministries as strategic opportunities for long term kingdom influence have the potential for shaping a new generation of culturally

5. Noffke and Hall, "Attachment, Psychotherapy, and God Image," 57–78.

6. Heb 13:7.

7. Notice the differences in the Hebrew words for "live" (55 times) in Ezekiel; see 33:11 (chay/alive)—God lives; 12:19 (yashab/lurk or occupy)—people exist; 33:3–5 (chayah/come alive)—people live and give life to others; Isa 40:10–11; Zech 11:17; John 17:18: Those who serve as the arm of Christ will gather their lambs and lead them to be the presence and opportunity of life to others.

8. Deut 6; John 13–17.

relevant and theologically significant churches."[9] Some teenagers just desperately need relationship. Cultivating an (appropriate) relationship with a young person can never hurt, but it also may never directly help some young people either. Pause and think about how, truth be told, often "relational" ministries seem to make no more difference than supposedly plagued traditional ministries.

Lastly, youth workers should be aware of Reactive Attachment Disorder (RAD).[10] This disorder describes youth who not only cling and have anger outbursts, but a way of interacting with others in which their negative feelings for caregivers often are projected onto others. These projections are designed to treat other potential caregivers in ways that will force them to confirm an adolescent's distorted self-beliefs as unworthy. This is one reason why many insecure youth don't get along with peers and drive caring adults crazy. RAD often shows as lack of conscience, developmental delay, acute anxiety and/or depression, eating disorders, violent actions, and addictive tendencies.

Youth Need Different Types of Relationships

Fritz has it right when he states, "if we are losing our young people in the church today, it isn't for the lack of effort."[11] Just like I implied in chapter 3, working smarter, not harder provides the most hope for everyone. We need prayerfully crafted strategic relational effort and mentoring, not just effort and mentoring. Some young people need a teacher more than an advocate, a friend more than a teacher, or an unsettling mission trip more than a friend. Those in youth ministry are in the helping business—sent as Jesus was sent—to make a difference, both temporal and eternal, being all things to all people (1 Cor 9). The difference youth workers make should be able to be measured in the present and future relationships of the young people. Relationships in ministry are not the end goal, but a means to the end goal of helping youth to mature in rela-

> The difference youth workers make should be able to be measured in the present and future relationships of the young people.

---

9. Senter et al., *Four Views of Youth Ministry*, 127.

10. Siegel, *Brainstorm*, 155.

11. Fritz, *Art of Forming Young Disciples*. 46.

tionship with Jesus Christ. We can't save anyone. Agenda free youth ministry falls short of our mission.

Neither, a pure "being with" (Keuss, 2014; Root, 2009) model, nor a pure, spiritual shaping "strategic influence" (Fields, 2013; DeVries, 2008) model, suffices in ministry. Both are valuable. Both are incomplete.

The most successful kinds of ministry will involve youth workers who are cultivating authentic relationship within the context of well structured, and intentional, purposeful ministry. An emphasis on "what God is doing in the kingdom here and now" can only be appreciated when one understands what God desires in heaven in the future.[12] Youth Directors need to cultivate relationships with young people as potential representatives of parental love and of God's love, and thus, as potential representatives of adolescent-human attachment and adolescent-God attachment.

More than any other need, every teenager needs a youth worker to represent tangibly the love of God and the love of humanity. How a youth worker proceeds in meeting the primary relational needs of a young person depends very much on how the love of God and love of humanity has been experienced by a young person. Depending on life scenarios, youth workers may be a young person's first aware experience of a "parentally" caring adult, or first aware exposure to God's love and truth. He or she may be a young person's first experience of both.

Additionally, while all teens need youth workers to "go" (Matt 28:19) to them in their own worlds, they also need youth workers who, like Jesus, say, "Come to me, all who are thirsty" (John 7:37). All young people need to find places that provide routine opportunity to experience retreat, safety, stability, unadulterated truth, mature guidance, and healthy peer social interaction. Some will realize these things for the first time, while others will find refreshing affirmation. From a context of security, all teens need to be able to "go" somewhere so they can feel some sense of self-responsibility, and thus, ownership and positive self-esteem, in individuating and taking steps forward in their own and others' maturation and/or recovery. (See illustration story in ch. 7 where my youth, in a "go" experience, bump into one of their friends selling drugs.)

---

12. Kimball, *They Like Jesus But Not the Church*, 237.

SUPPORTIVE ATTACHMENT RESEARCH ON RELATIONSHIP WITH GOD

Research indicates that people see and connect to God differently depending on attachment orientations, and doctrinal and experiential representations.[13] Attachment relationships with God show when people identify God as being personal, warm, interested, supportive, and responsive.[14] Anecdotally, most who receive Christ as Savior typically adhere to intellectual belief in these aspects.

Therefore, since this book presents a theoretical perspective, those who acknowledge Christ as Savior comprise those who self-identify as having a secure relationship with God. I know that not all professed Christians feel secure in their relationship with God. I'm calling it secure because once one has accepted Christ as Savior, security depends far more on God's grace and commitment than it does on His children's wavering emotions (John 10:28; Job 24:23). Was Peter less secure in his salvation when he denied Christ than when he died for Christ? Simple, faithful, confession means much to God. See the Prodigal son (Luke 15:21) and the saved thief on the cross (Luke 23:42). Other passages also contribute to a soteriology resting on the substantial significance of a simple statement of faith (Rom 10:9; Luke 23:42; Mark 10:15, Matt 5:20, Phil 2:11; 1 John 1:9)."[15] People's feelings relative to and fluctuations in relationship with God often have far more to do with their ability or inability to trust their parent(s) or traumatic childhood events than God Himself.

While youth worker-teen relationships are clearly moderated by the influence of previous parent-child attachment relationships, my research found that secure attachment relationships with Christian youth leaders positively relates to psychosocial adjustment in adolescents.[16] For youth who lacked secure relationships with parents, those who had secure attachment relationships with youth workers fared better in self-esteem and feelings of loneliness than those who did not, confirming findings on attachment and intrapersonal functioning in other research.[17] When considering associations between the use of Bible study and Jesus' mentoring

---

13. Zahl and Gibson, "God Representations," 216–30; Grimes, "God Image Research," 11–32.

14. Ellison et al., "Prayer, Attachment to God and Symptoms of Anxiety," 208–33; Rowatt and Kirkpatrick, "Dimensions of Attachment to God," 637–51.

15. Belsterling, "*Follow Me*, by David Platt," 103.

16. Belsterling, "Youth Work," 31–47.

17. Kelley and Chan, "Assessing the Role of Attachment to God," 199.

approach on the development of the secure adolescent-attachment, findings acknowledged the impact of the "Christ representative" piece of the relationship as playing a key role in the positive differences.

As has been stated, four distinct attachment profiles emerge with careful consideration of the fundamental needs of human beings and expressed desires of Christ. Depending on the numbers of youth, participating in one's ministry, perhaps this framework can help Youth Pastors to see a priority for indirect contextual ministry (see Search Institute's 40Assets) more than immediate direct (personal) ministry. Both the strategy and relational models are needed at different times, with different foci and interdependent emphases, all contingent upon a teen's core personal-relational needs. Depending on youth to youth worker attachment success, and teen profiles shifting, ministry priority to youth may also need to change. That is actually one of the goals. The ultimate goal is to see all youth as SGSP, secure in both key relationships.

A Quick Synopsis

The four quadrants (Figure 1) are identified by attachments to parents and to God. For the purpose of this model, attachment to God is signified by a student's confession of Christ as Savior. This approach seems consistent with research findings on the relationship between "God image" and "attachment."[18] It's understood that none of the boxes are airtight. Tempering influences could include traumatic events, mediating presence of uncles or coaches, and personality. There could be some young people who have "confessed" Christ as Savior, but don't have a relationship with Him. My hope is that readers will use these boxes as a lens to look through when listening to and ministering to a teenager, not as a fence which obstructs the view of other influential realities.

Boxes, Labels, Thinking Outside the Box

Why try to "fit" young people into a category, or a "box"? This seems antithetical to the *think outside of the box* trend of the last twenty-five years. But it's not and actually represents outside the box thinking. Thinking outside the box addresses problems from novel approaches.[19] The ARM

18. Moriarity et al., "Understanding the God Image," 43–56.

19. Arbinger Institute, *Leadership and Self-Deception*, 125–32.

model assists leaders who wish to be purposeful and authentic, and to possibly see some of the fruit of their labor. Anyway, I worry more about whether an approach works as to whether or not it's inside or outside of someone else's conceptual labels.

> The ARM model assists leaders who wish to be purposeful and authentic, and to possibly see some of the fruit of their labor.

In being good stewards of time and energy, youth workers can develop ministry which meets not only a few needs of a few young people, but also as many needs of as many young people as possible. The boxes provide clear starting points for addressing peoples' most critical needs. They confine no one to a label if they're used by a youth worker as a medical doctor uses a tongue depressor and a stethoscope—to see and hear the relational health of a teenager.

Ministry Leader Response

Several times throughout the course of the text I was reminded how necessary it is to be intentional in everything that is done in youth ministry. There should be a purpose behind everything. The entirety of the ministry should be focused on "strategic opportunities for long term kingdom influence." For a new youth worker, this is important. It is easy to make the urgent the most important, and even easier to be flustered, distracted and discouraged when things don't go as planned.

I love that emphasis on "value transmission" is included in this chapter. Value transmission is so critical at every level of ministry, especially for youth. We have the opportunity to step into that with the truth of the Gospel.

Danny Jackson, Middle School Ministry Director,
Mountain View Community Church, Frederick, MD

The goal for the youth worker using the boxes as a tool is to help youth alter their sense of self-worth (internal working models) and build hope for future relationships. The youth worker shares and lives God's story and his or her own story of transformation (see ch. 13), trying to help teens become aware of their own stories. As teens learn how to make sense of their own stories in the context of the unfolding of God's eternal plan for salvation for and through His children, they begin to find meaning. They begin to understand and see hope for reconciliation of past and present relationships, and to believe that perhaps future relationships might be successful, and that they actually can play a potential positive role.

As one at the beginning of Generation X, I did not want to get married; I never imagined I could effectively pull marriage off well. Rainer found in research on members of Generation Y, Millennials, that they wanted to get married but also feared an inability to be successful.[20] In studying Generation Z or the iGen, Twenge concludes that most don't value marriage as much as previous generations because they've seen so few good marriages.[21] This theme grows and not by "generational" differences but by scary attachment-issue similarities. This downward spiraling societal problem cripples communities, families, and individuals. It breaks my heart that so many young people hold out so little hope for the most important human relationship of their futures.

God desires to use youth workers to rewire adolescent brains, to help them to see hope in the ability to escape the norm of living insecurely in both sense of self and in relational context. The youth worker must try to recognize the unmet need boxes that fractured youth operate in and to free them to experience life and relationship outside of suffocating or nerve racking lifestyles. The aware youth worker will assist the secure teenager to take relational risks outside of safe comfort zones. Such assistance will move typically "good kids" to fervent maturity in Christ rather than towards religious lethargy and stagnation.

Considering these "boxes" can help programs to avoid being limited by one youth leader's personality, a church's penchant to take care of its own, or by the tyranny of the urgent.[22] Used correctly, these boxes provide a frame of reference to help improve accountability of the youth leader to the church and the church to the community. The church body can see intentional ministry efforts, feel encouraged, and find ways to participate in and support the efforts of a youth worker.

In the ensuing four chapters (7–10), youth workers will be guided along on how to work with youth representing each of the four boxes, addressing within the chapters the insecure-avoidant and insecure-anxious styles of insecurity. Since disorganized youth display random tendencies, behaviors thwart confident predictability. We will consider disorganized youth in chapters 11–13, where we discuss intervening issues.

The ARM model of youth ministry provides some answers to many "why" questions leaders in youth ministry often ask themselves. Knowing

---

20. Rainer, *Bridger Generation*, 117–32.

21. Twenge, *iGen*, 218.

22. Hummel, *Tyranny of the Urgent*.

why someone struggles with something or behaves a certain way may help to bring light to that individual, which may facilitate compassion, patience, healing and/or growth. Cathartically, awareness must first be experienced before healing occurs. Ministry relationships with teens should always rest on leaders' desires to help them to grow.

Adolescent Primary Needs	Key Need: Secure-Attachment with God	Insecure-Attachment with God
Key Need: Secure Attachment with Parents	Relational Need—To know, meet and minister to one's neighbor. Spiritual Need—Humility and Risk/Testing/Evangelistic Guidance/Missions and Church Leadership Parental Need—YL Support and Encourage Peer Need—To Lead Spiritually in Primary Roles and Relationally (think Elder)	Relational Need—To meet, get to know, and/or love God. (Some have met Him and Know about Him) Spiritual Need—Repentance . . . Spiritual Need (A)—Knowledge/Truth for those Outside the Church Spiritual Need (B)—Conviction and Service for those Inside the Church Parental Need—YL Clarifying Communication Peer Need—To be Led Spiritually by Peers
Insecure-Attachment with Parents	Relational Need—Restored relationship with Parent; To Trust God's Trustworthiness. Spiritual Need—Peace and Grace; Desire to Forgive Parental Need—YL Compassionate Interaction and Personal Reconciliation Peer Need—To Lead Practically primarily.	Relational Need—Demonstrated Presence and Concern (Unconditional Love, Interest, and Pursuit. Spiritual Need—Hope and Joy; Pursuit. Parental Needs—YL Prayer Peer Needs—To be Accepted and Led Spiritually.

Figure 3: Adolescent Primary Needs; YL stands for Youth Leader.

Research on attachment based family therapy suggests that one helps an insecure adolescent most by helping the adolescent to reframe relationships within the family.[23] Because most adolescents will never be able to go through family therapy (financial, lack of awareness, refusal—by teens and parent(s), etc.), youth workers can provide an opportunity

23. Diamond et al., "Attachment-Based Family Therapy," 595–610.

for relational-reframe within the context of a personal relationship and the family environment of a youth ministry group. The ARM offers suggestions for initially and coherently addressing both the relational needs of teenagers and how to help them mature in Christ via ministry programming.

All youth workers should see the adolescent profiles, presenting issues, and youth worker roles as shades of gray rather than black and white. As this chapter primarily introduces the second section of this book, it therefore only provides a cursory glimpse at the model. The ensuing chapters further delve specifically into each of these areas. And, note, that all suggestions reflect theoretical and experiential perspective, but are not steeped specifically in hard academic research.

Adolescent Issues Related to Profiles

As adolescents developmentally dance between the worlds of childhood and adulthood, their attachment patterns of relating to others becomes more transparent. This transparency sheds light on both intrapersonal internal working models (cognitive and affective self-understanding/ self-worth) and potential interpersonal issues associated with them. Autonomous (secure) adolescents reflect a balance between self-reliance and communal interdependence; avoidant adolescents guard independence; and anxious/ambivalent adolescents look to others to provide happiness, which never quite occurs. Disorganized adolescents often quickly "shutdown" as transference confusion subconsciously overwhelms them.[24]

Adolescents by virtue of their definition are in cognitive, psychological, and social transition. Spiritual and emotional maturation vacillate with physiological changes. Outliers always exist. With these points in mind, the Figure 3 presents social (both with humanity and with God) issues teens may be struggling through parallel to their developmental issues. Needs related to the issues are also mentioned.

While some needs and remedies may appear in only one quadrant, most would obviously benefit all (e.g., service, prayer, forgiveness, truth, etc.). Some of these are identified not to exclude their importance from others, but to highlight their dramatic importance to a particular

24. Transference: unconscious redirection of feelings for one person from the past to another in the present. See the works of Freud and Jung for more on transference. See Hughes, *8 Keys to Building Your Best Relationships*, for more regarding attachment styles and future relationships.

orientation. Considering all of the fore-mentioned, some issues presented as fixed in one quadrant may show up in some youth who might be in transition or drifting back and forth between two. Nevertheless, the identified issues seem very much to represent those seen in attachment literature and ministry experience.

ARM model	Discipleship Ministry	Evangelistic Ministry
Basic Initial Role of the Youth Leader	Secure—Attachment with God	Insecure—Attachment with God

Reconciling to God |
| Secure Attachment with Parents | Partnering with God and Parents | Representing God |
| Insecure—Attachment with Parents | Representing (and Reconciling to) Parents | Representing Parents and God |

Figure 4: Role of Youth Leader—essentially dictated by adolescent needs reflective of the primary relational needs. This breakdown suggests starting points and emphasized needs, but does not present ministry of any type as exclusively needed by one segment of the teen population.

CONCLUSION: THE YOUTH WORKER'S INITIAL ROLE

The ARM embodies the idea that was first presented at an Association of Youth Ministry Educator's Conference (1997). In the years since, many ministry workers have expressed both interest in the model and satisfaction in discovering valid reasons behind many of their unexplained frustrations or mysteries. Figure 4 presents the initial role of the youth leader at its minimal level. Each ensuing and corresponding chapter both adds additional specific steps and discussion regarding the extent of approach relative to each step. Order and slight variation of words intentionally emphasizes slight distinctions. One sees a division of youth into those needing discipleship and those needing to hear the gospel.

ARM model	Discipleship Ministry	Evangelistic Ministry
Advanced Initial Role of the Youth Leader	Secure with God (Within Christ Relationships)	Insecure with God (On behalf of Christ Relationships)
Secure with Parents	Essentially Secure (SGSP) Mostly require an intellectual discipleship approach emphasizing deeper or novel theological study (e.g., angelology) and opportunity to serve others through spiritual leadership experiences. Need real missional activity.	Relationally Secure (IGSP) Spiritually Insecure Mostly require an intellectual evangelistic approach emphasizing general revelation, apologetics, and opportunity to physically serve others outside of the ministry organization.
Insecure with Parents	Spiritually Secure (SGIP) Relationally Insecure Mostly require a socially, physically, and emotionally supportive discipleship approach (mentoring) steeped in patience, emphasizing opportunity to practically serve those within the ministry organization (youth group) and missional activity. Once these youth develop a secure attachment to the YW, apologetics grows in importance.	Essentially Insecure (IGIP) Mostly require a socially, physically, and emotionally supportive evangelistic approach, emphasizing general revelation, basic truth about God, and opportunity to physically serve others outside of the ministry organization.

Figure 5: Notice overlap of approach (and needs) between the cells on the vertical and horizontal axis.

For SGSP teens, the youth worker serves to complement parental efforts to reinforce and develop an adolescent's understanding of God, Christ, and self. For IGSP teens, a Youth Pastor needs to introduce Christ more theologically than personally, though lack of personal manifestation of the love of Christ will likely interfere with most young people's interests in God. SGIP youth have accepted Christ relative to either the overwhelming intellectual sense of God or out of an emotionally desperate craving to know how it feels to be loved, therefore work with this group may be the most confusing. They transfer their conceptions of fatherhood onto God and the male youth worker, often struggling with obedience. These difficult "personalities" need consistent expressions of unconditional love! IGIP teens will typically need to feel confident in the trustworthiness of a Youth Pastor before showing any interest in listening to one talk about Christ as Savior. Likeability opens a door to relationship but doesn't guarantee response. The Youth Worker must show perceptible love to these teens. The ensuing chapters explain and enhance the conversation related to all material presented in Figures 4 and 5, and in this chapter.

Jesus' Mentoring Approach

SGIP youth require mentoring from adult youth ministry leaders more so than do SGSP youth (See Figures 1 and 2). SGSP youth have greater opportunity for mentoring through their parents, and possibly the greater church family. It's likely that SGIP youth do not. I'm assuming that even those who were raised in the church and accepted Christ, if they're insecurely related to their parents, the mentoring potential from them isn't high. IGSP teens could certainly benefit from spiritual-specific mentoring as well as teaching, but requiring less time with a mentor (coach) than SGIP youth. IGIP youth need Christian practical mentors first, meaning someone who shares mutual interests (e.g., working on cars), and then when shifting over to SGIP, more serious spiritually focused mentoring. Certainly the practical mentor shares from the love of Christ, but not spiritually mentoring because these youth are not yet spiritually like-minded. As I believe spiritual mentoring is most required for SGIP youth, one can read more about Jesus' mentoring approach in that chapter.

I feel pretty adamant about some ideas presented in this book, and fairly open minded about others. While I'm adamant about Jesus' spiritual mentoring approach, who is more important to mentor than whom are more fluid considerations. I'm not advocating that youth workers cultivate an approach targeting teens representing separate youth quadrants for each and every aspect of ministry (e.g., youth group meetings, fun events, small groups, etc.). No doubt, all youth benefit by being around youth who represent the other quadrants. Experiencing God within a diverse group of people blesses. ARM only seeks to encourage youth workers to not miss fundamental needs of different types of youth. I advocate for sensitivity to varying needs and crafting some aspects of ministry relative to those distinct needs, not overemphasizing an aspect of ministry to one group while underemphasizing it to another. Youth leaders can use this model to enable deeper level conversations in one on one relationships; they can vary lessons and activities trying to connect with all different types of attachment style concerns; and, they can target and encourage each group with specifically designed activities (see Figure 5). In fact utilizing the model faithfully, requires all youth to be together for much of one's ministry endeavors.

Think about the type of ministry you provide to see if you are actually meeting core needs of all youth or not. See Appendix 1 for an example and a blank template of typical youth ministry approaches for which youth might benefit most from those approaches. After checking the template, consider the youth in your program and weight of representation by each quadrant. One quadrant looming larger than the rest combined suggests an imbalanced ministry, which probably reflects a youth worker's own attachment style, focus, and comfort levels. This exercise should assist reflection considering whether a youth ministry represents a generic approach for the ease of a youth worker or an approach sensitive to the needs of teenagers. If need be, can you adjust the way you minister to youth?

PERSONAL CHALLENGE AND DISCUSSION QUESTIONS FOR LEADERSHIP TEAMS

1. Somewhere in this book, write down some "why" questions you have about teenagers and how you and they relate or don't relate together. Come back to them after reading the rest of the book to see how some are answered.

2. Describe Attachment Relationship Ministry.

3. Copy the template in Appendix 1 and pass it out to your team. Fill it out individually, then bring it back to the meeting to brainstorm with each other to compile a final version. Do this before reading the ensuing chapters. After reading the next part of the book, revisit the ARM model you've constructed. Adjust as necessary relative to hearing my ideas spelled out more clearly and the interactive consideration of the team's thoughts. You'll want to do this every so often to see where other adjustments need to occur and to evaluate how things are going.

PART 3

Meeting the Relational Needs of Every Teen

These chapters focus on intentional relational approaches to differences in teen relational needs. Topics covered include student leadership potential, ministry to subcultures (LGBTQIA, etc.), spiritual formation approaches, and parents' needs. They also consider personal factors influencing ARM.

CHAPTER 7

Youth Attached Securely to Parents and to God (SGSP)

"In 1969, 48% of elementary and middle school students walked or rode a bicycle to school. By 2009, only 13% did. Even among those who lived less than a mile from school, only 35% walked or bicycled in 2009, down from 89% in 1969. . . . We protect children from danger, real and imaginary, and are then surprised when they go to college and create safe spaces designed to repel the real world."(Twenge, *iGen*, p. 164)

"Having a secure attachment to God was related to an increase in religious behaviours, fulfilment with one's prayer life and belief in a purpose for life. It seems that increases in these religious and spiritual variables are related to less emotional distress. This suggests that heightened connection with God, both through religious behaviours and heightened spirituality, is a beneficial pursuit." (Freeze and DiTommaso, An Examination of Attachment," p. 690)

"Studies suggest that regardless of the socioeconomic factors, the quality of the parental relationship is an important determinant associated with teen pregnancy. In summarizing the research in this area, the NCPTUP indicated that teens who are not close to their parents are more likely to engage in early sexual activity, are more likely to have multiple sexual partners,

and are less likely to use contraception on a consistent basis."
(Haley et al., "A Future in Jeopardy," p. 267)

LEADING SECURE TEENS

HAVING SPOKEN AT MULTIPLE youth retreats over the years, it seems obvious that SGSP youth make up at least the small majority of numerous
suburban and small town youth groups. This makes a lot of sense. The
youth enjoy the youth ministry. Many reveal godly character and prove
competent in academics, sports, music, peer relations, and leadership.
Parents encourage and support participation. Since chemistry with trusting SGSP youth often develops fairly quickly, youth leaders enjoy their
company. They also generally find their homes hospitable to the company
of the leader and other teens. For reasons cited above, and others, I believe SGSP youth have the most immediate potential to lead their youth
groups. (In the chapter on SGIP, I'll explain this in far greater detail.) In
this chapter we discuss some of the potentially strongest youth in our
youth ministries. We reap the blessings of their presence, but also have
to remember we're called to advance their maturity. SGSP parents often
provide model parenting, and those adults we probably lean on.

ADOLESCENT PROFILE: CHURCHIFIED OR CHURCHIFRIED?

SGSP parents also, due to their conscientiousness, success, and typical
leading personalities, can be our worst nightmares. For the sake of being
cautious, some work hard to limit potential growth and ministry. Many
worry reaching out to "less desirable" teenagers will interfere with their
child's safety (whose presence actually is needed to help foster maturation). These parents lead out of fear, not faith.[1] They often tie our hands,
then criticize us when their children find Youth Group boring or shallow.
Of all the chapters in this book, this one might be the best for the diligent
parent to read. Hopefully, God will inspire all readers.

How many times can a human being read one book about astonish-
ing adventure without yearning for and engaging in similar adventure? If
the Bible speaks to an open teen's spirit, and it always does, that soul will
be restless if it lacks corresponding adventure. With more time committed

---

1. FIC approach? Stollar indicates that teenage girls aren't allowed to leave the
house. Stollar, "6 Things You Should Know," para 7.

to thinking than acting, numbers of these youth develop serious questions, doubts, and frustrations. Many have been participating in church all their lives with seemingly no real Kingdom impact. Even the ones who aren't consciously frustrated possess unsettled spirits. Note, Jesus' discipleship group of teenagers left their homes, jobs, and lifestyles in order to follow Jesus. They encountered demons, hostile crowds, treacherous travel conditions, hunger, estrangement, people of tremendous faith, and more. We offer teens gaming nights, rock-a-thons, denominationally approved and pre-packaged Bible studies, and mission trips crafted by organizations who cross every t and dot every i.

And people wonder why young adults leave the church. While I believe this issue has been vastly overstated, one can't deny some truth in it.[2] We should also be concerned over those young adults lethargically staying. While numbers of young leaders are on fire for God, His church has stockpiles of moderately and severely bored adolescents. Perhaps bored youth reflect a laissez-faire manner of bored youth ministry and, dare I say, church leaders. Kids who've grown up in such ministries, whose spirits have been victimized by the church's careless (overly careful) spiritual-emotional negligence embody what I call, the *churchified*. Or, some are so ridiculously protected and/or poorly taught, they've actually been *churchifried*; it's like the difference between moderate and severe depression only its moderate-boredom and severe boredom. Bored teens indict the "living" church far more than the concept of youth ministry.

In the training of the young, we need to be aware of when we blur the lines between training in faith and controlling in fear. Those who never encounter an opportunity to make a moral decision out from under the watchful eye of an adult, lack developing the capacity to make moral decisions. Many youth

> In the training of the young, we need to be aware of when we blur the lines between training in faith and controlling in fear.

worship a God they do not know because obedience only comes within the confines of holy huddles, protected by helicopter parents. Training a child is a Godly pursuit and not easy. We need to appreciate and assist parents and churches who struggle to train appropriately. In some cases,

2. Youth ministries only entertaining teens reinforce that God and His church provide nothing distinctly special.

however, protection hovers at suffocating levels. Comfort[3] trumps suffering as a lifestyle target. But for the developing Christian adolescent, spiritual-emotional quandaries emerge when life proves potentially and practically completely comfortable and predictable. Games are fun because they're not those things. Life can be too.

What athlete prefers sitting on the bench to playing in a game? "Hey mom, I'm going out for the tennis team so I can wreak havoc on our schedule and my studies; I hope I get to sit the bench and watch all of the other kids play"! Even winning games loses its luster for one who never chips in. Though admittedly, there are clearly some who enjoy the prestige of being on a winning team without having the stress, or excitement, of producing, I'd rather lose trying than win watching. God designed us to want to contribute. Jesus told us we've all been sent as He was sent—on mission to reacquaint lost children with their Father in heaven. Lives not pursuing that mission will either sit on the couch forever or find other missions.

The Christian Home

For many children growing up in Christian homes, accepting Christ as Savior by or near the age of fourteen was never really going to be a difficult decision. Their parents consistently (enough) reflected God's love to them and modeled their love of God. For these young people it was relatively easy to see God as loving, provisional, and protective, and therefore, to develop a vicarious attachment to God. Sheltered in emotional openness to God, concrete-thinking spiritual assent was essentially a no-brainer.

But as children develop into their teenage years, they start naturally to crave to know God more intimately, to abstractly question whether their assent to relationship with Him was real or not. If not given any opportunity to test their faith in God, they'll become prodigal in their hearts. Most, because safety is what they know, will become prodigal like the older brother, not the younger brother, in Jesus' Luke 15 parable. The consistent ones will appear prodigal like the younger brother in Luke 15.

In the reality of life and by God's intent, secure (SGSP) young people need to taste risk on their Christian journeys (see Figure 1). They need

---

3. Stems from two Latin words meaning "joint" "strength." True comfort in Christ doesn't shield us from suffering.

to stop playing it safe. They need to stop being encouraged, directed, and/or allowed to coast. They need to be able to see God show up for them and on behalf of zealous ministry effort. Relative to physiological and emotional needs, "it could be that the only thing more dangerous than taking risks in adolescence is not taking them."[4] And if blame must be fixed on someone for this current crop of young adults leaving the church, it's more on the parents and the larger church than it is on the typical youth worker. I don't know how many stories I've heard of youth workers getting grief for ministry effort outside the bounds of the norms of expected activity.

SGSP—Essentially Secure	Secure—Attachment with God Primary Needs of Adolescent	Secure—Attachment with God Initial Role of Youth Leader
Secure Attachment with Parents Profile: As stable as a teen can be. Naïve-generous with trust. Many living on the extreme of either "on fire" or "bored/going through the motions."	Relational Need—To meet and minister to one's neighbor. Adventure; Freedom to express and explore doubt (intellectually); Leadership responsibility in ministry and peer leadership; Deeper exploration of truth/Scripture and social justice; Emotional assent; a Church's validation; Worship in their own language; Individuation opportunity; Going to neighbors; Fun; Parents validated; time with General Revelation; Christian role models.	1. RISK is the key. Offer uncomfortable ministry experiences: engage the heart. 2. Exhort and guide to own the relational and discipling leadership responsibility of the youth ministry. 3. Support, validate, challenge, and encourage the parents. Teach adult CE classes (validates self). 4. Model and cultivate loving concern for the lost—Mission. 5. Provide deeper level study.
	Figure 1: SGSP Youth	

Why make our young people settle for superficial fixes of adventure with special events?[5] We're (the adult population) wrongfully training them to believe that the fun of life occurs in fleeting weekend events,

---

4. Natterson-Horowitz and Bowers, *Zoobiquity*, 279.

5. Please don't misunderstand this to say that youth ministries should not plan fun events. They should—to compliment the fun of regular life for believers, to attract the lost, and to facilitate community for all.

when in actuality fun occurs in the minute by minute moments of surrender to God's desires. Why not lead them into a life of adventure? If someone is thirsty don't hand her a sweet tasting soda, which will only make her thirstier. Hand her a cup of water. Opportunities to experience God in action quench thirsty souls and energize His people like nothing else. Numerous youth ministries take youth out of their comfort zones and holy huddles, setting millions of young people on fire for the work of Christ.

PRIMARY RELATIONAL NEED? MEETING THE NEIGHBORS

"And who is my neighbor"? (Luke 10:29) Getting to know and love one's neighbor stands as the number one relational need of today's SGSP teenager (and adult). Christian teens, in a developmental stage and cultural era which fosters rebellious drive, thirst to move beyond yesterday's Christian status quo. They desire authenticity and want either to own their faith or abandon the façade of upholding fake Christianity. Those leaving the church more consistently mimic those of previous generations who also left, but never stopped attending. Since teens are the most predisposed to try new things and crave to participate in social justice, let's help them own ministry. Let's help them to see the face and the heart of their neighbor. The only guaranteed way to love our neighbors is to go to them, be with them, and love them in the midst of where they are, both literally and figuratively.

Youth leaders must model passion to go to the lost, meet the lost, and love the lost. And they must invite their youth to join them. Those who do energize following disciples. If we can mobilize teenagers to bring the love of Christ to those around them, the lost and the church share the hope of getting acquainted. Self-absorption fosters boredom; other-absorption fosters life. In answering the lawyer's question above, Jesus made it clear that often the lost neighbors who need us the most live right beside us, many of whom we intentionally avoid.

As a Youth Pastor in a church in Haddonfield, N.J., I knew full well who the people in our community avoided. According to the 2012 U.S. Census Bureau, Camden, N.J. stood alone as the poorest city in the country. Less than five minutes away, resides Haddonfield, recently identified by multiple real estate experts as one of the ten best family towns and suburbs of Philadelphia. Think Samaritans and Jews. In planning the annual youth group Mission trip, God clearly convicted me where He desired our youth group to go. I needed to introduce our teens to their neighbors in Camden and Philadelphia. Parents and teens were not as convinced.

Extraordinary Ministry via Ordinary Gifting

"You cannot take our kids to Camden—it's too dangerous," said multiple parents. More than a few parents were already irritated because the Golden Calf "Mission" trip to the Dominican Republic was laid to rest and their children had to apply (which included a testimony of Christ as Savior) to go on this "trip." The idea of meeting the neighbors filtered many vacation or "great experience" minded folks out of applying. About one dozen hesitant but convicted folks did apply. Of that group, the majority of the young people came from Christian homes. Almost all parents were careful and conscientious.

To illustrate *how careful*, one young man, a senior in High School, had only recently obtained permission to cross the main highway in town without an adult. Going on this trip stretched all of the parents as much, if not more than it did the youth. Philadelphia proved more scary and challenging than Camden. Within 5 minutes of walking on Kensington Ave., a homeless man crashed into our cloister, pushing some of the kids and demanding the sun glasses of one young lady. (I've been in the city hundreds of times and never had such an experience.) After moving between him and my pale faced young people, I gave him my shades and he left content. Our cloister got a lot tighter; no one wanted to be too far away from me. As we walked, we were praying for everyone we saw and over the community. Within another five minutes, the young people saw one of their friends from school on the upcoming corner.

He was high as a kite, selling drugs. A kid from an affluent community selling drugs in a rundown part of the neighboring city? Who'd guess that? Nevertheless, the whole world of awareness abruptly changed for all of them. All of a sudden, distant neighbors felt real close. Philadelphia and Camden weren't so far away. All of a sudden they realized that lots of people evangelize, it's just a matter of the message, "state,"[6] "drugs," or "Jesus." Sadly, we've all been deceived into believing that street evangelism

6. Both Richard Dawkins and Sam Harris (among others) have been literally identified as "atheist evangelists" in secular sources. Also see Augustus Caesar.

died as a relevant way to share God's loving truth. Perhaps we want to be deceived. Drug dealers clearly embrace the value of street evangelism.

To minister to one's neighbor means leaving comfort, but who is safer than one traveling with the Lord? Do teens see adults who believe that? All of a sudden, "go make disciples" feels possible when going allows travel to be closer than hundreds or thousands of miles away. How many miles legitimize "going"?[7] One works. To my

> How many miles legitimize "going"?

team, all of a sudden, desperate people had faces. When they saw their friend, their audible quietness and awestruck faces said everything. Dejection set in. After connecting with him we proceeded to the rest of the day of service.

Somewhere around midnight that first night, we were winding down, getting ready to turn in when we heard screaming from the street below. Rushing to the windows, we saw a woman lying on the ground, getting kicked hard by two men. I said, "We have to go down there and help her." Pale faces returned, "What can we do? We're just a bunch of white kids from the suburbs." I asked, "Good question, what can you do"? They said, "All we can do is sing." (Our church youth choir numbered about two hundred members.) "Then let's go sing," I urged. Running down the stairs I wasn't sure if they were following, but they all did. We burst through the front steel door—drawing everyone's bewildered immediate attention. We started singing.

The two guys, staring at us, stopped kicking the woman. From her fetal position, she looked up. For what felt like a long time we sang and all three did nothing. Then the woman crawled over, laid down at our feet, and went to sleep. The two guys looked at each other, said nothing, and walked away. Fear vibrantly transformed into faith. Faith blossomed anew. For the next couple hours we just kept singing and taking turns praying for and with anyone who was willing. We prayed over too many little toddlers, most wearing only diapers, left alone while their parents were scoring drugs. Interestingly, folks who started walking down the street on our side crossed the street to walk past us, and then back to our side of the street again. My teens logged that they seemed—afraid—of us.

---

7. Belsterling, "*Follow Me*, by David Platt," 103. Platt overemphasizes global missional travel; he underestimates his good fortune and others' lack of financial resources and the importance of local outreach and stewardship.

Do you think the exhortation that God gave to Joshua[8] and Jehoshaphat,[9] "Do not fear or be dismayed, for the battle is not yours but God's/for the Lord your God is with you wherever you go," took on any new meaning for these churchified teenagers? Just like God protected His people and gained victories in the Bible stories through marching, horn, and song, He protected that woman through those teens. They didn't just hear the victory has been won for the one-thousandth time, they played a role in ushering in His victory. "The Lord does not deliver by sword or by spear; for the battle is the Lord's" (1 Sam 17:47). No one enjoys the bench as much as playing in the game. Confidence dies on a bench and thrives on the field. In debriefing the experience, my partners in ministry became speechless, and shed tears, again—but in a very good way—they were in awe at the power and provision of God. "Sing to Him a new song" (Ps 33:3) meant so much more to them. These kids who had sung hundreds of songs in church, did sing a new song, and it authenticated their place in God's army, and they'll always know that.

SPIRITUAL FORMATION THROUGH BEING THE FEET, HANDS, AND MOUTH OF GOD

Fruit of the Risk

After our mission trip, we had a dessert with the church body to share the wonders of our adventures, which among other experiences, also included completing a VBS program in Camden with children who spoke no English and praying over teen prostitutes in the wee hours of the morning in Toronto. Adults attending were mesmerized by story after story. They were also convicted and invigorated. These youth fired up their peers. They took ownership of the youth ministry and the small group meetings. They invited that high young man and many others to youth group. He did participate randomly. Prayer and worship came alive. Random people not associated with the youth ministry approached me to donate *large* amounts of money to the youth group specifically. (I know, there are other issues there.) Our church started bussing kids from Camden to the church for after school study assistance. We also had follow up visits with

8. Josh 1:9.

9. 2 Chr 20:15–23.

those we worked with in Camden and in Philadelphia. All of these things and more happened within a one year time frame. God is good.

Taking Risk

Most in this field have had late nights playing Risk or Settlers or Exploding Kittens. And by the grace of God, in real life, many youth leaders lead their youth beyond the walls of programmatic routine, out of comfort zones, and into relational risk, in which "God always takes the initiative."[10] Countless young people have had their innocent trust in the person of God amplified into dynamic faith. I know because they major in Youth Ministry at College.

"You come to know God by experience as you obey Him and He accomplishes His work through you."[11] All the heroes of Hebrews 11 believed not only in God, but also that they were to be going with God into places where they could not see. They risked their reputations, and plans, and all other relationships on behalf of their relationship with God. Leading others well involves risk in the horizontal relationships. People aren't as dependable as is God, however, so risking relationally via vulnerability, and time, and effort requires much emotional and physical sacrifice. It often leads to trials we could have avoided. But we know that the testing of our faith produces endurance.[12] Youth workers, making these sacrifices, forge attachment relationships with their youth, reinforce parental-attachments and help build confidence in God. We'll only know the extent of these efforts when with the Lord one day. And God, who knows fully, continues to draw others to Himself through ongoing ministries, personal or professional.

As for us, taking risk bolsters our ministry interest and energy. Take back "the call" from "the job." Leading others without being able to predict the future fires up a pumping heart. That means not falling into the trap of youth ministry becoming simply one's occupation, being tossed here and there by every event, whim of a parent, youth ministry blog, or effort to avoid a criticism. We need to lead beyond the ordinary. The ninth footnote of the last chapter points out that another way to translate

10. Blackaby and King, *Experiencing God*, 85.

11. Blackaby and King, *Experiencing God*, 50.

12. Jas 1:3.

the Hebrew word "occupy" is the term "lurk," both poor versions of what it means to live. We need to lead teens, not lurk over them.

We need to pursue prayed over, discerning, spiritual, intellectual, emotional, and possibly even physical risk opportunities if our youth are to live.[13] Who will change if everything in their life stays the same? To live is to change. So perhaps, risky leading requires a willingness for self-change as much as a desire for others to change. "The Hebrew word, *lamad*, the most common word used for learning in the Old Testament, means to 'stimulate and exercise in' and denotes that learning requires readied integration of knowledge into life that includes a change in action and commitment."[14] In what ways have you noticed your own maturation in Christ?

What teen click personalities (jock, geek, freak, pop, etc.) dominate the youth group? Are not present in the youth group? Any wrong-side of the tracks kids at youth group? The answer to these questions reflect the youth leaders' social comfort levels. Youth leaders must love Christ not only with all their hearts and souls, but also with their minds.

Relative to varying lessons on youth group nights, my youth groups have met in stairwells in the winter, graveyards, at local schools, and more. I challenged my youth to replace some of their social media and entertainment choices with choices for God. We read C. S. Lewis books as a youth group . . . *Mere Christianity* . . . *The Great Divorce* . . . I ordered those books by the box loads. Remember the family who started doing that too because the parents were so enamored by the passion of their daughter? Teenagers are family system change agents. Youth leaders model to youth, parents, and church leaders how to be system change agents.

Modeling Risk in Our Leadership

Youth leaders taking risks in multiple ways show their teens how exciting (scary, fun, exhilarating) ministry transforms lives. Risks involve sacrificing the golden calves of traditional program. Keeping tradition has value, if one knows why it fits relative to vision. Risk means knowing some will

13. Don't misinterpret this encouragement to take foolish risk lacking in wise counsel, prayer, and Godly inspiration.

14. Belsterling, "Scriptural Basis for Teaching," 26; 1 Pet 3:15, "but sanctify Christ as Lord in your hearts, always being ready to make a defense to everyone who asks you to give an account for the hope that is in you, yet with gentleness and reverence."

be offended. Possibly volunteer adults especially.[15] Risk means creatively taking old ideas and using what one has at disposal to adjust relative to climate conditions.

For example, the youth in one of my ministries needed to ramp up their confidence in defending the gospel. When planning the student leadership retreat I approached a local Cru leader at Syracuse University, to see if he could provide about ten young men to crash my retreat. Their purpose was to dramatically disrupt our meeting, to discover that we were a Christian group and then to make fun of Christians, God, and the Bible. I briefed the female adult leader. (This might not be a good idea to try without having the strong confidence of parents.)

It was a dark winter night and we were in a remote camp lodge. My team of about ten young leaders, consisted almost entirely of SGSP youth, with clearly one raw SGIP leader. We were discussing cultivating a heart for the eternal state of the lost when tons of snowballs cracked hard on the floor to ceiling windows. Everyone jumped. I left to check out the situation and told the youth group to fill in the gap by praying that God would move through our time together. After several minutes, BOOM, those guys plowed into the room with obnoxious energy. My female adult leader left to find me, telling the youth to stay in the room. Alone with these young men, my team admitted later, they were confused and terrified.

As this group zoned in, isolating my students with questions and insults, my young people responded. They intuitively teamed up, distinctly relative to personality and knowledge strengths. Instinctively, they defended God and their beliefs. One tense situation transpired as one guy knocked my Bible off of the music stand. John, my raw SGIP, jumped in front of him, picked up my Bible, poked the guy and told him to keep his hands off of my Bible. As Cru leader, Nick had been warned, about John,[16] his people were told to back off if he got upset. They did.

---

15. In the first few months at one church, my adult volunteers participated entirely unpredictably. I provided them with contracts, where they needed to commit to predictable youth meeting attendance and some particular responsibility. They refused. I said it was nonnegotiable. They said, "We'll quit." That idea was preferable to not knowing who was showing up when. Their reply, "You want to run this ministry by yourself?" "No, but I will," I said. Every one of them quit. Within a year, all of them apologized and some of them applied to help.

16. John, from the inner city, kicked out of two high schools, rough around the edges in every way, was fiercely loyal and used to fighting. He embraced the Lord and grew deep and zealous fast. He could not get enough of God.

And we all laughed together afterward, discussing the situational fears, successes, mistakes, invigoration, challenges, hope, etc. This evening moment spurred a movement in and through our youth ministry, similar to the other story.

Ministry Leader Response

For the past several years I have been asking myself how to disciple and train youth in a hypersensitive cultural landscape? This chapter answers this questions with a simple word, RISK.

We separate the youth from the rest of body of Christ because we know that a lot of adults don't want to interact with youth, so we fail to risk and we take the path of least resistance. If we are not willing to take risks within the body of Christ, we are certainly not going to take risks outside out if. It is impossible to talk to youth about sex and other issues devoid of risk.

The problem with taking risks is that either way we are taking them. We can either risk difficult conversations, or we can risk the youth that God has entrusted to us to become prodigal. Not risking difficult conversations is a blind risk, the Word of God calls us to take faith-filled risks instead. Those risks are the ones that change us, those are the ones that change those around us, and those are the ones that a watching world needs to see more of by the church. This is the call of the chapter, take faith-filled risks and let God.

Rev. Marco Requena, Associate Pastor, Birmingham International Church; Birmingham, AL

Now I realize some believe the new apologetic today should be much more about "embracing the mysteries of God and life and discovering what it means to reveal the illogical and unreasonable truths of Christianity."[17] First, I can't agree with calling any truth of God's "unreasonable." According to Folmsbee adolescents aren't mature enough to "handle a conversation in which a 'defense' of the faith is required."[18] Based on watching my youth on multiple occasions, I disagree. Based on the success of Jesus' disciples I disagree. Based on God's word, He totally expects such wrestling of His disciples.[19] Folmsbee argues we should teach teens how to serve first, then articulate their faith after-

> While the youth often complained that their voice was not heard by church leaders, they never chose to speak the language of adult leaders. They never considered participating in the places where their voices had more probability to be heard.

17. Folmsbee, *New Kind of Youth Ministry,* 59–60.

18. Folmsbee, *New Kind of Youth Ministry,* 59.

19. Isa 1:18; 2 Pet 1:5; Heb 2.

wards. I wonder if his teens ever get to the "afterward" part based on his belief that they can't.

Retreats like the one we had energized me way more than typical church committee meetings. When I first started in youth ministry, I abhorred just thinking about joining larger church committees or leadership teams. After serving with countless teams, many of my fears were realized. And, I learned valuable lessons along the way. While the youth often complained that their voice was not heard by church leaders, they never chose to speak the language of adult leaders. They never considered participating in the places where their voices had more probability to be heard.

Owning Youth Ministry

As far as I can tell, most youth ministries involve young people in some form of leadership. Youth feel empowered when given leadership opportunity within the youth ministry, be it church or parachurch ministry. Leading brings owning. I've also noticed that most teens respond well when their peers lead. SGSP youth need relational leadership opportunity for several reasons.

Most leaders feel more energized by relational responsibility than practical responsibility. In my experience, they also typically prove more competent and committed in relational leadership. A mutual accountability within the teenage subsystem seems to extract more out of both the leaders and the rest of the youth. With leadership opportunity, student youth leaders develop awareness, skills, and resilience which grow to accompany successes, mistakes, and failures. (Can we risk letting them make mistakes? Fail at something?) Fellow students feel inspired and begin to realize their own potential possibilities. Practically, during the day, many youth share close proximity with other ministry participants (or could-be participants). Relational ministry on their part also relieves some of the burden of relational leadership on the adult youth workers. This allows the Youth Pastor or Director to relationally focus on the core disciples, not exclusively of course, but making the most of limited time and energy. Relational responsibilities varied relative to situations, availability, maturity, program structure, and other factors.

Leading Beyond Youth Ministry

Several genuine reasons exist why some youth leaders want nothing to do with guiding their young people into leadership within their churches. First, some say that the landscape of current culture presents as too fluid and unpredictable for past ministry methodology to work.[20] Second, others believe their church leadership runs the church too formally and archaically, through hierarchy and committees. Third, others ask, "Why"? Because they know that the adult leadership (not all) of the church, if they were being honest, prefers not to have to hear, and worse yet, consider, the input of the young people. Fourth, they don't trust the behavior of the adults. Most hold to these views based on past and current experiences. All reasons have merit. Not enough merit, however, to deny the effort as worthy.

After being at the church in Syracuse for a couple of years, the leadership of the youth ministry decided that individual youth on my Youth Cabinet (student leadership team[21]), should represent the youth community (church and neighborhood) on our church committees. Yes, at first some cringed, and initial meetings substantiated low expectations. But eventually, most of the young people actually learned to enjoy participating. Feedback from multiple sources suggested most of the adults started enjoying having the youth participate too. Church committees actually listened to, discussed, and applied some of the young leaders' ideas.

As an example, the CE committee agreed to let us make the Library more teenager friendly. I grabbed a book display wheel from a local Christian book store and filled it with catalogues of Christian colleges. Parents loved this section. We started a subscription with Interlinc[22] and

20. See Morgan, *Youth Ministry 2027*; and Bolsinger, *Canoeing the Mountains*.

21. As indicated by testimony on applications, all of these youth had secure relationships with God through Christ. Most also had secure relationships with Parents, but not all. As an example, one young man, SGIP, grew so fast and so passionate in his zeal for God and His word and His leading that he became a part of the spiritual leadership team with barely one year of involvement in the youth ministry. While he became open to trying to restore family relations, his situation was such a wreck that I never saw any progress there. Other SGIP teens also ended up in spiritual leadership in a couple of my youth groups. In one youth group, if I didn't include SGIP youth on the leadership team, I'm not sure I could have had a leadership team. Though not exclusively, their responsibilities focused more on the practical elements and program than the relational. Student leaders need more than secure relationships, see Sonlife key criteria: faithful, available, teachable, and responsive to authority, at sonlife.com.

22. Interlinc music resources adapted well to twenty-first century realities: http://

filled the shelves with solid Christian music that the kids could explore without having to buy. Teens loved this section. Rotating the music provided me with in-demand door prizes at Youth Group. Yes, it's a digital world today, but you'll come up with your own good ideas. Changes occurred for the larger church as well.

The broader church developed a vision for youth ministry. Trustees who lamented the wear and tear of youth ministry on our property started granting previously ignored or denied youth ministry oriented requests (gym use, parking lot signs, etc.). They happily completed the security and parking teams for youth events. Long time participants in other ministries sought to become involved in the youth ministry. I literally had to talk some fantastic people out of helping us. The Nifty-Fifties (the Senior citizens—for those confused) agreed to become prayer partners with the youth ministry. Literally every kid associated in any way with our ministry was prayed for regularly. One woman wrote her youth and continued writing one troubled, churchifried young man when he left for college. She helped lead him to Christ. Years later I heard this fellow who had never connected with any youth ministry leaders, became a Youth Pastor. Trust me, families felt and continued to feel the positive impact of youth ministry.

Sunday night worship services were points of contention for all leaders and families in the church. Attendees included those from the Builder Generation and those who felt obligated. Many desired to eliminate the service. That is until Sarah (SGSP through and through) took ownership of a once a month Sunday night Youth Worship service. As a Cabinet member and our rep on the Worship Committee, she accepted the challenge to own the youth ministry of our church.

Sarah quit the soccer team to organize and run this monthly service during her senior year in high school. Our church had been averaging somewhere around forty in Sunday night attendance. On the evenings the youth led frequently choppy worship services, we started to average over two hundred. More of every age group started attending and enjoying that evening worship. And despite the Pastor's insistence that I intervene more (admittedly, sometimes there were awkward moments), I refused to do more than consult with Sarah and be available to her on those nights, should she want my assistance. She never did, and I didn't think she needed it. Sarah heard God. God invigorated Sarah and

www.interlinc-online.com/

everyone else because she listened and obeyed and was given the freedom to lead in the church. If everyone would stop pointing fingers we might get more done through our churches.

PEER NEEDS

As has been alluded to often, SGSP youth need opportunity to lead others, primarily their peers, in both getting to know God and in representing God. In that, they need the guiding assistance of adult youth leaders who love them and model for them as Jesus modeled to His disciples. We also suggested earlier, that most teens feel more compelled to listen to and follow confident and, yet humble, contemporaries. They see their own possibilities more easily. According to research, people influence each other more between the ages of thirteen and fourteen than during any other stages of their lives.[23] Don't misunderstand this to say that they all don't want or need adult guidance! They do on both accounts. But adults and teens working together provide for more potential for positive peer influence.

PARENT APPROACH

With contemporary culture and school pressures, parents are in the middle of a draining fight the moment they have children. As soon as most parents start to develop some sense of comfort in being able to guide their children well, the children turn into teenagers. Very few places and people offer trustworthy, Christ centered help. Parents can't even count on other parents. The local church and/or parachurch youth ministries purport to be places of encouragement and refuge. They need to be. They can be.

More than anything, most SGSP parents need their kids to hear their same God given wisdom from a different voice. They need to feel confident that a ministry will not just entertain their children, but also will link arms with them to partner in molding their children in the image of Christ.[24] They need someone who has a thumb on the pulse

> Parents need to believe that while a youth leader knows how to be child-like, he or she avoids acting childishly.

---

23. Steinberg and Monahan, "Age Differences in Resistance to Peer Influence," 1531–43.

24. Burns, *Partnering with Parents,* 209.

of youth culture to inform them what they do not always have time to discover alone. They need to know that the adult their child goes to when complaining about them actually has their back and will support appropriate expectations.[25] Parents need to believe that while a youth leader knows how to be childlike, he or she avoids acting childishly. They need occasional push back by the Youth Pastor to cooperate in the equipping of their children for ministry in the world.

They need to be invited to partner with a youth ministry in allowing some missional risk into their children's lives. They need a YP to challenge them where they have become lazy or controlling relative to their system lifestyle. They need teammates, filling different roles, in the goal of winning souls to Christ through their children. Other church staff can assist here.

CONCLUSION

SGSP youth probably are on fire for the Lord, or are bored in and by the church. A few might actually be both. These young people need challenge on all levels and leadership opportunity. Socially they deserve the opportunity to teach and lead other children and youth. No student ever learns as much as one does when teaching. Physically, habits, patterns, and total safety assurance must be replaced by new relevant to Christ ideas, activities, and mission. If these areas are relevant to Christ, they'll be relevant to the youth and everyone else. Spiritually, youth leaders and youth must supplement reading about God's adventure by living adventurously. Parents and church leaders need to be encouraged verbally and experientially to join with youth leaders in providing such opportunities. Ministries who do will find God showing up beyond imagination. He'll revolutionize the spirit of the young people which will transform families, churches, and communities.

25. Not everything. One parent called a Youth Pastor (a former student) demanding that the YP endorse his discipline method of filling his son's guitar case with the dog's "business." I advised the young YP that supporting parents relies more on cultivating healthy communication than on agreeing perfectly with everything they say or do.

PERSONAL CHALLENGE AND DISCUSSION QUESTIONS
FOR LEADERSHIP TEAMS

1. What makes you a risk-averse person? In what ways has risk shown up in your ministry?

2. What are the barriers to taking risks in your ministry? Have you seriously prayed about God turning barriers into open doors? Pray now.

3. How can you help SGSP parents see you as a partner? How do you invite, encourage, allow, or equip parents to support your efforts to equip their children?

CHAPTER 8

Attached Securely to Parents, Insecurely Attached to God (IGSP)

"So when He was raised from the dead, His disciples remembered that He said this (would happen); and they believed the Scripture and the word which Jesus had spoken." (John 2:22)

"The comprehensive social practice of science demands that we weigh into dialogue between scientific findings and faith—it reveals that actually the social practice of science is not science at all . . . with Scientific findings, we can show that the personal commitment of Israel's laws and the incarnation of Christ are not primitive fairy tales." (Root, *Exploding Stars, Dead Dinosaurs, and Zombies*, pp. 48–49)

"Adolescents who described a secure attachment to their parents were more likely to report a gradual religious conversion than those who were less securely attached." (Schnitker, Attachment Predicts Adolescent Conversions, p. 211)

IN THIS CHAPTER, I put some heat on the typical youth worker and those who oversee them. This chapter parallels Hebrews' demand that we get past drinking milk. As I'm well aware many in youth ministry are often theologically untrained, through fault of their own and those hiring them. I believe this problem keeps many youth ministries from being more effective, and actually makes a few dangerous. Adolescents have impressionable minds and spirits. Charisma attracts adults and teens alike, no matter theological competence. Charisma is not enough though. While I realize not all youth workers, especially the many volunteers, will enroll in Seminary, I do hope chapter 5 and this chapter nudge readers toward developing their own theological understanding.

Can we get too theological? Yes, but only if we turn simple truth into complicated matters. Not if we learn more than our mature teens know. Does the average middle schooler need to be able to define and explain "propitiation"? No. But if the youth worker wants to help the average adolescent get to know God better, the youth worker should.

ADOLESCENT PROFILE: THE POTENTIALLY PRESENT INVISIBLE OM_YOUTH

Insecurity with God for the IGSP reveals far more about one's uncertainty with God than about one's own tussles with self-esteem or problematic family dysfunctions. Many IGSP teens are intellectually capable and oriented[1] and will quickly respond to teaching with difficult questions and challenges. These young people, owning satisfied internal working models (assured views of self), chiefly face only developmentally initiated struggles with self-worth. Due to lack of emotional turmoil and strong parental guidance, these secure (and SGSP) youth comprise the majority of high school students taking college courses, filling AP classrooms, and performing well on SATs and other academic measures.[2] In short, they're an academically oriented group.[3] The IP youth working hard, determined to succeed in college, represents the minority among IP teens. Some IP-Anxious teens seek approval through grades. Many will go to college, but just with much extra personal resolve and less emotional support.

Though typically respectful (possibly arrogant, personality issues in play) IGSP youth with little or no church background voice their

---

1. Escobar et al., "Brain Signatures of Moral Sensitivity in Adolescents," 534; Arain et al., "Maturation of the Adolescent Brain," 449–61; Belnap, "Current Trends in the Diagnosis and Treatment," 179–86.

2. Twenge, *iGen*, 62–63, 111; Ramirez, "More High School Students Take College Classes," line 120.

3. What I mean by "academically oriented" is that even if they're not in AP classrooms, intellectually, they try harder than typical IP students and probably intend to go to college. Some IP-Anxious students strive hard academically.

disbeliefs and doubts about God, the Bible, and the church, with no reservations. They also trumpet their strong faith in the validity of science, which many believe opposes God's truth. With their expressed doubts, these teens stimulate deeper level conversations for everyone. They articulate what SGSP youth might think, but politely don't say out loud, strengthening the faith of the SGSP youth if the youth leader(s) articulate God's truth well. IGSP youth provoke the beginning of faith in the IGIP to SGIP youth because they probably ask questions before IGIP teens even think about them.[4] If the youth leader struggles to capably present God's truth, this potential positive assist spins negatively instead, failing the youth and the parents of the IGSP youth raised in the church.

What about IGSP youth who attend church with their families? Embarrassed by doubt, most don't want to be known as not connected to God, therefore, they'll lay low. Because they're well behaved, we take for granted many of them trust the Lord.[5] Because of the greater masses of them in most suburban and small town youth ministries, individuals among them don't obviously stand out, unless it's by charismatic or distinct personality. Most IGSP don't draw attention to themselves through complaining or by randomly disappearing. Youth workers generally find this group of youth easy to work with like the SGSP youth. They're relatively confident, not demanding, say "Hi" at football games, and come from homes where parents' primary concerns include safety and communication. Parents outside of the church put little pressure on a youth worker to do more than entertain their children in a wholesome environment.

Weaknesses often include God being flippantly disrespected, i.e., through the cultural nonchalance of an OM_youth culture, caught up in being popular and up to speed on the latest technology, slang, and social media broadcasts. Most of these young people see material gain, physical beauty, fun lifestyle, and well-paying jobs as the epitome of success. The aim for these ideals interferes greatly in a willingness to surrender these gods to Him, especially if God isn't real. Believing in science and not God

---

4. I'm not saying IGIP are not intelligent. The problem is so many have so much emotional baggage to deal with.

5. Convicted of my ignorance on this matter with a large youth group, I decided to ask each and every young person, one on one, where he or she stood in relation to Jesus Christ being Savior and Lord. I was definitely surprised by some who admitted not being sure about God, Jesus, and/or the Bible, or about one's desire to embrace discipleship.

provides what seems far more appealing rewards. And this is where the youth worker must start: the reward of relationship with God. Win them by presenting the wonders of creation, purpose and heaven, and sharing His joy and peace.

PRIMARY RELATIONAL NEED: MEET, GET TO KNOW, AND LOVE GOD

Meeting God

Old man Marley murdered his family with a shovel, according to Buzz, Kevin's older brother in *Home Alone*.[6] As kids, we've all had the unknown neighbor the older kids in the neighborhood told stories about. I had two in two different places. "Willie" lived across the street when I was five and "the Crazy Lady" lived right next door when I was seven. When I saw either one of them I literally ran at first sight. In this era, humanity receives credit for all that is good and God receives the blame for all that is bad. Children have been conditioned to avoid God and any "foolish," "cultish" person who represents Him.

While many youth today consider themselves to be atheists[7] or agnostics, many have not truly thought their theological positions through carefully, ignoring proofs God provides. Based on shared details in many conversations and books, most angry atheists intellectually resist God because of past emotional pain.[8] Cloaking intellectual ignorance, the IGSP (see Figure 1) young person resists God from a culturally vogue, rebellious, and puffed-up apathy in addition to possible pain. Peer pressure advances resistance. These youth have no need of God. Parental representatives of God's unconditional love and holiness provide the love minus the holiness. Teenagers believe their needs are met without God's help. "Lower God attachment for middle adolescents may suggest that these adolescents have achieved an identity that marginalizes or excludes

6. Columnus, *Home Alone 1*.

7. Pew Research Center, "Atheists." Forty percent of today's atheists are between 18–29 (the largest block among generations). Considering 30–49 year olds make up 37 percent more, our nation is in serious trouble.

8. While I'm in a dry season on Twitter as I write this book, I've had many online discussions with atheists and believe that the majority of them have been significantly hurt by an authority figure who misrepresented God's love. This seems apparent in some of the leading writers' texts as well—no matter how much they try to make the argument an intellectual one, it's obviously an emotional one.

God."[9] It would be best if we could introduce teens to God before the joy bandits catch them for good.

With IGSP youth we need to share of our love for God in the same way as I share about my love for my wife. I've never oversold how wonderful my wife is to anyone. I speak truth about her and let my admiration of her show itself. I'm motivated to share about her because she impacts me and others so greatly. Another motive is to inspire students with an awareness of God's kindness and wisdom personified in Christ. Quite naturally, and without solicitation, students often tell me, "I can't wait to meet your wife." They watch us interact and seem excited to meet her when I invite them to my home and when we attend campus events. It's easy because she wants that as much as I do. I don't feel pressure to make them interested. Though I communicate as best as possible they would benefit by meeting her, I have no desire, or ability, to force their interest. Some students introduce themselves and engage her in conversation. Others wave. After four years of possible interaction and hearing all about her, some show no or marginal interest, some appease me with interest, and some get to know her. And a few develop friendship with her; those who do realize the blessing of the friendship.

IGSP—Socially Secure Spiritually Insecure	Insecure—Attachment with God Primary Needs of Adolescent	Insecure—Attachment with God Initial Role of the Youth Leader
Secure Attachment with Parents Profile Interest in God is likely complacent (agnostic—just don't care) or skeptical; Physically, Socially and Emotionally—essentially content.	Relational Need—To meet, get to know, and love God. Knowledge; Teaching basic doctrinal truth which is straightforward, clear, and compelling; a Church's compassion and interest in social justice; a YW's Theology of science; Exposure to Christianity in action (service); Definition reconsideration (of success, living, purpose, Wth, DOC, S2R, etc.); Healthy peer community and modeling; Individuation; YW-Parent interaction; Worship	Representing God 1. Truth/Doctrinal teaching. 2. Know and Utilize scientific discovery (not theory) as a teaching ally (engage head). 3. Address life purpose topics (career, college, marriage, etc.) 4. Model loving concern for social-justice. Involve in service to community (engage heart). 5. Share the Gospel, aimed at the head and heart. 6. Befriend and minister to parents.
	Figure 1: IGSP Youth	

9. Sim and Yow, "God Attachment," 276.

Getting to Know God through Revelation

Knowing God feeds the human spirit more than knowing about God. Many have pointed out that even Satan knows about God, but he doesn't know God. Ray Vander Laan states those truly knowing God describe Him as, "My God."[10] In *Wasting Time with God*, Klaus Issler writes that to know God is to be friends with God.[11] If God is not personal to us in our daily walk, it will be very difficult to introduce Him to someone.

Sometimes when I preach on this topic I choose several folks from the audience to describe one of my children. There is the "volunteer" who never met my child, who struggles mightily to say anything, sometimes saying nothing, other times bluffing with random guesses. The second person may have met my child or has been in a class with me and heard me describe my child; this person usually shares some basic information. Lastly, I start to tell the audience about my child, telling them I could continue for several hours if they so desired. Most get the point. In helping others to know Him, faking it becomes obvious quickly. Knowing basic information may be helpful to a few, but elementary to others. Knowing another intimately, from much time together, makes it much, much, easier to introduce Him as "I am."[12]

The two best ways to help others enjoy getting to know God are to mutually enjoy the wonders of His creation (see Job 12) and to share God's word with them. When one combines ministry efforts to bask in both God's general and Special revelation, impact potential escalates. Why? Because ultimately we're challenging their complete sense of security in their parents alone. Yes. We need to challenge the security of IGSP youth, moving them into feeling less secure. Not so as to doubt the love of their parents, but to see the strength of love behind the love of their parents, and to perhaps one day help their parents to allow the love of God more profoundly and clearly speak to them and through them.

Parental love only dimly presents true security. Without God, self-worth wrapped up in parental security ends up being eternally meaningless, somewhat like a mirage in a dessert. Hope is in what is seen, caring not about what is unseen.[13] With security in Christ, security in the love of one's parents becomes rightly understood as that which successfully,

10. Vander Laan, "Follow the Rabbi Lectures," lesson 1.

11. Issler, *Wasting Time with God*, 37–66.

12. Exod 3:14, "I Am has sent you."

13. 2 Cor 4:18.

but only faintly, exhibits the magnificent grandeur, appeal, and solid reliability of God. That which is unseen provides hope for that which is
seen. God is infallible and infinite. Parents are fallible. If parents who
loved their children rightly, not knowing Christ, ultimately divorce, what
happens then to the self-worth, the internal working models of the IGSP
teenager or young adult? Hope in the love and strength of God *potentially*
provides one with a foundation of security which never fails to speak
love back into other secure and potentially secure bases, like relationships with parents (and future spouses and children) which fail in small
and big ways with more regularity than preferred.

The Pew Research referred to earlier, regarding atheist teenagers,
also mentions that more than half of all atheists marvel at the wonders
of the universe.[14] Hiking trails, canoeing rivers, swimming under water
falls, watching ocean waves crash, sleeping under the stars, and sitting
around a campfire all penetrate most people deeply and facilitate both
awe at God's general revelation and valuable discussions about self-
worth, purpose, and creation, order and beauty in the universe. "The
more we comprehend of the sheer scale of the universe, our biochemical
makeup, and the contingencies of human history, the more elusive any
sense of human dignity becomes. . . . Divine intention bestows human
significance in ways that cosmic coincidence never could."[15] "When I
consider Your heavens, the work of Your fingers, the moon and the stars,
which You have ordained; What is man that You take thought of him"?
(Ps 8:3–4). One can't help but to feel vulnerable before the beautiful, ex-
pansive, power and creativity of God.

Curiosity in the written record of God's working in the universe, the
history of humanity, and with each of us personally, develops as naturally
as a craving for something sweet after eating something salty. "If nature
had never awakened certain longings in me, huge areas of what I can now
mean by the 'love' of God would never, so far as I can see, have existed
. . . (but) nature does not teach (and only) hints of the uncreated, for the
one is derived from the other."[16] God's word shared and read captivates.

"For as the rain and the snow come down from heaven, And do not
return there without watering the earth And making it bear and sprout,
And furnishing seed to the sower and bread to the eater; So will My word

14. Pew Research Center, "Atheists."

15. Meynell, *Wilderness of Mirrors*, 114–15.

16. Lewis, *Four Loves*, 20.

be which goes forth from My mouth; It will not return to Me empty, Without accomplishing what I desire, And without succeeding *in the matter* for which I sent it (Isa 55:10–11). For those with no experience in God's word, clear communication of it entices dormant spirits.

> For those with no experience in God's word, clear communication of it entices dormant spirits.

While a wayward teen, I did attend a youth group meeting once in 9th grade so I could play basketball for a church team at the YMCA. I have no idea who the speaker was, but I remember he explained the Lord's Prayer relative to Jesus' agenda, the original language and cultural context, which fascinated me (though I didn't show it). The same thing happened once while attending a church camp. The same allure stirred in me when I read large amounts of God's word for the first time as an older high school student.

In an intentional teaching environment, IGSP youth can discover the relevance of God's word. Even comfortable teens face developmental trials; all teens "flip their lids"[17] emotionally; the Psalms speak so well to them. Youth from good homes still must make many difficult decisions and navigate difficult relationships. The Proverbs offer so many pithy statements of encouragement. Luke and John's Gospels share many stories of Jesus loving and helping the underdog. We'll explore this subject a little more deeply in a few pages.

After several years in one ministry, my youth (lots of secure and insecure kids mixed together) sent some delegates to me to tell me they wanted more teaching! We had initiated small group ministry every other week with leaders and apprentices, all carefully trained and each group having at least one adult advisor/presence. They enjoyed these as they fulfilled the intent behind their initiation, the developing of community. They also enjoyed the teaching and discussion variety of the regular weekly night meeting. What they stated they wanted more of though was not more trips, not more discussion, and not more small groups, but more hard-core teaching. I was able to teach fifty to eighty youth on a Wednesday night (depending on the year, week, night, etc.) and they ate it up.

17. Siegel, *Brainstorm*, 107.

Teens Covet Truth

By sharing God's truth, we can make a huge impact in a short time with securely attached youth. Remember the young man, Chad, who wanted his parents to sell their home, buy a smaller home, and give half of the money to the poor? (see ch. 4). Most parents in his church loved and provided for their families and most of their kids felt secure in their parents' love. Many of them (adults and youth), however, had no idea what a relationship with Jesus Christ looked like, the group of kids perhaps reflective of those in many mainline churches. While teenagers may not be aware they're interested in Jesus, they are tired of living vague lives.

Teens want to make their own decisions, but they also want to make them knowing the truth. They're tired of fake and ambiguous and meaninglessness. They want teachers who aren't afraid of them or the status quo. I had only been in Chad's church for a couple of months when he connected with my teaching rather quickly, as had most of those who regularly attended the weekly youth meeting. I did not have to work hard for their trust. The biggest issue among them was that none of them really believed that Jesus Christ was the Son of God. They didn't doubt the possibility, but they also never deeply contemplated living as a disciple of Christ. And they had read very little Scripture. There were fifteen to twenty high school teenagers willing to participate in youth group who did not know the gospel. After pouring into God's word fairly heavily right away, their questions and expressions of doubts and curiosities grew weekly. Their thirst and adamant passion to drink once they realized they had never drunk at the well of Christ inspired me and each other.

This young man, Chad, made decisions to trust and follow Christ after just a few months of God's truth being intentionally taught. His name is made up as I can't even recall his name. That is how close we were . . . honestly, not very. He didn't need me to be Jesus in the flesh. He needed someone to tell Him God's truth more than he needed a mentor, friend, big brother, etc. He then took God's truth home and shared it with his parents. Praise God that they were open to hearing it as well. Changes in Chad initiated changes in his relationship with his father, a strong subsystem in his home. Changes in John also then meant changes for the whole family unit. Family ministry occurred in a very natural, probable, and beautiful way.

Serving God by Serving Others

Guided opportunities to provide service to one's communities make Scriptural truth come alive. As the last chapter emphasized, Jesus made it clear, we show love for God by showing love to our neighbors. Helping teens to love their neighbors helps to open their hearts to the Holy Spirit's pursuit, voice, and power. We not only love God by loving our neighbors, we can learn to love God by loving our neighbors. Which enables and enhances which, attitude or action? The answer is both. The same holds true in loving God and loving one's neighbor. Missional work helps those who know Christ to mature in Christ, service work helps those who don't know Christ as Lord to mature in knowing Him.

Helping communities and individuals personally makes young people feel the joy of contributing, which embodies scriptural admonitions to feed the poor, remember the prisoner, and visit the weak.[18] Service can be eco-friendly, cleaning up garbage around the neighborhood; elder-friendly, visiting nursing homes; or community-friendly, collecting food on Halloween[19] night for a local food bank. Countless idea books on service ministry exist. My youth ministries assisted retired missionaries, local camps, senior homes (not just at Christmas), widows, young parents, and non-Christian agencies doing positive work in the community.

These projects represented service ministry, not missions. All youth often receive more love, appreciation, and encouragement than they give in these projects. For IGSP youth it grows difficult to ignore an awakened spirit, feeling in touch with one's purpose to manifest God's love in this life, even if God has not been verbally recognized. One time I approached a young lady, active in our service ministry, to see if she desired to accept Christ as her Savior. She said, "Oh, I did that one night when I was praying a couple of months ago." She saw that decision as more important to talk over with God than with the relational broker, me. You gotta love that kind of surprise. The blessings of serving have a way of boomeranging around back to us.

18. 1 Cor 13:3; Matt 25:36; Heb 13:3.
19. In an effort to redeem All Saints' Eve, rather than ignoring what it has become.

SPIRITUAL FORMATION THROUGH GROWING IN KNOWING GOD

Getting to Know God Knowledgeably

Before one can know someone, he or she must know of that person, even if what is known is minimal. Before Julie, my wife, could get to know me, she had to know that I existed. And even if she was interested in knowing me, if I had no interest in knowing her, her ability to know the true me would be very limited. She would have to gain her understanding of me from a distance or only through second hand information. To confound that situation, I have an identical twin brother. We're quite similar in looks, mannerisms, and histories. But we are two different human beings. He is not me, but many have assumed a great deal about me based on knowing him. Learning about another outside of the context of a personal relationship may help one to learn some details, but learning remains incomplete, and depending on who the resource(s) is/are for the information, potentially, completely inaccurate. From a distance, what one finds out is always filtered through another's perspective.

Have you ever met someone that others told you about, like Willie or Marley, and discovered that the person was completely different than you understood him or her to be? Considering the true God, most of those who disbelieve do so because they're uninformed, under-informed, or misinformed about Him. The average unchurched IGSP young person knows almost nothing about God. They only know relative to what they've been told, with no first-hand consideration of Him. They've never read the Bible, gone to a Christ centered worship service, or prayed. Most of their "truth" sources (social media) describing God bluff, as they've never met Him either. Or what the sources do know is tainted by past bad experiences with "Christians" or marginal and suspicious effort to get to know Him. Many rejecting God assume things to be true or false based on what they've learned about other deities in other religions. Under the conviction of the Spirit, we need to share the real God and Jesus with them.

Repentance

IGSP youth need to repent more than anything else. They're fine for now but not for eternity. And that is if their parents don't surprise them with a divorce during their adolescence. Youth workers represent God most to those within this attachment style group, likely having more proximity to most of them than any other Christian adult. Those in youth ministry should think about and prepare a few ways they might challenge these kids so when opportunities arise, they'll be ready in the moment. Ultimately, these next few sub-sections zero in on key focus areas for youth leaders who want to competently and meaningfully minister to this group with their need for understanding of self and God and repentance in mind.

The Bible

Accurate knowledge of God lacks today among everyone. Most non-churched youth in this era have little to no understanding of the biblical God. Specific reasons include the obvious: God's "Theologians" malign, dismiss or second guess the historical credibility of almost every doctrine, person, and event in the Bible;[20] God's Pastors preach and teach from unabashed subjective perspective rather than exegetical study; Prominent Christians trade integrity for wealth and fame; God's people share less about Him, fearing an imperialistic label; School teachers disregard or flippantly dismiss Godly principles and theories; Media mocks and misrepresents God and godly Christians; Science explains and Technology reduces contingencies; and the Christian religion lacks the hip factor. Notice, those on the inside and outside receive equal blame. The only thing Satan hasn't been able to utilize in blocking the young from God is the still small voice of God inevitably speaking through His eternal Word and the

> The only thing Satan hasn't been able to utilize in blocking the young from God is the still small voice of God inevitably speaking through His eternal Word and the remnant who show they trust His Word.

remnant who show they trust His Word.

We must teach His Word well to provide well-informed knowledge.[21] Based on Paul's writings, Ortlund suggests those who are zealous without knowledge actually perform sinful deeds, not spirit-led deeds.[22] Zeal without knowledge celebrates one's sense of one's own righteous-

20. Keller, "Insistence that Doctrine Does Not Matter."

21. 1 Kgs 19:12.

22. Ortlund, *Zeal without Knowledge*, 23–37.

ness. Spirit led deeds celebrate the righteousness of God and the purity of His truth as conveyed from His Word.

God, the Bible, and Science

According to author Duffy Robbins, "Every truth to be learned must be learned through a truth already known."[23] Robbins believes since truth is sequential, "we can't usher students into truth C until they understand truth B and . . . we have to start where they are."[24] Just like I used different leadership applications with different groups based on the level of communal Christian maturity, we need to consider what we teach based on the level of what our current and potential youth group knows, or, does not know. In today's world, with IGSP youth, that probably means most of us have to start at the beginning.

Relative to God Himself, we start teaching in Genesis. "To speak intelligently about the existence of God, we need to know the whole story . . . without the story of creation we would not have the context necessary to understand good and evil in the world."[25] Three key thoughts relate to that point. First, relative to this group of teens especially, youth workers must not only be proficient in handling the word of God, they must also minimally be able to discuss the differences between scientific theories and scientific discoveries. Theories may contradict the scriptural record but no scientific discovery contradicts, and many do validate, the scriptural record (e.g., biochemistry-humanity/impossible protein sequences in macroevolution; geology-age of earth/cyclical radiometric dating and the flood/catastrophic plate tectonics; archaeology-historicity of Scripture/merneptah stele; astronomy—see *Indescribable* by Louie Giglio; paleontology—fossil records and fraud; mathematical laws—prophecy; etc.).[26] Second, if the subject of good and evil weren't fascinating to the lost, most book and movie plots wouldn't revolve around that topic, so teach about the historic clash between God and Satan. Lastly, relative to both God and Christ, the books of prophecy would particularly challenge IGSP youth.

23. Robbins, "Teaching the Bible," 219.

24. Robbins, "Teaching the Bible," 220.

25. Evans, *God Speaks*, 49.

26. See Root, *Exploding Stars, Dead Dinosaurs, and Zombies.*

Relative to Jesus and the New Covenant, teaching would start with the Gospels, and probably John in particular. "The disciple whom Jesus loved"[27] communicates Christ's heart more personally than do the other gospels, though it's not like they are bad options. Romans explains salvation in Christ and would be a good text to consider early on as well. From those two beginnings, Genesis and John, see where God leads based on conversations with the youth and diligent, prayerful conviction. God's Word must be understood and taught competently if IGSP youth are to be intellectually stimulated, intrigued, drawn to God, and capable of making other disciples glorifying God. The transformation of one's "mind shows itself in the transformation of one's character and awareness of opportunities to love others."[28] We want to fulfill our mission to build the kingdom.

Theological Responsibility

Earlier I made it clear that we can't teach about whom we do not know. My question right now is, how much of what we know about God is based on what the Bible teaches and how much of it is based on our denominational histories, pastoral teaching, and familial beliefs? Now, perhaps much overlaps. But perhaps some does not. And here is the killer point. How theologically literate are many of today's youth workers? Almost all have surrendered hearts. What about the minds? In our research on youth ministry education in the United States, we sadly found some ministry leaders believed it was not essential for youth pastors to have theological training, but others, feeling the theological clumsiness of previous youth pastors, believed it to be essential.[29] I concur with those who believe it to be essential.

If a youth worker is not theologically sound, it's possible more damage than good will be done to our sheep and the relationship between our sheep and God. Keep in mind that thorough interpretation of our "stricter" judgement (as identified in Jas 3:1) conveys our judgement as the "more important" judgement. Not because we're more important to

---

27. John refers to himself as that not because he was haughty, but because he understood that to be the essence of who he was and his meaning in life, and that to be the reality for every disciple of Christ.

28. Belsterling, "Scriptural Basis for Teaching," 30.

29. Hampton et al., "Survey of Youth Ministry Degrees," 20.

God than others, but because our competence in our consecrated roles relate to their judgement. We all like to think that God will just send someone else to successfully teach another to conviction if we fail, but what if their eternal state rests in our hands because God has chosen to let Himself depend on us? Jesus did say, "As You sent Me into the world, I also have sent them into the world."[30] Jesus was sent with responsibility not just a message. He also stated, "Of those whom You have given Me I lost not one,"[31] seeming to imply He could have. I dare not say it's a probability others' eternal fate rests in our hands. But considering the possibility increases a sense of burden. We who teach better understand God's word inside and out, upside, and downside.

Research shows that teaching frequently from the Bible enhances the likelihood of teens developing adolescent attachment relationships with their youth workers. The more frequent the Bible study, the greater the probability of developing an attachment relationship.[32] Ortlund tells us we better be teaching competently as well as frequently. As we represent God in this era and through the conveying of His Word, we help IGSP to vicariously attach to God through their Holy

> Through the Spirit's illumination of His Word, our teens stand to realize He is so much more trustworthy than we are. That's the goal.

Spirit influenced relationship with us. Through the Spirit's illumination of His Word, our teens stand to realize He is so much more trustworthy than we are. That's the goal.

PEER NEEDS: TO BE LED SPIRITUALLY BY PEERS

IGSP youth are more likely to consider God's truth by seeing excited friends and other teenagers leading the way. While they possess little aversion to adult leadership, they suffer minimal absence of it. And, they need to realize loving God is not out of date and not unscientific. These adolescents particularly need to realize God is not dead, eternal life is real, and a relationship with God proves beneficial; They can see it's not out of the realm of possibility for teenagers to admit and want to live by

30. John 17:18.

31. John 18:9.

32. Belsterling, "Adolescent Attachment," 337–52.

God's truths. And watching people their own age publically enjoy growing in relationship with God and being willing to encourage and guide
others to do the same, escalates potential of success. What better way for
safe youth to rebel today than to acknowledge God's truth and receive
His love? Now, of course, we hope they receive the love and forgiveness of
Christ for more reasons than simply to rebel, but why not take advantage
of individuating desires to expose them to true freedom? True joy? True
peace? True purpose? True measures of success?

PARENTAL APPROACH: CULTIVATING COMMUNICATION

I've discovered many good, unchurched, parents of IGSP middle and
high school students appreciate their children dipping their toes in the
pool of a religious youth group. After all, most church youth groups
provide wholesome activities and attract "good kids"; knowing about
God rounds them out. Some panic, however, when their children wade
deeper into Christ and start wanting to swim with Him. I've had parents
creatively re-arrange schedules with the specific intent to interfere with
youth group nights (at least according to their children). That happens.
I've also had parents who adapt and hope it's a phase, adapt and grow
interested themselves (see illustration), tolerate, or grow more supportive
without personal interest in Christ or the church. One desire common
among all of them: *communication.*

Ministry Leader Response

*This chapter really provoked me to the think of who are my IGSP's, and it is pretty clear cut,
they have secure home lifestyles but care little about God. The students whom God has given
me, are all secure in finances—Lake houses, boats, friends/family with money etc. My IGSP
teen's security in parents is transmitted through material things. It's not that they are IGIP but
rather their "S" is translated in a different way.*

*You definitely hit the bullseye in the Theological Responsibility section, answering questions
about the different generations. Generations change. Too many of us (Youth Workers) focus
energy on how we can make our program trendy, keeping up with the culture, but it's more
about what am I doing to go deeper in my relationship with God. What does Jesus want us to
know more about Him? Instead of chasing the changes, stand firm in the Truth.*

*Thank you for reminding me and assuring me through this chapter. I should not be discour-
aged if parents or volunteers are not communicating well, or if youth are not showing up to
youth group. A relationship is an organism that needs intentional care. From the lead pastor
to the youth worker; to the volunteer, to the student, to the parent, to the neighbor, and so
forth. I can't rush relationship, but I can cultivate and nurture it.*

Shin Kang, Student Ministry Director, Journey Church, Huntersville, North Carolina

The parents crave effective communication. First, all parents of this age group are busy, very busy. The larger the family the more complex the schedule. Intentional parents often encourage over activity. Passionate organizational (athletic, academic, social, religious) leaders demand too many participation hours. Most expect better communication from the youth worker than they're willing or able to accomplish themselves. It is what it is. Youth leaders need to post ministry agenda far in advance several times, in several different locations, utilizing several different methods.

Such communication efforts help to thwart off suspicion. Let's face it, we live in a culture where lots of strange things occur and many in the religious sector have abused their proximity to vulnerable youth. We help parents to feel better by not ignoring this fact and by trying to be as obvious as possible with our ministry agenda and efforts. So while these parents may be cooperative, it doesn't mean they're not suspicious. And when questioned or grilled actually celebrate that a parent cares enough to ask questions beyond what may have been announced. When we started a Young Life ministry in our community and held the first club night at our house, we had a number of phone calls from carefully curious parents who wanted to know who we were, in addition to many other pieces of information. Praise God. We should have received more calls. In patiently addressing concerns, some of them stated more curtly than politely, we built immediate connection with parents we had never before met. These parents often end up as allies in defending or explaining a ministry to other unchurched and potentially apprehensive parents.

Youth workers need, however, to do more with this parental group than communicate. As far as enhancing the possibilities of reaching IGSP youth on behalf of God, youth workers increase the likelihood by developing positive relationships with parents. Like all teenagers, these youth want some distance from their parents and don't want to think the youth worker is their parents' new best friend, but they typically respect their parents, and subconsciously desire parental approval in all endeavors. Therefore, youth workers should make efforts to cultivate friendships with these parents. Instead of walking the stadium with youth at every football game, take some time to sit in the stands, chatting it up with the parents. Provide parental support through coffee-shop meetings, educational seminars, and participation in occasional family nights and/or retreats. At parent meetings, announce a willingness to eat dinner in the home of your youth, and accept the few incoming invitations.

CONCLUSION

Intentionally targeting IGSP youth means placing a premium on the planting and reaping parts of CPR.[33] If "C" is to be emphasized, it's more so in the effort of the youth worker trying to cultivate relationship with parents. For many youth raised in the church and having heard the gospel story often, the youth worker may have to do not much more than invite a young person to receive Christ as Savior to fulfill his or her minimal role responsibly. I know early on in my ministry, "reaping" efforts definitely lagged behind cultivating and planting efforts.

For unchurched youth, planting is a non-negotiable. Youth workers must focus on clearly and creatively sharing the plan of salvation. Critical to young people understanding the role Jesus plays in their salvation is knowing they're sinful and what sinful means. They must know what the straightforward blessings and costs of relationship are and what the definitive consequences of what a lack of relationship means.

Clearly we should disciple youth beyond conversion, but one reason discipling doesn't always occur successfully relates to the reality that some youth workers do not have clear ideas as to the spiritual status of varying adolescents who participate in their ministries. So, ensuing conversations that could take place, in between youth talks and Bible lessons, never do, therefore leaving young people possibly confused as to their own spiritual status. Hanging in spiritual limbo keeps us from knowing and taking necessary maturing next steps. Limbo also allows more freedom from accountability. IGSP youth need to be kept intellectually accountable. If they are, spiritual growth stands a better chance.

PERSONAL CHALLENGE AND DISCUSSION QUESTIONS FOR LEADERSHIP TEAMS

1. How prioritized and protected is the time that you have in God's word during a week?

2. Do you know exactly where each of your teens stands with Christ?

3. How important is it to have an Eschatological position? Why? How about the five points of Calvinism? How do your positions influence your views of evangelism? Heaven? The lost? Discipleship? Bible study?

33. See Sonlife: c—cultivate relationship; p—plant seeds of the gospel; r—reap the fruit.

CHAPTER 9

Attached Insecurely to Parents, Securely Attached to God (SGIP)

"For those who come from insecure backgrounds their greatest strides in spirituality will come about through their involvement in the religious community." (Lanker and Issler, "The Relationship Between Natural Mentoring and Spirituality in Christian Adolescents," p. 95)

"It may well be that safe haven processes are activated when adolescents are depressed or have lost hope, which is when they feel particularly attached to God." (Sim and Yow, "God Attachment," p. 275)

"*Divided* implies that youth ministry is not working and therefore should go away. Instead of adhering to this unspoken conclusion, I think parents should recruit and work with youth workers. They are incredibly valuable. They seek out students who don't live in Christian homes. They come alongside those who desperately need loving mentors. And they want kids to walk with Jesus." (Breakey, "Divided")

THESE YOUNG PEOPLE PROBABLY irritate youth workers more than any other group of teens. I'll make that point in various ways in the following material. If we're going to minister to those who are just easy to minister to, then are we in ministry for the right reasons? Sure, we get tired. I know, that's why I hope this chapter encourages readers to fight the good fight, and provides some ideas on how to fight the good fight. I'll describe some teens and share some stories to which many will immediately relate. In chapters 9 and 10, more than any previous others, we'll highlight differences between teens inside and outside the church, and how to hear teens. I hope the main point jumps out of the chapter at readers, SGIP teens need to be heard. Youth workers must hone their listening skills if they want to be Godly competent.

ADOLESCENT PROFILE: GONE AND PLEASE GO

SGIP youth in many ministries represent the efforts of children's and youth ministry leaders who have helped them to move from IGIP young people to those acknowledging Christ as Savior. Relative to the ARM model, initially, this realistically is the only direction for IGIP youth to go. Philosophically, the youth worker connecting with IGIP teens represents Christ first in their eyes. While a youth leader may be providing parental oversight, he or she first presents as a Christian and will likely be better received as a representation of God than one's parents. Smart youth leaders initially avoid encouraging associative connections to a lost teen's parents. When SGIP youth accept Christ, we obviously need to switch gears mentally as to their need to be discipled; note, however, SGIP youth possess some different discipling requirements than do SGSP youth.

Teens growing up insecurely, essentially feel unheard because they were unheard in their homes. They live with an interpretative filter that says, "No one listens to me," subconsciously assuming they're not worth being heard, while desperately desiring to be wrong. It's a war within. They behave so as to provoke others to reinforce their maladaptive beliefs about themselves. That's why they require so much extra patience. Historically they've been referred to as EGRs (Extra Grace Required). I don't like that term though, because no one truly needs more grace than any other.

These young people struggle with a self-concept built on a sense of inadequacy and shame. As a therapist, I occasionally prodded clients into admitting they "won't" do something instead of "can't" do something. Youth insecurely attached to parents, apart from timely intervention or the miraculous, literally can't trust that others love them. Their brains were rewired very early on to mistrust.[1] Under the leading of the Holy Spirit, and with the sword of Christ, we can surgically rewire those brains back to their original design. Or, at least, cut the faulty wiring and hope that maturation into adulthood reboots back to original default settings. The period of early to mid-adolescence provides the open window for when that work has the best chance to transpire.

Listening to SGIP remains critical. At first, modeling Christ and listening benefits SGIP teens more than teaching about Christ and what He taught. Continued receptivity to God primarily indicates a desire to believe that someone cares. Confidence in that doesn't grow overnight. While all youth like to be heard, these youth especially need leaders who make consistent, intentional effort to listen. And even though they've already accepted Christ as Savior, they'll still struggle with continued, longings to be acknowledged. The feelings are healthy; the ways those feelings manifest themselves socially typically will not be healthy.

Insecure Anxious/Ambivalent Youth: Please Go

"If I'm too unworthy of others' love I'll drive them crazy until they give it to me." Perhaps the most difficult aspect of that rewiring job relates to a youth worker's dislike for or frustration with those in this group. This SGIP-anxious group probably unnerves leaders more than every other group combined. We enjoy the company of secure people. If IGIP youth are around, we're grateful and probably acquiescing to "sloppy agape",[2] expecting less of them, tolerating more bad or awkward behavior than the average youth group member (hence, why church parents might not be excited about their presence).[3]

---

1. God designed all children to intuitively trust their parents. If they don't, that means parents negatively rewired a child's circuitry during his or her infancy.

2. A Dave Busby phrase: see http://www.davebusby.com/ and go to the Youtube channel.

3. I led an urban youth ministry in Syracuse, NY and at first was accused of not showing love while displaying contextual misunderstanding by not tolerating typical problematic, common social customs (pants below the butt, groping one another, f-bombing each other out, use of the n-word). I tolerated these things when I was on their turf (court, home). When they came to youth meetings, they followed the rules, or were excused. I started using adults whose only role was to chaperone the excused until parents arrived or until the end of youth group. In community, inappropriate behavior by anyone compromises feeling safe and belonging by all. Many youth adapted, enjoying the only space in their world which was safely predictable and lacking in

News Flash: when an IGIP adolescent accepts Christ, he or she becomes an SGIP member. Don't provide too much latitude on expectations, or everyone pays a long term price. When adolescents confess Christ as Savior, youth leaders subconsciously expect automatic affinity for responsible Christian living from them. They shouldn't.

An insecure person accepting Christ's love accepts Christ far more to address personal present sadness than from eternal concern. Many people, knowing little about Christ, accept Christ selfishly, not selflessly. SGIP teens want what they've always been missing and if they have to go to God they will. They feel emotionally lost, but probably do not entirely comprehend the depth of their lost sin nature, nor the personal sacrifices required to living a life pleasing to God and beneficial to society. Christ as a life-jacket works, but Christ as a "piercing as far as the division of soul and spirit" challenge?[4] That's a little different. Someone with a weak self-constitution will not immediately adapt. Salvation depends on God's conviction, not complete understanding or adequate behavioral execution. Just because someone accepts Christ doesn't mean views of self-worth automatically change and thus, it doesn't mean life-long practiced behaviors automatically stop. If they do, it's God's gift of miracle.

> An insecure person accepting Christ's love accepts Christ far more to address personal present sadness than from eternal concern. Many people, knowing little about Christ, accept Christ selfishly, not selflessly.

Youth leaders sometimes wonder about and get tired of an SGIP youth's re-confessions, clinginess, and/or obnoxious interactions. They find themselves exhausted by the constant turmoil with other youth group members, left in the wake of the SGIP's presence. We all have those young people. When they graduate we breathe a sigh of relief only to discover we never run out of others to take their places. Externalizing (aggressive behavior) and insecure anxious youth end up being the angry, provocative, and intentionally testy ones. Internalizing (depressed behavior) and insecurely anxious (see illustration story) youth drive a youth worker crazy too, just not as much on purpose as the externalizing teen.

The immature youth worker, or the spent youth worker, can start to ignore this teen, silently hoping he or she goes away. It may or may not

---

chaos. Others did not (see Matt 10:14). Church parents learned to appreciate and support reaching out to lost teens in our community.

4. Heb 4:12.

be subconscious. We silently celebrate when such a youth can't make certain events. Gunny sacked comments[5] might even escape a youth leaders mouth and obvious non-verbal language makes it clear to the SGIP youth and everyone else that he or she isn't truly welcome, and at the least, his or her company is not enjoyed.

And that teenager gets exactly what he or she wanted, yet hoped beyond hope would never happen. These youth see themselves as unworthy of another's attention and love. They subconsciously do everything they can to sabotage potential relationships to confirm what they dread they know about themselves. Their consolation? At least life is easier to predict when, "Even the one who is paid to like me doesn't." I've observed this type of interaction and experience too many times. It is definitely not easy for anyone.

I had an SGIP young adult in one class a few years ago, who by his behavior made it difficult to show him the friendship of Christ. I tried and prayed. I challenged others to do the same. I enlisted another person to provide some one on one mentoring. And for about a year, by God's mercy, experienced some degree of success. Then one day, unexpectedly, as almost always occurs with these cases, he chose to act out, publically challenging a previously assigned grade and sacrificing a group project presentation to do it. To my chagrin now, he finally won that day. I was so livid I didn't want to talk to him for fear of what I might say. I found that I retreated back to how everyone else dealt with him, to stay away from him as best as possible. He graduated and we never did connect again. Praise God there have been several other success stories over the years. I shared this story to show that we've all blown it. SGIP youth require patience and wisdom.

Please Go to a Friend

Paige showed up at my home or office almost every day of the week, every week of the year. She wasn't trying to be rude or intrusive. All she knew was she enjoyed feeling the love that she received through the youth ministry and my family and therefore, she was never separating from it.

---

5. In the counseling world, "gunny-sacking" means that people get angry about something but say nothing and just put their emotion into a "gunny-sack." The sack gets heavier and heavier the more one does that, until finally, the bag pops, and one's anger shows up almost uncontrollably, sometimes in response to a situation that might have been pretty docile in nature.

Subconsciously, her fear was that if she did, she just might lose any sense of worth. She was going to make sure she didn't.

When we went on youth trips, she was already typically sitting in the passenger seat beside me when I got into the van. The small majority of the other kids didn't mind because they wanted to sit with friends and they thought she was odd, so better not to have to sit next to her. There were others, however, who did mind, relishing potential one on one time with me. She spent holidays with my family because on Christmas day, who can turn away an insecure young person from a broken home showing up at your door. And when she came, she didn't contribute to playing with the children, she just sucked out whatever attention she could. Honestly, I was enabling her distorted approach to relationship and it had to change, for her sake and mine; compassion was giving way to frustration. With a youth group close to one hundred and fifty (total participants), she was dominating my time everywhere. Her presence was also sometimes awkward, as I couldn't just stop doing whatever I was doing (maybe prepping for a message) when she showed up. It didn't matter that I told her not to come by every day, she did anyway.

But thankfully, compassion and strategy won out. I knew it was healthy for her to not want to be in her home as much as possible; the condition of her home life was not good. So, I identified a group of about five or six youth group girls who agreed to have Paige visit them at a rate of almost once per week, with Paige routinely showing up at varying girls' homes relative to a fluid-premade calendar. All parents were on board. In this arrangement, she found friendship instead of fixation, which at first was sympathetic, but eventually became genuine. As time progressed, the girls saw strengths and gifts in Paige and encouraged her. Now being able to breathe again, I didn't turn the other way when I saw her. Now, on what became the occasion rather than the routine, when she sat in the front passenger seat, we enjoyed talking together. After a couple of years in the youth ministry, Paige truly blossomed into "normal,"[6] more so than anyone, apart from God, could have ever rightfully expected.

6. The idea of normal has also come under fire lately, with folks suggesting there is no normal. No matter what anyone says, it's not necessarily wrong to believe in and support "normal." Normal helps life to have some stability and predictability to it. Without normal, nothing is wrong or creative. Most of us subconsciously operate and perceive with social ideologies of "normal." Those who don't quite qualify as "normal," through no fault of their own, often know it, and find great comfort and motivation in being able to feel normal and to be perceived as normal. I'm not talking about LGBT youth here, we'll discuss them in chapter 10. If God uses us in some peoples'

Insecure Avoidant Youth: Gone Like the Wind

"If I'm too unworthy of another's love, why try"? These youth disappear in plain sight. They're not like the personally-easy-to-miss typical, likeable, generic teen in the IGSP group. They're just gone. When they come to youth group you might feel like you totally hit it off with them, but then never see them again. Maybe you bump into one of these guys at a lacrosse game and he seems friendly and happy to see you, but again, unless you make some tremendous effort to reconnect—he's gone. He's not shy. He's not stealth. He just avoids deeper level relationships which means isolating himself away from relationship. He is more pragmatic than the insecure-anxious teen. If he finds worth, it'll be through himself, without the help of anyone. He represents what we think of as apathetic teens, even if after possibly acknowledging Christ's saving grace. He might intellectually concede to a relationship with Christ, but emotionally is still unlikely to be invested in that relationship or in any other one. If involved socially, he'll use people for what he can get and be gone when done. I know this person well. It was me as a teenager.

I grew up as and still occasionally behave insecurely avoidant. I'm a classic example. Early elementary years were all about making decisions relative to how I had learned how to survive up to that point. In second grade, I laid in a neighbor's yard and deduced the only person I trusted implicitly was myself. Not including my brothers, I had no friends until midway through fifth grade. Getting in trouble frequently, both at home and at school, and receiving what I considered to be unjust beatings, I decided I would never let myself show sadness. My mother frequently said that I would let someone kill me before I would cry. I didn't express inner needs because I wouldn't let myself have them. During my elementary years, because my family went to church religiously, attending a coming Billy Graham crusade event was a given. It was there that I accepted Christ as my Savior. As an IGIP child-in-progress to SGIP, I could have a relationship which was "beneath awareness" and would meet my true need to be close to someone, but wouldn't require any risks

---

dysfunctional worlds to help them arrive at a place where they feel "normal," we've produced some fruit. Dismissing "normal" provides the façade of caring, but not caring. It's an academic elitist's way to condone chaos from a seat in the "ivory tower," without having to help.

or show obvious signs to anyone.[7] These are reasons why IGIP youth are willing to consider relationship with Christ.

As a young teen, two teachers and one coach tried to connect with me. But I shunned them. Even though I liked throwing javelin, when the Track Coach told me I needed to pay more attention to his rules or I'd have to quit, I started to walk out, but he stopped me. I've always been happiest when alone. In tenth grade, my mother paid me to go to youth group at our local church. So, I took the money and went. The evening was superficial, with basically no structure. Nothing about it felt compelling. I never went back, even though my mother offered to pay me every time I went. I had zero interest. I never received a phone call from that youth leader. I knew Christ as Savior, and that was enough for me, even though I hadn't really given any of myself over to Him.

PRIMARY RELATIONAL NEED: TO BE HEARD AND VALUED[8]

Youth leaders legitimize teens' continued insecure feelings of SGIP youth when they guide them by prioritizing listening above most other ministry efforts. While, as stated earlier in the book, Jesus earned the right to be heard for us, this refers to boldly proclaiming His name. If we're to imitate Jesus modeling concern for others, we'll take time to listen to all, especially the marginalized. We can't expect a teen with a fifteen year long, dysfunctional self-belief and behavior system to change overnight. It's possible, but not probable. Youth workers displaying minimal patience may jeopardize representing God adequately to SGIP teens. I'm definitely not advocating that youth leaders have to yield to co-dependent demands. Some teenagers will not only drain every minute a youth worker has, but also every ounce of energy. Some hurting adolescents incessantly revel in bitterness and blame. Patience and wisdom are required.

At some point, competent listening moves from hearing a teenager out to helping a teenager to hear himself and to try to hear God. Skillful and wise assistance helps this to occur. Capable listening does not result in giving advice; it results in a teenager beginning to be able to check circumstantial self-talk and to make cognitive-emotional adjustments

7. Siegel, *Brainstorm*, 183.

8. As you might detect, much overlap exists in terms of approach between the SGIP and IGIP young person. Perhaps I should have put IGIP youth before SGIP youth in chapter order because for insecure youth, the youth leader's approach will build from suggestions for IGIP youth toward SGIP youth.

mid-stream. Perhaps not right away, but over time. A degree in counseling isn't necessary, but one might benefit by reading a book or taking a course. All youth pastors should either know or learn basic listening or counseling skills. Yet, skills alone don't suffice.

Time with God means so much to both the teen and the youth leader. As God frequently speaks in whispers, such as hinting at opportunistic moments to encourage moving past bitterness, only the youth worker who diligently listens to God will effectively listen to a teen. When alone, the unsaved or newly saved adolescent may not yet be immersed in God's word. Thus, a youth worker must also skillfully teach, helping to develop a deeper interest in new disciples to want to hear what God has to say.

Youth workers who only listen to a young person without teaching her, enable a consumer oriented leader-student relationship. The youth leader slothfully ignores relational responsibility and work. The better a relationship, the more work required. Leaders who sacrifice God's missional expectations re-victimize adolescents, essentially feeding off of the adoration and affirmation.[9] Consuming rather than giving. Whether inside or outside the church, SGIP teens' parents mishandled past opportunities to demonstrate love and trustworthiness. This occurred to such an extent that these children developed insecurity in self and lack of trust of all people, especially those in authority. In close proximity to teenagers diligent youth workers take advantage of a phenomenal opportunity to break historically bad, relational patterns.

SGIP—Outsiders

Teenagers not from a church background may, as one quote at the beginning of the chapter indicates, seek within a relationship with God what they never had with their parents. Instead of fully intellectually contemplating God's truth, they emotionally accept Him as Savior, like making a wish on a four-leaf clover, lots of desire, but little confidence present. Repentance probably ignores the Romans Road,[10] taking the option to jump off of a cliff instead. Most teens emotionally decide to trust God. But in reality, they're hardly ever entirely either-or decisions.[11] Maybe the

---

9. Rambo and Bauman, "Psychology of Conversion," 879–94.

10. Rom 3:23; 6:23; 10:9–13.

11. Rambo and Bauman, "Psychology of Conversion," 879–94.

Romans Road isn't ignored after all. Cliff jumps typically involve *some* calculated consideration.

Actually, accepting the forgiveness of God in Christ is an either-or decision in one way, but not another. They're not either-or decisions relative to either emotional or intellectual. Most choices involve at least some minimal aspects of each. Supportive of Christian conversions, Rambo shares that decisions steeped in only one area, devoid of the other, might suggest pathology.[12] I would say "decisions" steeped in one area exclusively, suggest deliberations, but not decisions. Deuteronomy, which exhorts awareness of and obedience to God's statutes more than any other book in the Bible, indicates that knowing and feeling God are inseparable considerations. "Know therefore today, and take it to your heart, that the LORD, He is God in heaven above and on the earth below; there is no other" (Deut 4:39). Most successful commitments do show either-or, fork-in-the-road turns, in which one chooses to walk one way and not another way, imperative to growing in Christ by reorganizing of all of one's life patterns. With fruitful teaching, SGIP youth learn "to interpret life with new metaphors, new images, and new stories."[13]

As confirmation, several recent research efforts show that while conversions start with emotional bonding (attachment) between a convert and an "advocate," the jump off of the cliff isn't as hasty of a decision as might appear.[14] While an SGIP young person may not be able to direct another to or recite the verses making up the Romans Road, the experience of jumping off a cliff metaphorically most likely relied on a journey up the road together with friends, and within a community like a youth group. The decision made easier with opportunities to see previous jumpers reaping blessings, minus any pressure to do likewise for the sake of retaining friendships.

Sadly, many teens growing up insecurely have found no solace for emotional repair, at least not until they've encountered God's remedy—one's local youth ministry. The potential for belongingness we offer is so critical.

12. Rambo and Bauman, "Psychology of Conversion," 879–94.

13. Rambo and Bauman, "Psychology of Conversion," 888.

14. Schnitker et al., "Attachment Predicts Adolescent Conversion," 198–215.

One time when I asked my Pastor to say one positive thing about my ministry, he said that it was stable. Being in an unsettled urban community, I took that as the best compliment possible. SGIP adolescents need the availability of stable ministry.

SGIP—Insiders

If a church going teen fits in this category, chances are he or she is frustrated, depressed or angry, probably coming from a home life with at least one controlling parent. The parent operating on the unhealthy cohesion-extremes of either demanding family enmeshed codependence or totally disengaged self-absorption (job, social media, fitness, entertainment, addiction). Or, they lead from the adaptability extreme of either dogmatically rigid, or chaotically unpredictable.

These youth need to be able to come to a place where they feel safe and secure, where roles and rules exist within the context of relationship. "Going" to estranged youth is not good enough. We need to provide them with shelters, more now than ever. So many advocate go, with seeming hostility to the idea of "come." Jesus went, no doubt. He also was approached and loved by many who came to Him. We need to know what we believe theologically as primary and what we believe as secondary. For example, I would be willing to die on a rack claiming we are eternally secure and cannot lose our salvation. On the other hand, I would relinquish my belief that women ought not to be ordained before even contemplating dying on a rack. Youth need to learn from adults who are flexible though not chaotic, and relationally interested by not codependent.

SPIRITUAL FORMATION NEED: TRUSTING GOD'S TRUSTWORTHINESS THROUGH A TRUSTED MENTOR

As you first read in the ARM chapter, SGIP youth require mentoring from adult youth ministry leaders more than any other group. This is where youth leaders step into the gap, hoping to facilitate affiliative attachment as a bridge between insecure youth and their parents. I'd like to briefly describe Jesus' mentoring approach, advocating utilizing it to mentor SGIP adolescents. The five central qualities of Christ's approach were gleaned from Jesus' farewell discourse in John 14–17, in the context of the rest of the book of John. To be sure I found five distinct aspects of Jesus' specific mentoring ministry with His twelve disciples, multiple statistical analyses were performed. In my research I wanted to see if attachment relationships between teens and youth workers were impacted by whether or not youth workers imitated Jesus' emphases in their ministries. The results not only indicated meaningful and significant effects, but also progressive effects on the intrapersonal feelings of teenagers.[15]

If an adult youth leader mentors youth in the five following ways, the probability increases in a teen's developing an attachment to the adult, which helps a lonely teen and increases the possibility of reconnecting a teen with at least one, if not both, parent(s). For that to happen the youth worker must have that as an agenda, showing the teen that he or she wants or has a relationship with the teen's parent(s). The five critical coaching pieces include:

1. Personal humility; modeling humility in person and in relationship.
2. Personal honesty; speaking truthfully to a teen, even if the teen doesn't like it.
3. Showing care to and for a teen (loving a teen).
4. Conveying to a teen that his or her concerns are important (listening to a teen).
5. Helping a teen to understand purpose of life, developing vision for life.

At first, when these approaches of Jesus jumped out of the pages to me, I wondered if caring for another and showing concern for another were essentially the same thing. They are not. Many parents love their children, but children don't feel it because the same parents don't know how to express their love. They direct the child more by their own concerns than by what concerns the child.

A perfect example is when a parent chooses a career path for a child instead of a teen choosing it. I once had a mother email and call me, instructing me to talk her daughter out of being a Youth Ministry Major and into being an Education Major. I told the mother to give space to her daughter. Within the next year, the young lady "decided" to become an Education Major. Resentment builds here, which will explode at some point.

---

15. Belsterling, "Youth Work," 31–47.

Teens want to be guided by someone who humbly and honestly helps them to discover God's unique inspiration and plan for each of them. Advice givers often don't listen, haven't learned how to listen, and don't truly care to listen. Adolescents know the difference between being heard and being patronizingly pacified, brewing internal hostility and resentment when not heard repetitively. Youth workers must love out of an agenda to free a teenager to pursue partnership with Christ by cultivating a life course relative to one's own ambitions, skills, and gifting's. Mentoring Youth Pastors help teens chart personal life adventure in partnership with Christ and the community of Christ (See Figure 1).

PEER NEEDS: PRACTICAL LEADERSHIP AND PARTICIPATION IN A YOUTH GROUP

At risk literature constantly points out the need for teenage delinquents to develop responsibility. Working a job flipping burgers can turn a life around. When people meet responsibilities, they feel good about themselves and their contribution to community. That is how we were originally wired. I can usually see differences in the expectations, attitudes, and behaviors of typical adolescents who were raised in homes where pitching in was required and where it wasn't. Therefore, as soon as possible, all insecure youth benefit by the opportunity to serve. Actions sometimes determine attitudes, meaning that some youth invested in helping another human being will find spiritual thirsts met, facilitating greater identification with Christ and greater desires for serving as His ambassador. Putting youth in safe and sensitive serving situations, like cleaning up or painting an older woman's home, actually stimulates growth of teenagers' prefrontal cortexes and insulas which develops one's ability to empathize. Action determines attitude determines action determines attitude.

In my youth ministries, at all events, everyone understood they were supposed to help set up, maintain comfortable and clean atmosphere, and clean up afterwards. Young men let young ladies eat first. With cots or beds or couches, all youth deferred the most comfortable spots to adult leaders, to respect those serving them. There are many other practical ways for youth to serve.

What Not to Do

Youth Leaders who distinguish between being an adolescent's adult-friend from being a peer-friend provide the type of relationship with an adult these youth desperately need. Many restless teens come from homes where parents act like friends. Teens do not need more adults in their lives who act like kids. Early on in my ministry I failed some great youth relative to this topic. Thankfully, all three were SGSP youth, and the cost primarily impacted me. But what if one had been SGIP? Feel free to laugh, but please correct possible similar tendencies.

My Senior Pastor clearly disregarded God's ways. Scripture, family, integrity—none of it mattered. When I enlightened him that the church's last Youth Pastor provided beer kegs for an out-reach event, which he kept bragging about, his response was, "So, he had over two hundred kids here, didn't he"? He made fun of me with the other staff because I would not curse. He consistently pressured me with double-bind decisions, criticizing me no matter what I did. The list goes on. And on. I grew to dislike him greatly. Every week our church's weekly bulletins had little pictures of his face on them. One day I picked up a bunch of them, cut out his pictures, and taped them to some old golf balls. Then I asked three Senior High youth group members to go golfing with me. Yep. Those balls were intentionally driven into every pond on a golf course with lots of them. We all laughed hysterically every time we launched one high up to come straight down—PLOP, gurgle, gurgle, down into the water. I took many mulligans. They took their swings too.

What a poor example I was. I modeled disregard for authority, an immature approach to conflict resolution, and the same lack of integrity I detested in the Pastor. And all because I had lost sight of the fact that these fellas were not my friends, they were those God and their parents had trusted to me, to make disciples of them. I was—but on this occasion to teach them to be more like me than Jesus. What if those guys had been SGIP youth? How would my example have encouraged them to initiate reconciliation in their homes? One of the three, about twenty years later, approached me regarding a fairly petty rumor he'd heard about me from when I was in college; no matter my insistence on the falsity of the claim, he struggled to believe me. The sacrifices we make in ministry for the sake of a laugh hurt more than we know. What we send out has a way of boomeranging back to us.

Spiritual Leadership?

Due to difficulty in selection processes, political correctness or impatience with church politics and/or adolescent emotional ups and downs, some youth leaders may not even acknowledge teen leaders formally.[16] Reflecting on these points, I've wondered if choosing leaders via an ARM grid-filter might possibly pigeonhole youth or label them. Ultimately though, it doesn't; ARM frees youth from potential experimental effects of those who work with adolescents, but don't understand adolescent development. Those working with teens better understand more than the Bible.

> ARM frees youth from potential experimental effects of those who work with adolescents, but don't understand adolescent development. Those working with teens better understand more than the Bible.

First, young people who have not confessed Jesus Christ as Lord of their life should never be considered for spiritual leadership. For any who disagree, please read two stories in chapter 10 about how satanic teens tried to undermine two different youth groups of mine.[17] Eliminating insecure non-disciples automatically reduces the field of potential teen spiritual leadership candidates by at least 50 percent (assuming Siegel's estimations are correct).[18]

While I would never say don't ponder the possibility of an SGIP youth for spiritual leadership, I would say proceed with extreme caution. Adopting such a position protects the ministry and all youth involved from making unreasonable mistakes.[19] (Read the footnote.) As opposed to insecure youth, secure youth report more altruistic reasons for

16. A mistake which negatively effects the whole youth group and wider community.

17. In one situation I inherited a youth leadership team whose core leaders were not there to glorify God.

18. Siegel, *Brainstorm*, 148: Though Siegel postulates that one-half to two-thirds of the general population are securely attached, I disagree with the high side of that estimate.

19. Hughes indicates, "the neurological processes active in social engagement are the same as those that are central to mindfulness . . . a mental awareness of relationships where we move from me to we, that enables us to see that we each are part of an interconnected flow, a wider whole." Hughes, *8 Keys to Relationships*, 169. There are benefits to making mistakes, but calculated mistakes. That which occurs without careful and deliberate process, when it comes to potential inappropriate embarrassment of an already troubled youth, is not a mistake; it is carelessness.

volunteering.[20] According to neurologist, Stephen Porges, when relationally engaged, their brains trigger a "social engagement system," enabling them to care for others and to notice another's tone, volume, facial expressions, etc.[21] Due to their own dysfunctional tendencies and related difficulties in personal spiritual growth, SGIP youth generally don't have the capacity to notice, consider, or minister to others' needs.[22] Because they subconsciously feel un-safe in relational situations, their autonomic nervous systems trigger self-protective, fight (mobilize) or flight (immobilize), panic responses, and shut down warm, empathetic, compassionate, or, essentially, other-sensitive (I-Thou) responses.[23]

This is why insecure people find it difficult to forgive another person or to celebrate in another's success. This is why a youth worker's best efforts to "politely" tell a clingy teen to back off do not work. These poor children do not hear verbal or read nonverbal cues correctly. Every relational interaction gets interpreted though their insecure-style filter. Anxious youth get defensive and competitive. Avoidant youth shrink away, retreating fearfully, and spinning thoughts and feelings as one who has just been victimized. These realities show up in personality and conflict style inventories, which, however, do not acknowledge the deeper root level issue of insecure attachment. Note also that peers typically don't enjoy relationships with SGIP youth or see them as preferred leaders. Perhaps as God uses us to short-circuit their fight or flight responses and create warm and safe environments for them, they will emerge as tremendous spiritual leaders.

I've had a few very successful experiences with SGIP teens as spiritual leaders, but when I did put them in spiritual leadership roles, because I misread their level of insecurity or because I felt heat from other leaders, I usually regretted it.[24] Calculated mistakes occur in healthy ministry

20 Canterberry and Gillath, "Attachment and Caregiving," 207–19.

21. Hughes, 8 Keys to Relationships, 47.

22. Canterberry and Gillath, "Attachment and Caregiving," 213. Because of early neglect, SGIP youth may have even experienced serious mitigation of neural development, such that they literally lack cognitive ability to coherently notice and/or respond to another's emotions or behaviors.

23. Huges, 8 Keys to Relationships, 169.

24. My hunch is that the successful experiences I had were with SGIP youth, who had actually securely attached to myself and/or another adult leader more quickly and/or subtly than I realized, moving them more into the same realm of an SGSP adolescent. Most movement will be gradual, not black to white, as my research shows stark differences in two year and four year adolescent youth leader relationships.

risk, but that which occurs without deliberate process, especially when it comes to potentially embarrassing an already troubled youth, describes carelessness more than it does a mistake. Rarely considering SGIP youth for spiritual leadership roles, reduces the possible potential of future escalating issues.

The only condition that would let me consider an SGIP youth for leadership revolves around evident success of God's ARM between someone on my adult leadership team and a teen. Signs of attachment developing include:

1. An adult and a teen being on the same wavelength. The adult's perceptions of how a teen thinks and feels proves accurate according to the teen.

2. A teen's sensible proximity seeking behavior. A teen expressing reasonable desire for and responsibility to time together.

3. A teen's vulnerability increases in consistency of appropriate expressions and allowance for others' feelings to be expressed increases.

4. A teen's attention seeking and/or provocative and/or depressive tendencies, expressions, and behaviors, decreases, even slightly.

5. A teen contacts her preferred caring adult when a difficult scenario arises and contacts an affiliated adult when the preferred adult is not available.

6. The teen displays some movement in the ability to correctly discern facial, verbal and nonverbal cues from others.

7. The adult notices oneself and others enjoying the teen's company.

This means that relative to the ARM model, probably no more than about 25 percent of your young people probably qualify for spiritual leadership. Without considering ARM, that sounds reasonable. While the ARM approach will never prove full-proof, using it does contribute to making scripturally consistent, calculated decisions.[25] Spiritual leadership requires surrender to God's ideals and, as best as possible relative to adolescents, stable and other-oriented-capabilities in relationship. Before proceeding with an illustration of my being proven wrong, readers should know that all youth in my programs were annually notified of leadership application and selection processes. Every year, some specific

25. Luke 6:39; Prov 15:1,18; 18:2–3,6–7,13; 26:6–7; Eph 4:26–31.

youth were individually encouraged to apply by adult leaders. Selections were approved through several tiers of leadership up to the Elders.

One year, a young SGIP-Avoidant lady, Amy, a rejected applicant, made an appointment with me to clarify why she was not selected. She was polite as always, but showed more determination than I had seen before. She told me we were wrong not to choose her. We had a good conversation about living to please God and leading without a title, with me suggesting for her to prove us wrong. She began regularly bringing new unsaved friends with her to youth meetings. She also arranged for follow up visits with me personally, so we could thoroughly discuss all of their questions about God on a deeper, more personal level. Week after week, downcast teens who probably never would have initiated a visit to the local youth group, were discussing the gospel. Amy grew in social confidence, boldness to proclaim His word, and theological understanding. She modeled leadership to everyone connected to the youth ministry. We were wrong. When encouraged to apply the next year, she declined, enjoying her evangelical focus.

We still must proceed with caution relative to even practical roles assigned to SGIP youth, especially when the lines between spiritual and practical roles prove fuzzy. For every youth leader who thinks that drumming for a worship team involves spiritual oversight, there exists another arguing the opposite position. Whatever one's position, if a drummer for the praise team drops F bombs during worship songs, the mood of worship suffers.[26] No doubt God feels disrespected. When it comes to choosing leaders and tasks for them, I suggest insulting a young person or a parent before insulting God. If I'm going to err, it will be on behalf of making too great an effort to esteem God. Nevertheless, since opportunities for and success with responsibility has proven central to helping develop competency, imperative for insecure and at-risk youth to possess if healing is to occur, Youth Pastors must provide some opportunity for responsibility.

PARENTAL APPROACH

Parenting orientations probably reflect spiritual immaturity and dysfunctional personal attachment styles. As youth leaders we ought not to bond with teens by resenting their parents with them. Parents with

---

26. I inherited a drummer of a youth worship team who did just that.

avoidant orientations shy away from most youth workers, shamefully embarrassed by failure, probably self-blaming failure. Youth workers shy away from anxiously oriented parents, shamelessly avoiding another potential onslaught of complaints about the inadequacies of the youth worker or program. Been there, done that. One influential church leading parent once cornered me in my office in between Sunday School and the worship service, telling me that his son's spiritual apathy was my fault and my responsibility to correct. Somehow these folks often end up leading ministries.[27] That exchange inspired compassion in me for his anxiously insecure, antagonizing son. God uses everything to His glory.

We need to intentionally try to cultivate relationship with SGIP teens' parents for several reasons. First, while we're in youth ministry, God hasn't limited us to caring only for adolescents. We need to care for everyone who crosses our paths, especially those we're tempted to despise. I prayerfully realized in that situation identified above, that in addition to my calling to that community by God, I had a unique calling to that family.[28] Both parents, with entirely different self-schemas (beliefs about self-worth), as best as each could, eventually and appreciatively noticed.

---

27. I say "somehow" tongue in cheek. Such people target leadership opportunity and steam roll others, desperately trying to appease their own senses of self-inadequacy. It's like materialism, the more they get, the more they want; enough is never enough. It never will be until full surrender to Christ, not just of one's intellect, but also one's own shame, fears and narcissistic self-deceit and self-aggrandizement. I've had too many conversations with youth workers who wonder why so and so has so much hostility toward them.

28. If you're not praying over and for everyone associated with your ministry, and if you haven't enlisted others to pray for you and your ministry, you might as well quit. Ministry is tough. Without prayer? Impossibly tough.

SGIP– Spiritually Secure Socially Insecure	Secure—Attachment with God Primary Adolescent Needs	Secure—Attachment with God Initial Role of Youth Leader (w/ assistance of other leaders)
Insecure—Attachment with Parents Profile: (SGIP) Trust in God is intellectually volitional more than emotionally stable. Manifests with anxious youth as extremely clingy and/or critical. Manifests with avoidant youth as unavailable or in communicational difficulty.	Relational Need—Restoration with Parent(s); Christian adult mentoring via availability, modeling, integrity, interest, and support. To be patiently mentored and cared for; Freedom to express and explore doubt (emotionally); Reconciliation assistance; Belonging; Unconditional love and forgiveness (relative to mistakes [note; not unlimited opportunities for failure]); Parental role model; Healthy peer community; Opportunity to express grief; a Church's integrity.	Representing and Reconciling to Parents 1. Love backsliders unconditionally. 2. Persistent Pursuit of those who disappear (avoiders). 3. Persistent patience face of critical spirit (agitators). 4. Help to repair broken relationships w parents (as best as possible). 5. Cultivate Community (via Small Groups, or other) 6. Mentoring 7. Provide practical and outreach leadership opportunity for youth ministry. 8. Listen—pray for wisdom

Figure 1. Primary Needs of SGIP Youth and Roles of Youth Leaders.

Thirdly, when we love all others, indirect associations between them and one's flock of teens show up constantly, affirming one's love of and integrity in Christ. Youth and parents see someone who loves like God, not just to get a paycheck (vicarious learning). Such love inspires them to prayerfully (self-regulating) offer the same love (positive mastery), perhaps with the same difficult people. It's the same love because it's the abundant overflowing love of Christ. Teens and their parents benefit alike. Lastly, lonely onlookers notice and want to experience that kind of love.[29]

29. See ch. 5, Bandura's Social Cognitive Learning Theory, Triadic-Reciprocal-Causation.

Ministry Leader Response

We all agree that relational ministry is important, but we can't find any proper blueprint that seems to make a difference. This seems like the Youth Ministry book I've been waiting to come out for years. I'm reminded of the special students who exhaust at every turn. Some youth groups are filled with teenagers struggling in these ways.

Some of the best advice I ever received is, "you can't hate someone you understand." Understanding SGIP teenagers in this light makes me far more empathetic towards their needs, to better love, equip, and cherish them. Candidly, I now see where I have struggled in the past with SGIP teenagers. Instead of grace upon grace, I gave frustration and resentment. Often avoiding them, or speaking poorly about them. Now instead of avoiding them, I feel better able to engage them.

Jack Hein, Youth Pastor, Renaissance Church, Decatur, Illinois.

We need to love disconnected parents mercifully, ministering to them intentionally, listening to them and gently encouraging them to keep trying. Any slight effort at adjustment a parent makes, even if not competently, improves the chances, even if minimally, of a noticing teen's willingness to attach. Such home life experiences may assist possible self-perspective development of a teen. They'll certainly complement how a youth leader operates and the successes a youth leader has via one's ministry. The home and youth ministry settings, working in tandem, multiply potential influence on a teen. Should a parent actually make a slight adjustment, he or she might realize other or larger adjustments are possible. Parents might also develop an affinity for a youth worker. In cases of insecure anxious parents, a welcome prospect.

CONCLUSION

A 1990s youth speaker by the name of Dave Busby shared a story that impacted me profoundly. There was a girl in his youth group who nobody liked, including himself. Her demeanor was obnoxious. She chewed gum loudly with an open mouth. She swaggered with a chip on her shoulder. Then one day God convicted him as to his dislike for her. So he prayed for God to help him to like her. And he prayed. And prayed.

And then one day, about six months after that first prayer, the youth group went on a trip which required a lot of time on the bus. At the end of the trip and back on the bus, everybody was fried and had fallen asleep. Most of us completely understand the mood of that moment. Dave was falling asleep too. And then he heard movement from the back of the bus coming forward. By the chewing of the gum, he knew exactly who it was. When this young lady arrived she asked Dave if she could talk to him. He repositioned and invited her to sit in the seat next to him.

She said, "Dave, I need to ask you a question." He replied, "Ok, shoot." She wanted to know if Dave liked her. And fairly quickly, as God answered his prayers, he was able to tell her, "Yes, I like you." She then said she really wanted to ask him a different question. He told her to, "Shoot." She asked, "Dave, honestly, do you love me"? Dave gratefully replied, "Yes I do, I love you." She cried a little. Then after a little while she said, "Dave, my parents don't love me. My friends don't love me. And the kids in this youth group only tolerate me. As far as I know, you are the only person on planet earth who actually loves me." They cried together, Dave grateful for the conviction and empowerment of the Holy Spirit. Her grateful to be loved.

Who desperately needs to know your love? Love the obnoxious kid. Train up leaders who will also love that young person. Seek those who stray away with fervent spirit. Train up young leaders who will do likewise. We are here on mission, not vacation. Our mission is to do more than assist in redeeming souls, we're also here to redeem others' time on this earth, so they can help redeem others' time. Jesus sent us the Holy Spirit to help us to do that for others, and for ourselves.

Some may be wondering about personal insecurity issues and fearing that the time for healing has come and gone. Don't despair. I believe in the miraculous more than these theories. God provides millions of small miracles daily. Reframing self-talk helps. Simply say out loud, "I am worthy of being loved," and pray to believe it. Enlisting loving others to provide the self-talk you need, not necessarily want, helps too. Just don't make them responsible to accommodate your insecurities—that is called enabling, which is the last thing healthy relationships need. Realize though, it's possible that some insecurity will be a thorn in the side forever. Thorns help us retain humility.

PERSONAL CHALLENGE AND DISCUSSION QUESTIONS FOR LEADERSHIP TEAMS

1. How does your youth ministry define spiritual leader and which positions qualify?

2. Who drives you crazy? (Feel free to include other adults here, staff and volunteers.) How diligently do you pray for him? Her? Pray right now.

3. How can you incorporate more specific mentoring into the ministry? Who can help? When would it start? How long would the relationships be encouraged to be? How would supervision occur? Accountability? What five teens need it?

CHAPTER 10

Attached Insecurely to Parents and to God (IGIP)

"Avoiders tend to score very low on all measures of religiosity. . . . We call this group Avoiders because it seems as if they
are avoiding being either religious or irreligious. . . . They are
uninterested in having religion be a part of their life." (Pearce
and Denton, *A Faith of Their Own*, p. 53)

"A lot of people come by to talk to me, but I make all their words
sound like the clicking of insects in the jungle. Meaningless and
distant. Dangerous, but only if approached. Whenever the words
become distinct, I moan until they give me more painkiller and
that fixes things right up." (Collins, Katniss in *Catching Fire*, p.
390)

"Poor peer relationship, fighting for control, stealing, and lying may characterize children with attachment disorders. . . .
It seems that infants with attachment disorders can grow into
children with conduct disorders and subsequently may become
adults with antisocial personality disorders." (Borgman, *Hear
My Story*, p. 191)

I COULD HAVE DESCRIBED this group as the either-or group. Most youth
ministries either target these youth or ignore them as much as is possible.
I think AELA works too though. We need to *go* to these youth. But please

remember, if we don't invite them to come, listening to the "experts," assuming they won't, we'll ignore some of their primary needs. In this chapter we discuss why going and coming are essential. These folks present complications similarly to SGIP youth, we just typically expect less of them.

Children who are to be seen and not heard are never really seen. If SGIP youth need to be heard, IGIP youth need to be seen before they can be heard. We miss them if we neglect to intentionally pursue them. I've definitely noticed seasons of my life and ministry in which I've ignored this population. The kids already in the church kept me busy. But we weren't called to fulfill business. Whether church, parachurch, or Christian camp, we all need to be consciously noticing and loving lost IGIP teens.

AELA—APATHETIC EXPLETIVE-LACED ACRONYMS

Acronyms make messaging so much easier and quicker, and they offer an additional clandestine benefit, concealing certain feelings and thoughts from uninformed onlookers. Almost a new language has been created by the plethora of hopeless and sex laced abbreviations, overwhelming me as to the depth of pain, confusion, and distorted perspectives of today's teenager. While all teens use these, the IGIP adolescent, the AELA poster child, uses them to emotionally undress rather than to impress. The supposed apathy conveyed through these, and the classic "*whatever*" comment, actually convey true feelings, hate is in the middle of all of it. Adolescence is difficult enough, but with no relational anchor whatsoever, navigating the world and its ways leaves the average IGIP adolescent in nothing but drifting survival mode. Most disguise their distressed search for a buoy as its opposite, apathy, hoping someone somewhere sees the obvious.

Research indicates that juveniles seek God more out of emotional desperation than awareness that He is trustworthy.[1] When comparing youth with minimal church involvement, one study found that insecure youth were 20 percent more likely to turn to Christ as Savior than were secure teens.[2] And of those who acknowledge committed interest in developing a relationship with Christ, 20 percent of secure youth identify

1. Ellison et al., "Prayer, Attachment to God and Symptoms of Anxiety," 208–33.
2. Schnitker, "Attachment Predicts Conversion," 205.

parents as a factor, whereas only 2 percent of the insecure youth do.[3] Representing the majority of the juvenile population, IGIP youth have an easier time than IGSP accepting the love of Christ; the requirement for one to reject oneself as one's own god is much easier for the parentally insecure than the parentally secure person. For the IGIP youth becoming more like the Son of God presents as an easy decision.

If the church doesn't bring God to stressed teens, they'll find other gods on their own. How many teens in a church's youth group? In the local CRU or Youth for Christ chapter? The answer is, "How many teens live in the community"? Because of their God designed curiosity in the spiritual world, self-doubt, impulsive decision making, and defiant leanings, teens are willing to engage in the absurd. Religiously, becoming an atheist or dabbling in the occult meets every angry or hurt adolescent prerequisite toward that end.[4] And those in the occult have noticed and organized aggressive evangelistic responses.[5] So emotional interest in God is better than no interest in Him. An emotional decision to accept Christ at least gives God a chance to connect with a teen through the work of the local youth leaders.

Elements of the maligned idea of "program" in ministry actually address very serious needs of insecurely attached youth and model both the just and merciful sides of God's love, cultivating a safe space to learn the details of God's plan. Schedules and spelled out philosophies and mission statements offer predictability. IGIP youth need to experience a sense of structure; they want systems with clearly spelled out limits and boundaries, most of their push-back serving to save face and/or test the resolve of a leader. On the surface, for the moment, IGIP youth cele-

> IGIP youth need to experience a sense of structure; they want systems with clearly spelled out limits and boundaries, most of their push-back serving to save face and/or test the resolve of a leader.

brate a leader's relaxing of a rule. Down deep, they disrespect it. Leaders who do that too many times, lose potential for trust from IGIP teens. Inconsistent doses of structure and enforcement of clear expectations show inconsistent results, at best.

---

3. Schnitker, "Attachment Predicts Conversion," 205.

4. Urban, *New Age, Neopagan, and New Religious Movements,* 1–13.

5. Alupoaicei and Burroughs, *Generation Hex,* 13–14.

Most youth ministries have set guidelines, if not originally by intent, then out of necessity to control resulting chaos when no clear rules existed. Without enforcement of them, rules have no meaning. Making and enforcing them demonstrates love to insecure youth, despite their resistance to them. As many IGIP people adeptly challenge boundaries, youth leaders must hold authoritatively firm in the face of conflict.[6] After inevitable conflict, youth leaders show IGIP teens they're valued by communicating desire to resolve the conflict, and by taking ownership of any mistakes made during it. Youth leaders model reconciliatory importance and communicate to a teen that he or she is personally important.

RELATIONAL NEED: TO BE SEEN AND VALUED

Avoidant IGIP Youth

Most success in connecting to IGIP youth will happen through peer friendships. I've had more avoidant teenagers associated with my youth ministries than I will ever know. I'm confident some came to a youth meeting once or twice and never showed up again. I did not pursue relationship with them. Not because they were around, yet invisible. But because they weren't around. Such youth are the prototypical candidates who commit suicide and only then do other teens think about who they were. These kids might only be reached by a youth worker who goes where the young people spend time. I tried to meet as many kids as I could through other kids in whatever responsible ways presented. Though not as frequently as I should have, I intentionally looked for kids who seemingly had no friends.

When meeting an avoidant teen, it's not always obvious. There may be some signs to the astute youth worker, such as less eye contact and more emotionally flat than the average person. If attending a youth meeting, an avoidant person would probably have been invited by someone. I've always encouraged soft hospitality from our leaders. Meet, greet, and don't smother. If I obtained contact information I followed up by trekking out to find them, but only after they came to youth gatherings a couple times. Pursuing too quickly might feel stalkerish to teens. Some avoidants will eventually come around, but patience, perseverance, and wisdom in pursuit is required.

6. Authoritative—Rules and Relationship; Authoritarian—Rules, No Relationship; Permissive—Relationship, No Rules.

Non-personally-threatening-relational activities, help connect with avoidant kids, like building puzzles or playing cards or video games together. At retreats, we often had a puzzle set up. I'd invite a teen on the fringe of the youth group to grab three friends to spend a night playing video games together. Conversations start and stay at surface level longer than they do with most other teens. That's okay. Help avoidant teens share generic details of their days with a leading question but don't threaten emotional space verbally until sensing openness to it. Allow silence together. Make deliberate hand motions or facial gestures which match what you're saying. These recommendations will stimulate them to use the right sides of their brains, which hard core avoidant personalities do not use. Helping them to engage that side might just help them to start to go to that side of the brain on their own a little more frequently. For anyone thinking this is a bit much to remember, I ask is it really that hard to tailor our communication efforts to better reach someone? Is it too much work?

Anxious/Ambivalent IGIP Youth

When a young person complains about the youth ministry, he illustrates a tendency of all anxious youth, who see God as judgmental, demanding, and controlling.[7] An insecure, anxious person thinks, if I criticize first, I have the advantage. After getting beat up pretty badly in first grade, I decided I'd throw the first punch to the face, as hard as I could, in any future possible confrontation. Resulting scenarios typically affirm one's subconscious sense of social worthlessness and conscious social frustration, asking, "Why is everybody always picking on me"? Throwing the first blow in anticipation of a confrontation, creates confrontations where none may have existed. Often, egocentric teens not logging their own offensive attacks as problematic, nonchalantly engage youth leaders a day later as if nothing happened.

When I first went to one ministry, I had three annoyed IGIP teenage guys and one quiet (floating SGSP, looked more like a IGSP) follower of them, who were pretty defiant. Our ministry was in a local school, using the gymnasium for fun activity for the first hour, then classrooms for the next hour. Being short on volunteer adult help, they found a way to

---

7. Zahl and Gibson, "God Representations, Attachment to God, and Satisfaction with Life," 216–30.

escape sometimes after the fun and before the spiritual side of the night. Though worship and discussions went better with them gone, escapes ended after speaking to their parents. I tried to befriend them and not to give up on possible connections, but they had no interest. The old, "You can make me go, but you can't make me try" teen approach was obvious. I faced many teens forced into counseling who initially made the same stands. Their belligerent behavior infected the whole youth meeting, for everyone. Being realistic, I didn't blame these four guys. They honestly expressed, no interest in being there. They attended only because they were forced.

One night, I kept them after a meeting for five minutes to discuss our shared dilemma. I told them when I was their age I probably would have been more obnoxious than they were if I was forced to go to a youth meeting. They thought that was pretty funny. I stressed I did not want anyone attending who did not want to be there and that I would defend them with their parents. And we all agreed their parents would not agree. We made a deal. They would come for four more nights and actually try to participate. At the minimum, they could not interfere in the evening's flow. If after that they didn't want to participate, their parents would let them not. They agreed, thinking this to be a fair approach and great road out. In this endeavor, we had become allies.

Parent negotiations turned out to be more difficult. With diligent effort and explanation that their sons would never want to attend as long as they were forced, all parents finally, and fearfully, conceded. The four cooperated with the deal. All four kept attending after the four weeks expired. Eventually, we lost one. His little brother stayed as a regular attendee and eventually accepted Christ as his Savior. The SGSP youth renewed his childhood commitment. The other continued to present some rocky times, filled with anger, raised in a home where going to church was more important than loving Christ and living consistently in His call. Eventually, one of our youth ministry's prayer warriors (a seventy-ish woman) deeply connected with him through committed snail mail, post high school, and he changed his college major and went into youth ministry.

Churchified IGIP-Insider Youth: Ron, You Suck!

The youth meeting night was proceeding as usual. We played for an hour, worshipped together, and then broke up into High School and Middle School groups. As we were starting, with about forty-five to fifty youth sitting in a large circle, one young man, sauntered into the middle of the room, drawing my and everyone else's curiosity. He turned to me, pointed his finger at me, and said, "Ron, you suck"! And then turning around, he said, "And so do the rest of you." Then he walked out. Wow. We hadn't even interacted together that day, or recently, relative to my recall. We didn't have a great relationship, but we did occasionally have good-natured deeper level chats here and there. He called me on more than one occasion for help, which I always provided. Then why?

Why shoot me down in the middle of everyone? I was tempted to react immediately that evening, but God led me to act first by taking some patient, responsive steps, for the sake of everyone involved. Then by guiding my prayers that night and answering the why questions. This IGIP young man just said and did to me what he truly wanted to do to his father. His father, however, was unsafe. Had he done that to him who knows what might have happened? His father never loved him as he ought to have been loved and the pain of that reality embittered him. He took his anger out on me.

Ministry Leader Response

In youth ministry, we see all sorts of attachment issues with both teens and parents. One of the most frustrating issues for me in this arena is the smothering mother who desires her child's youth minister to "fix" her child. What that mother doesn't get, that Ron explains, is that in smothering her child to meet her own needs, she may have formed an attachment disorder.

Ron expertly defines what an insecurely attached youth is and explains through research what such a youth tends to be tempted by, how such a youth acts out and how to speak to a youth who is insecurely attached. This information gives youth leaders insight with an in depth knowledge of the psychology of the teens who display these patterns in their youth or young adult groups. I know this insight has given me fresh perspectives on how to see and approach parents and their teens with insecure attachment issues.

Marv Nelson, College and Campus Plant Pastor, Allegheny Center Alliance, Pittsburgh, PA

Author of: Unleash, Empowering the Next Generation of Leaders

It was a win-win risk for him. If I reacted, and rejected him, like he provoked me to do, I would justify his bitterness and reinforce his beliefs that he was not worthy and that all Christian adults were hypocrites. A win. Or, if I didn't reject him, if I didn't pull back on my unconditional love of him, then maybe, just maybe, there was something valuable about God, Christian relationship, the church, and himself. A win in another way. Clearly, his deliberations happened at a subconscious level. Teens need multiple right wins in these tests to break disillusionment. The trick is for them to stick around long enough to get them. I tried to connect with him and saw glimpses of success here and there, but he never let it develop. He wanted to be angry and alone. The same could have been said about me. Don't ever give up. Trust what you can't see.

NO CHURCH BACKGROUND IGIP-OUTSIDER YOUTH: I'M NOT INTERESTED IN GOD

There were two brothers, Jake and Scrappy, who grew up in a broken home, from a hard part of the city. The older brother, Jake, in his late teens, said he liked hanging out, but told me he had no interest in God. As a teen, he dropped out of school, moved out of his house and bounced from place to place. Scrappy actually moved into my home, for almost a year, and accepted all that Christ had to offer. He faithfully cooperated with demanding expectations (for him), which resulted in earning a GED, keeping a job, and maintaining a supportive network of Christian friends. Together, we got Jake to attend youth group sometimes. Then I helped them move into an apartment together.

One day, after about two years from our first chat about God, Jake and I were sitting in front of the apartment, when I brought God up again. He looked surprised, and said, "Ron, I told you, I'm not interested in God," his demeanor, flat and resolved. Led by Christ, my best efforts, equal with both, changed one life but not the other (as far as I know). Jake and Scrappy represent the classic IGIP teens who ultimately make their own temporary and eternal decisions. We can only try. We love teens as our offering to the One who truly appreciates what we do.

SPIRITUAL FORMATION THROUGH FRIENDSHIP AND PLAY

When I was young, kids from all around town would ride bikes to a central grassy lot to play baseball on a Saturday morning. Sometimes we played a game and sometimes we played made up games. Even as teenagers, we did the same. My children grew up in an era where open lots were taken by adult organized, formal baseball games. Today's teen grew up in world that discourages play. Most of them desperately need it. We shouldn't distort the idea that making disciples excludes a child-like enjoyment of life. I don't doubt for a minute that Jesus and the boys goofed off quite a bit together.

In *The Four Loves*, C. S. Lewis laments that adults no longer can play as children play. Adolescents, on the verge of adulthood, get one last chance to be a kid with no judgement. As IGIP adolescents grow older, one sees numerous amounts of them clinging to mindless play, rejecting adulthood. Possibly because they never experienced full childhood, securely, the way God intended it to be experienced.[8] Let me restate that, many young adults reject adulthood today, *probably* because they never experienced full childhood, securely, the way God intended.

"The playing adult steps sideways into another reality; the playing child advances forward to new stages of mastery."[9] Play helps children to directly explore, discover, see sequences, and notice patterns.[10] It also helps the young learn about their bodies, become interpersonally attuned to others, fend off obesity and the physical and social-emotional consequences accompanying it, grow in risk-assessment competency, and ultimately, to socially mature.[11] "The decline in play may be the factor that has most directly caused the decline in children's mental health" and "restoring children's free play is not only the best gift we could give our children, it is also an essential gift."[12]

"Playing may contribute to the enhancement of adaptive systems, mind and body capabilities that enable life to thrive, building the capacity to cope better with uncertainty through refining stress response pathways and building a network of strong attachments to other bodies, spaces and materials. The fun and pleasure of playing generates positive

---

8. That sounds like a needed research project to me.

9. Erikson, *Childhood and Society*, 209–46.

10. Ginsburg, "Importance of Play," 182–91.

11. Ginsburg, "Importance of Play," 182–91.

12. Gray P. "Decline of Play and the Rise of Psychopathology," 443–63.

affect, which has considerable health benefits.[13] Playing has been described as the deliberate creation of uncertainty and as a state of "being in control of being out of control." As a society, we are guilty of forcing children to grow up too early. The church should not contribute to that cultural phenomena.

> Playing has been described as the deliberate creation of uncertainty and as a state of "being in control of being out of control."

Youth Group and Fun Social Events

How is it a bad thing to offer IGIP youth wholesome fun and opportunity to escape and laugh and get silly? Youth workers serve God by making disciples of His and our sheep. Youth ministries only entertaining teenagers discredit the field and work of youth ministry. That being said, intentionally fun activity, in the context of regular youth group meetings and through youth ministry events, has a significant purpose. Having clean fun together contributes to a hospitable atmosphere for the lost and to discipling the saved; the children must play.[14] Contrary to what some naysayers' suggest, some youth ministries need to ramp the fun time up a notch. Unless of course, IGIP youth are not wanted.

Youth ministries offering fun social activities attract and relax the average teenager, two exceptional reasons for continuing to do that. When having fun together, young people learn to laugh at themselves and each other and to feel comfortable feeling uncomfortable with each other. They get to risk and lose with no real consequences. And most of that occurs while the walls between subcultures and attachment styles tumble.

A principal told our Young Life Committee that a major reason we won favor among school administrators was based on teachers' marveled reactions to a new, friendly, interaction of teens across subcultures. Youth who hadn't even acknowledged Christ as their Savior were being used

13. Lester and Russell, "Turning the World Upside Down," 14.

14. After preaching a sermon at a church where I preached often, one woman told me afterward that she enjoyed my message more than any of the others. I asked why. She replied, "because you didn't laugh today, I don't like it when you laugh." (Literally!) Some people have in their mind that becoming a true disciple of Christ demands sacrificing enjoying life. There just isn't enough time for that. How tragic.

by God to draw the eyes of a supposedly hostile adult community to our Lord. What reward it was when a neighboring School Superintendent asked us to bring Young Life into his school district. A key aspect of YL Club night and Camps is to offer hysterical games or skits each week. Serious disciple maker wannabes want to get rid of these types of activities. Some have said the weekly youth meeting format has to change. If we don't reduce the regular worship, teaching, and prayer time, or community/small group time (which we shouldn't), the only thing left to reduce is the fun time together. This also would be a mistake. Why must we strive to such extremes? For the sake of successful ministry or because we need "new" ways?

Lastly, when at Nyack College, another Professor was making fun (in good humor) of Youth Pastors getting to heaven and throwing their crowns at the feet of Jesus like a Frisbee. I agreed we would, and suggested because we know Jesus will leap up, reach behind his body, between his legs and catch it while doing a flip. And then they'll give each other a big bro hug. We will play in heaven! Count on it.

The Allure of the Occult

Counter culture subcultures allow angry and dejected teens to be where they believe they belong. Unfortunately for the extremely insecure teen today, just about every subculture pocket has been normafied, making it difficult for the disassociated teen to be counter cultural or rebellious. In other words, making it difficult to be noticed or for the depth of their pain to be heard. Skaters perform in the Olympics. Potheads indulge legally. Gay is cool. Grandmas have tattoos and piercings. So, in the last ten years teens are turning to the occult.

One knows there is spiritual interest among the lost simply by the plethora of movies, games, programs, and books dealing with zombies, witches, the devil, vampires, and many other pagan ideas. In a survey of mostly Christian youth, we found almost 20 percent believed in the possibility of zombies being or becoming real.[15] Our respondents might have been playing with the survey, but if anyone saw the video of the young woman convinced by her brothers that the zombie apocalypse had arrived, maybe they weren't. Assuming they were being honest, what might that say about those who don't know Christ? We have teens organizing as

15. Belsterling et al., "Religious Lives of Alliance Youth," 1–20.

werewolves. Wicca grows faster than any other religious movement right now. Teens have blood-letting parties and file their teeth, as they literally drink one another's blood. I know some of what's going on because I've personally counseled wiccans, warlocks, and vampires. Those involved in these activities, whether for play or serious exploration, typically end up being entangled in evil, becoming serious even if they didn't plan on it.

God is real. Heaven is real. Satan is real. Hell is real. Satan's agenda is real. His evil presence through demonic influence is real. Every demonic or occultic program and game are tools in his hand. Those who minimize evil agenda and reality by frivolously indulging in its entertainment, mock God and His Word, especially those leading youth ministries.

In one youth ministry of mine, a young, IGIP, committed to Satan, attended only with the mission to interfere. He never hid his intent. After a year of building relationship with him, I realized he meant it and finally told him not to come back. We maintained one-on-one time. Once he suggested that sometimes he wanted out. But he was resigned that he could not get out. Sad details made it clear this was no game that he could put down. I've seen Satanic worship spots in the woods of several communities. I've been called at two in the morning to meet with some teens because one girl who had been participating in séances in her home freaked out because all the doors in her home were opening and closing non-stop. If she made it up she was psychotic because she was visibly horrified to her core. When I was a teen I engaged in some similar activity that scared me away from that world of evil.

Satanic youth were running my youth group in another church. Inheriting a youth group leadership team, I decided to meet the team in my home, having every member testify to Jesus Christ as Lord, with a past or present story.[16] One girl refused on grounds that we didn't know each other well enough. What was supposed to be an enjoyable evening turned into a hostile night. After the meeting, my wife said God's spirit welled up inside of her when a woman came to the door to pick up her daughter, and my wife had never said anything like this to me before, as

16. Anyone heavily into Satanism will not honor Christ with a testimony. Satan conspires against God and we ought not to take that for granted. Note, I'm not someone who sees Satan behind every rock. I do not endorse deliverance ministry with professed Christians. I am far more logically than emotionally oriented—a good rep of someone who grew up avoidant, though I am grateful to God for giving feelings back to me.

we don't endorse spiritual drama. That woman was that girl's mother. Red flags fired up.

Since I discharged that young woman from the leadership team, she and some other leaders, those with marginal testimonies at best, left the youth group and started their own weekly youth meeting on the same night that our church's ran. Those in the occult often, purposefully run their own activities on the same nights as Christian meetings. As an example, a Wiccan group in North Carolina annually runs a Wiccan Witchcraft School parallel to when churches in the community run VBS programs, promoting it just like they do in the religious sections of local news sources.[17] In the next month or two, threatening phone calls and letters arrived, tires were flattened, and NOR showed up constantly, written on windows, my car, and office door. I was actually glad they did that, as it confirmed for me their Satanic affiliation. Since blasphemy reverses what God describes as good and bad, those involved in Satanic worship spell the names of those they hate (Ron) backwards. The NOR thing came in handy at the first hostile parent meeting.

Sadly, millions of teens today dabble in the occult at earlier and earlier ages. Too many Christians make up part of the vast viewership of programs like the *Walking Dead* and *Evil Lives Here*. What will it take? Those who know Christ cannot be possessed by demons. But IGIP teens don't know Christ. Demonic presence is real. If God has a plan, Satan has a scheme. How much do we care about fringe IGIP teens? They're the most vulnerable to evil. Let's meet their spiritual thirst with the real thing, the living water of Jesus Christ (John 4:10), and with integrity. Fight evil, don't minimize it or evade it.

LGBTQIA . . . X, Y, Z[18]

Lesbian, Gay, Bi, Transgender, Queer, Intersexual (historically-Hermaphrodite-born with unclear biological gender), and Asexual. The X, Y, Z, portion identifies the reality that sexual perversions demanding acceptance and sensitivity, once welcomed, only increase in number and

---

17. Alupoaicei and Burroughs, *Generation Hex*, 13–4.

18. For more on these terms, depending on possible, personal, temptations, see the following site, which tracks, identifies, and compiles alternative sexual language and approaches. For instance, they claim twenty variations of the term Intersex itself: https://lgbtqia.ucdavis.edu/educated/glossary.html.

demand.[19] Proving the point, LGBT no longer shows good enough to represent the sexually deviant community. Attending to twenty-first century teens' sexual identity dilemmas brings opportunities and challenges to the Christian youth worker like those never faced before in the United States.

Gender Stability and Sexual Identity

Based on Kohlberg's early work, by age three or four, children grasp "the basic ideas of being a boy and girl as defined by their culture. . . . As children's understanding of gender matures they begin to develop gender stability . . . seek(ing) out same-sex models."[20] Essentially, a five-year-old girl with short hair who prefers blue to pink knows she is a girl. Due to the absence or unpredictability of primary role models and resulting confusion as to one's self-schema, many children with insecure attachments, suffer normal development of stable gender comprehension.

Therefore, distorted sexual curiosity and experimentation for these teens occurs right beside the heterosexual curiosity of "normal" teens. Secure heterosexual teens may also be tempted to consider deviant sexual ideas because of sinful-rebellious inclinations, culture tells them they should, raging hormones, and/or to alleviate guilt they feel for sensing such behavior to be wrong. But they're not as thoroughly tempted as the insecure teen who never obtained a gender identity during childhood. These insecure teens face the struggle for *Identity Achievement* with twice the angst and typically much less parental support than the secure teen.[21]

As teens experiment sexually outside of heterosexual norms they risk enjoying the encounters (any sexual activity is better than no sexual activity) and thus more confusion, not to mention other possible physical and emotional consequences. So, in the desire to be seen as an adult and strike back at parents, many teens who are too young to competently decide, identify as LGBT. This is known as *Identity Foreclosure*, selecting an identity before one is truly ready. These decisions are received and welcomed by those with evil and political agendas, despite the harm to

19. The fight over Bestiality should be an interesting one when PETA and GLAAD square off.

20. Underwood and Dailey, *Counseling Adolescents*, 336–37.

21. Not all insecure teens struggle with perverted sexual interests, because many achieve gender identity during childhood, even if they never achieve a secure attachment.

the children. Physiologically speaking, teens can't really reach *Identity Achievement* prior to late adolescence. Parents and adults encouraging or allowing anyone under the age of eighteen to undergo reconstructive surgery on genitalia should be arrested for child abuse of the greatest magnitude.

LGBT Challenges

Many states have multiple anti-discrimination laws which range from illegalizing refusal of involvement to discouraging remedial counseling.[22] Be aware, while helping teens into destructive lifestyles may lead to public praise and job advancement for some, helping teenagers out of destructive lifestyles may create dire financial and social repercussions for youth workers. Discerning youth leaders will prepare for the probability of future difficult LGBT situations and decisions. Leaders need to prayerfully discuss, record, and revise key tenets of a youth ministry's theology, philosophy, policies, rules, boundaries, approaches, and acceptable terminology, anticipating and describing many possible LGBT scenarios/solutions.[23]

Key deliberations include the following fundamentals. All youth must feel welcome, loved and safe within the context of the youth ministry, meaning LGBT youth and all of the rest of the youth, regardless of anyone's personalities or personal struggles. Behavioral respect of and obedience to God's Word must not be compromised within the context of youth ministry time together and on ministry property. All parental concerns are vital to consider. Communication must be careful and clear.

All written material and planned verbal statements, must be approved by one's supervising authority, and posibally, publicly posted. Doing so not only protects youth workers, but also should serve as an initial guide, enabling teams of leaders in providing consistent and caring

22. The most difficult states reside on the West Coast, South West, North East, and North Central areas of the country.

23. See Yarhouse, *Understanding Sexual Identity*, and other works. They help provide terminology and material to consider in the building of one's theology, philosophy, and ministry approaches, even if the larger body (organization) has its own policies and statements. There might be a gap or contextual factor that wasn't considered by the authoritative bodies. After finishing, compare documents. If yours includes valuable material, not on the other, ask if you can include a special Youth Ministry oriented addendum.

ministry to teens in the LGBT community. Before faithfully assisting the hurting and confused LGBT teen, youth leaders must take proactive steps, tangibly demonstrating to families and supportive communities, concern for their concerns and security as well. The LGBT youth only pose more warranted attention than drug users or band buddies because of the potentially political and awkward dynamics, not because these teens should be treated as more sinful than any other teens.

LGBT Opportunities

Out of all quadrants, IGIP youth are clearly the most at-risk for developing deviant interests, which in today's culture, is best represented by epidemic engagement with distorted sexual activities and drugs, the two often experienced together. IGIP youth who particularly wrestle with sexually deviant interests pursue them, subconsciously venting anger or lonely despair at an unresponsive attachment figure. Somebody has to suffer! Many take out their frustrations on themselves.[24] Some take them out on each other, sadomasochist sex dominates wiccan ceremonies and homosexual encounters.[25] Hurt teens also target adults because they represent authority. On the surface, sexual expressions and experimentations stimulate physical responses, generating and satisfying sexual appetites, and seeming to address craving to be loved. Thus, allowing one to deceive oneself into believing that these activities truly fulfill. Eventually, however, every person learns, superficial experiences fail to compensate for the lost love of a mother and/or father or for supernatural longings. So they try more of what they know satisfied at some point, perpetuating cycles of reach for the, ultimately, unsatisfactory.[26] I pray we more intentionally reach out to these teens earlier than later.

People move from momentary high to momentary high, lacking contentment in between, developing cycles of addiction.[27] Addiction occurs relative to a broad variety of objects: drugs, relationships, attention, control, sexual expression, and more. "Addiction is a particularly

24. Nathanson, "Embracing Darkness," 272–84.

25. Pearson, "Inappropriate Sexuality," 31–42.

26. Heschmeyer, "Neurology and C. S. Lewis' Argument from Desire." Read Lewis, *Mere Christianity*, for more on the topic of a person's life appetites and satisfactions; also read C. S. Lewis' *Argument from Desire* at www.strangenotions.com.

27. Most literature on helping addicts out of addiction describes the common paths by which all people develop addictions as a cycle of addiction. Read on.

modern habit, and can be viewed as a mirror reflecting back to us aspects of modern culture. . . . Persons with severe addictions are among those contemporary prophets that we ignore to our own demise, for they show us who we truly are. Christians must heed prophets."[28] These teens are telling us loud and clear, they need to know and feel the love of an invested parent and the love of God! Authentic vulnerability stands a much better chance in the context of a youth ministry than anywhere else in their world, or at least it ought to. Interaction with youth leaders, peers, and other aspects of youth ministries allows teens to freely admit to self and others repressed and anxiety provoking thoughts and feelings, relating to both original insecurities and current indecencies. Awareness and acknowledgment providing relief more than embarrassment.

LGBT and So Many Others

Awareness and insight are not enough, however, to propel an anxious teen, tempted by substitutionary fonts of "love," toward healing from habitual, destructive, life choices; the real source of anxiety-causing pain must be addressed. Connecting young people to professional therapists represents one advisable way that youth workers assist distraught teenagers. During such a process, youth workers ought to walk beside teens, possibly as a young person gets professional counseling. Walking with a youth definitely means actively expressing concern and interest, not just watching from the sidelines.

Relative to LGBT youth an invested youth worker might be a young person's sole or best hope for restorative life. Many youth and their parents believe they have no need for therapy and, based on social and legal encouragement, actually feign happiness with current lifestyle choices. Youth workers must help these teens, ultimately feeling shamefully rejected, to feel loved, safe, and welcome—no matter who they are, what burdens they bear, or what addictive, lifestyle pain-killers they use.

Loving them doesn't mean telling them they're making bad decisions, nor does it mean telling them they're fine just the way they are, as most in Hollywood and politics would like. Loving someone means accepting another as imperfect. Loving them means guiding them to achieve an identity consistent with the character of Jesus Christ, leaving their decisions of what that entails up to the convictions of the Holy

28. Dunnington, *Addiction and Virtue*, 10.

Spirit. We must focus our efforts on dealing with core issues, not distracted by (scarlet or rainbow) *letters* by which our teens might historically or whimsically label themselves.[29] We help LGBT youth most in the exact same ways we help

> Loving them means guiding them to achieve an identity consistent with the character of Jesus Christ, leaving their decisions of what that entails up to the convictions of the Holy Spirit. We must focus our efforts on dealing with core issues, not distracted by (scarlet or rainbow) *letters* by which our teens might historically or whimsically label themselves.

all teens through adolescent turmoil: offering the traditional elements of youth ministry. Offer a rock of refuge, a safe place of shelter, which provides: love, positive peer encounters, caring adults, and teaching from God's holy, convicting, and healing, Word.

When a young man asked me if he had to give up smoking to be a Christian, I told him three things. First, research shows that smoking ruins one's lungs and causes cancer, but no research shows it prevents one from wanting or accepting the love of Jesus Christ. Second, the decision to quit smoking was between him and God, and even though I thought quitting would be the healthier choice, smoking would not keep God or me from loving him. Third, if he did sense and want to surrender to God's desire for him not to smoke, I would do what I could to help him achieve that goal. He decided he wanted a relationship with that kind of God. Sometime later he decided to quit smoking, though he found it a difficult decision (not in desire, but in ability to achieve). Enveloped in the arms of the youth ministry's adults and teens helped him to feel less alone in his struggle. I've counseled several others struggling with sexually perverse fascinations the same way.[30]

Practically, a youth worker almost automatically helps a young person slow down one's cycle of addiction, the best way out of addiction. No matter the symptom (sexual deviation, chocolate, alcohol, isolation, pornography, popularity, success, gaming, drugs, social media), consuming

---

29. Isa 1:18; see Nathaniel Hawthorne's novel, *The Scarlet Letter*.

30. One struggling with deviant interests compares to one struggling with a variety of problems, therefore, not necessarily prohibiting one from going into ministry. However, since youth are vulnerable, and youth ministry settings offer more than typical intimate opportunity, those actively struggling with sexually deviant desires need several sources of accountability and much more carefully drawn and honored boundaries. An unwillingness to follow these and possibly more steps indicates a lack of mature awareness and invalidates one for ministry.

habits follow behavioral cycles. They're initiated by emotional triggers, which solicit escape fantasies, which foster obsessive craving, appeased only by acting out, typically leading to engorging in actions, resulting in one feeling frustrated with self, and desiring and vowing (at first, more to self than anyone else) to stop. The cycles continue and get worse because normal joys in life can't competitively create the dopamine releases into one's system that one's body demands. Tolerance develops when targeted consumption becomes the norm, thus meaning actions have to escalate, homosexual interaction expands to multiple partner interaction, controlling environment expands to controlling people, a spoonful of ice cream becomes a quart of ice cream. For those entrenched in sexual fixation, eventually no sexual deviance satisfies alone.

Symptomatic experimentation allows one to dysfunctionally express pains at "non-retaliatory" enemy stand-ins, one's self. Ironically and sadly, though, addicts destroy themselves, perpetuating the effect of the negligence or abuse against them, to a worse degree than the original violation(s). By continuing in a pattern of self-abuse, a person gets to hate oneself with regularity, endorsing one's lowly opinion of one's own self-worth. I decided to stop my deviant adolescent ways when by the grace of God while experimentally reading His word, I realized that I was harming and threatening my own potential present and future more than anyone else ever had. An incredibly difficult moment, yet the spring board toward fuller healing.

IGIP-Spiritually and Socially Insecure	Insecure—Attachment w/ God Primary Needs of Adolescent	Insecure—Attachment with God Initial Role of Youth Leader (w/ other leaders)
Insecure—Attachment with Parents Profile: Extreme Internalization (quiet/avoiding—the potential cutter/SI) or Externalization (potentially agitating, rude, bitter, or loud/attention seeking). No spiritual assent to God. (Those raised in the church are typically more difficult to work with than those not.)	Relational Need—Unconditional Love and obvious interest; Availability; Interest-Contact; Belonging and ability/freedom to come to a safe place; To observe other youth trusting and partnering with adults; Healthy intimacy in healthy peer community; Small-Group ministry; Youth led worship; Heard; Bible character stories; Adult role model; Healthy social fun; Practical expressions of support/love; a Church's hospitality; Peer receptivity and leadership	Representing God first, then, depending on the development of a relationship, parents. 1. Evangelism aimed at the heart. Loving the youth and meeting individual physical, emotional, and social needs first. 2. Listen; Pray with in compassion. 3. Befriend without judgment, as a confident adult. 4. Teaching simple truth and stories of the Bible. 5. Give basic practical ministry responsibility. 6. Offered a structured, safe place for IGIP teens to come.

Figure 1. IGIP Youth Needs with Youth Worker's Initial Role

Slowing an experimental, struggling teen down, involves several normal emphases in youth ministry. First, reflect on stated and implied action steps in the chapter up to now. Second, share the gospel, regularly. Pray together. Read and/or study the Bible together. Validate the worth of a person. This occurs in common interactions, but not normally with unintentional effort. These interactions can and should occur among groups and in individual connections.

One on one conversations should focus on foundational, emotional loss and pain, and not the symptomatic behaviors (sexual expressions) of those pains. As discussed in the last chapter, listen (see Figure 1). Help a teen to feel heard, from the inside out, not from the outside in. Allow silence in conversation. Ask one or two questions, but not so many they feel grilled by questions reflecting curiosity more than concern. When a teen talks, reflect back just one or two key words or phrases, often strong emotional words, like, "I *hate* it when," or "it gets so *lonely*." For a rejected and rejecting teen to be heard in such a manner is rare. Obvious behavior and clutter comprises the façade of most lives and the bulk of most conversations. Let superficial chat take a back seat to one's buried and hidden, failing roots. Start with surface level conversation, but encourage, the teen to move deeper verbally and nonverbally. Pray together at some of these connections.

Teach teens how to pray, modeling it and explaining it. Pray in your youth meetings. We usually prayed together for twenty to thirty minutes, in varying forms on most of my weekly youth meeting nights, and in most of my ministries. Many IGIP youth only know prayer as something someone does before a meal or at bedtime, if they have a concept of prayer at all. Prayer is the best answer to slowing one down. When one's emotional triggers fire, or when fantasies start, the Holy Spirit nudges one to pray, and stands waiting and wanting to work with one in prayer. Praying can intervene at any point in a habitual cycle. Reading God's Word can intervene at any point too.

Valuing God's Word shows in one's own lifestyle actions, modeling the impact of His word. Teaching the depth of His word helps teens to see depth to life and to self. Letting them see one turning to God's word at difficult junctures or slight quandaries or in celebration shows regard for His word. Memorizing God's word can serve as a great inhibitor to cycle continuity. Quoting a verse from memory might block a normal fantasy related to a typical trigger, and lead to a teen picking up a Bible to read instead of engaging in a normal pattern. It's possible that trigger emotions will call certain scriptural passages, instead of past imaginations. Literally provide teens with Bibles. We kept stacks of them to give away in all of my ministries.

Give unsolicited attention to a teen as a human being worthy of interest, not to what the teen uses to bring attention, like weird hair, tattoos, provocative dress, and more. See below one's façade and help the teen to see oneself the same way. And for teens who have historically entertained and cultivated distorted sexual identities, pray for hearts to change. Don't expect behavior to change overnight, or even ever. Let the change be up to God and the person. We in youth ministry are required to feed another with His love and ours. We challenge IGIP much differently than we do those who acknowledge Christ as Savior. We must be more gentle and patient. Until one steps into a relationship with Jesus Christ, whatever changes occur are only steeped in human effort anyway. The Holy Spirit will work the rest of it out.

LGBT Nuts and Bolts Issues

Youth leaders cannot let any deviant person dictate a flow of ministry that impacts many others. Being sensitive to another and indulging another's dictums are two different approaches to working with people. One cannot sacrifice the standards of God or the inclinations of one's own common sense judgements to appease anyone. On retreat, I would not allow a teen to smoke in a cabin with other teens, nor allow a young heterosexual teen couple to display affection. Thus, using the same moral logic, I would not allow a boy who thinks he is a girl to sleep in a girl's cabin or to use a girl's restroom. I would not allow a father who had an addiction to alcohol to serve as a chaperone and neither would I allow a mother in a lesbian relationship to serve as a chaperone. Realistically, we often might not know about people's closet issues until after we've used them to help. Making an unknown mistake is different than making a known one. Once one spells out a theology and philosophy relative to LGBT issues . . . the nuts and bolts of how to deal with them fall into place.

Peer Needs: Their Last Hope

IGIP avoidant youth simply need to be seen by their peers. Many of these youth sit next to everyone else in their classrooms, yet remain nameless to most unless they do something drastic. Some seem to be the center of attention, known as the class clown. Whether wearing a Bozo nose or not having a name, all of these young people want to be seen. They just make different distorted efforts. They need to be noticed below the surface. Most class clowns end up exhausted by entertaining peers and feel disappointed when no one seems to see them as more than a clown. They're popular on a surface level, but more as a sideshow. They crave someone to befriend them and they have no idea how to do that normally. Class clowns force laughter trying to cover their internal tears. See comedian and suicide victim Robin Williams' life story of childhood

> Class clowns force laughter trying to cover their internal tears.

emotional neglect (CEN). If a secure young person does not reach out for deeper level friendship to an IGIP first, then a relationship is unlikely.

Due to their resistance to adults, most IGIP youth will need peer friendship to meet Jesus and youth workers.

Parental Approach: Prayer

You might have noticed I said nothing about ministry to parents in the fourth quadrant identifying a Youth Pastor's initial role. I discovered that a lot of these adolescents feel tremendous disappointment or rage against their parents. And unlike the SGIP youth, they don't feel any compulsion to forgive or reconcile or to even want anything to do with their parents. I started to build a decent relationship with one young man who represented these insecurities. He was actually probably Insecure Disorganized, at times very anxious and aggressive and at others incredibly difficult to reach. But he started expressing interest in God and participating in the youth ministry. And he was beginning to enjoy life.

One day his mother showed up in my office and asks if she can help with the youth ministry. Well aware of this fellow's disdain for his mother, I encouraged her greater participation in the church and not in the youth ministry. She persisted. She was observing dramatic changes in her son that she desperately wanted to experience herself. She knew God was working in our ministry and wanted to be a part of it. So I gave her an administrative role, a very helpful one as it turned out. When I told her son that his mom wanted to help and that I gave her a position that would not interact with the young people, he went ballistic. He told me it was either him or her. I explained that I could not turn down anyone who expressed a desire to grow in a relationship with Christ and that I found a way to help her while not interfering in his experience. I asked him to pray about being receptive to the idea. Despite extra effort on my part, we never connected again.

Our ministries are to youth first. Don't deny parents who become attracted to Christ, but also don't make them a priority to reach when working with IGIP teens. At least not at first. We must communicate with and be available to them, but not intent on discipling them until rapport and trusting confidence is first clearly established. I had rapport with this teen, but not confident trust. Pass adults' names off to other ministry leaders. Though that boy's mother did grow in her faith, had I to do it all over again, I would have more strongly encouraged her into a different ministry in the church. And at the least, delayed her work with the youth ministry.

CONCLUSION

Extensive evangelism was the main priority . . . with the youth who had grown up in the church in my first professional ministry. Years later in another church, 60 percent of the youth group had made confessions of Christ as Savior, supposedly, but only 20 percent demonstrated any evidence of belief.[31] The world has closed the mouth of the Christian in the marketplace and the church has ignored the words of Christ in His own home. Anecdotal evidence tells me that the IGIP teens raised in the church start the walk away from God long before they ever get to the Youth Pastor.

We must restore a right understanding as to who God is, with integrity, to the non-parented youth. The single-parented home represents about one-third of today's families, the fastest growing family in the country. But there are more absent parents than those stats indicate. We must stand in the gap and become a bridge to the many who don't know their parents.

Having done previous research with youth to find out what factors contribute to an attachment relationship with a youth worker, I found that in addition to Jesus' mentoring approach, the frequency of time in God's word made significant differences in the formation of attachments to youth workers. Seventy-three percent of the youth with the highest attachment relationships to youth workers had the most frequent interaction with Scripture in a week, while those who had the least interaction with Scripture only represented 14 percent of that same group. This is a significant consideration when thinking about IGIP youth, as another finding in my research demonstrated attachment relationships with youth workers helped teenagers to feel significantly less lonely. Yes, IGIP youth need physical and emotional needs to be met, perhaps before they care about the gospel, but the gospel brings spiritual significance to them. What good is surviving in life, if one survives alone? If one survives without purpose? Represent Jesus.

> What good is surviving in life, if one survives alone?

31. These are estimates.

As a wayward lad, walking to the Pittsburgh Pirate game during a day "at school," I stepped on something. Being environmentally conscious, I picked it up; it was an evangelism track. Before throwing it away, I read it. It mentally slowed me down for just a minute. Don't discount sharing the gospel in any way that one can or in any way that it's ever been done because certain methods seem outdated or squirrely. God speaks through many awkward, sincere efforts. At least those who give tracks out try. I'd rather share Jesus in any way than simply criticize others for using a wrong approach. We need to make sure we're sharing the Jesus of Scripture too, not of our own making. Thirsty youth need the real thing, Living Water.

PERSONAL CHALLENGE AND DISCUSSION QUESTIONS FOR LEADERSHIP TEAMS

1. Do you believe that God and heaven are real? Satan and hell? How does your ministry acknowledge those realities?

2. In what ways is your ministry IGIP friendly? Pursuant? Growing?

3. What is the balance of the youth ministry right now relative to fun and evangelistic and discipleship focus? Where and how can it improve?

CHAPTER 11

Youth Leader/Ministry Context Influencing ARM

"We don't know how to be with our kids. We don't know how to be with ourselves. We don't know how to be with God. We move from activity to activity, with few real relationships and little introspection." (Yaconelli, *Contemplative Youth Ministry*, pp. 19–20)

"The unspoken assumption in nearly every Christian is that our cultural activity will change the world for the better. . . . There is one crucial way that all culture is local: all culture making is local. Every cultural good . . . begins with a small group of people." (Crouch, *Culture Making*, pp. 199, 239)

"Leader one-on-one time was the only significant predictor of conversion among the Young Life program variables . . . more time spent with the Young Life leader predicted increased odds of a gradual conversion at camp." (Schnitker, "Attachment Predicts Adolescent Conversion," p. 211)

"[D]ata shows that the longer an adolescent participates in mentoring relationship with a youth-worker, the more likely he or she is to be attached to the youth-worker. Significant differences were found between adolescents who spent two or less years together with a youth-worker and those who spent four or more years together with a youth-worker." (Belsterling, "Youth Work," p. 42)

Multiple contextual issues impact a youth leader's ability to lead. These may restrain, constrain or unleash a youth worker trying to apply ARM. Most churches focus on discipleship, while parachurch ministries tend to concentrate on evangelism. What room exists relative to these matters and the flexibility and cohesion of the system where one works makes huge differences. How open and able is one's organization to support and encourage a more fully rounded and balanced approach? Attachment styles of a Youth Pastor's leaders matter. Relative to personal issues, what is a youth leader's own attachment style? Availability? System preference? Educational training? Experience? One's own spiritual maturity, relational priorities, and notions of biblical authority sway ARM effectiveness. This chapter considers all of these issues.

ORGANIZATIONAL CONTEXT AND PHILOSOPHY

All systems have written and unwritten rules and roles within an identified context and structure. For instance the supervision scheme usually works far differently for a Youth Pastor than an Area Director for Young Life, which works very differently from an Intern for Young Life. Know the system. Know the hierarchy of authority and who dictates the flow and expectations on the youth ministry by written and unwritten factors. Identify the key supervisors, whether direct or indirect. Consider their approaches, communications, strengths, and weaknesses.

Without formal analysis, pinpoint the overall slant of each key person or body (most bodies have one to two major power players). When all lead from a balanced, yet different perspective (see Figure 2, ch. 5) this still sends some conflicting signals and may create tensions, but at least everyone desires healthy ministry. The more they overlap, the more likely a youth worker's role and expectations have been clearly articulated. Of course, if one sees multiple leaders leaning toward far and different corners, the youth leader probably bounces from one's disfavor to another's scorn. "For am I now seeking the favor of men or of God," proves difficult enough in healthy environments. Trying to seek favor when one's leaders' desires diverge on different ends of a dysfunctional spectrum literally drives many out of ministry.[1]

1. Gal 1:10.

Into an interview for about fifteen minutes one time, it appeared that several power players on the committee disagreed with one another as to what the church wanted or needed from a Youth Pastor. After another fifteen minutes of giving questions and answers designed to test my theory, they confirmed it. At that point, I pulled out of interviewing and offered to consult. Working there would have been a disaster. We constructively spent another hour together, the committee realizing the need to table hiring anyone until outlining unified goals. (I hope Lead Pastors are reading this.)

Some work for organizations where one's position requirements flow neatly out of a national or carefully constructed template. Just because a piece of paper says something it doesn't mean a youth leader's supervisors follow it. It provides leverage when they don't though. I've called supervisors back to my job description multiple times relative to how my time was to be spent relative to which tasks. If one's job description suggests the possibility of an eighty hour work week, ask supervisors for their priorities to see if they match each other and one's own. If working without a job description, write one and submit it for approval. After several years in youth ministry I discovered all volunteers, adults and youth, work better when they have a job description.

Ministry Leader Response

Ron, I love the direction you've decided to go with this book and am glad you are calling youth workers to intentional relational ministry. People need to hear that youth ministry is not dead or outdated or ineffective. This welcome perspective and unapologetic call will change whole perspectives and the lives of teenagers. Done right, ARM can break the doom and gloom mentality so many have assigned to the role of youth ministry in the church.

Having the support of the leadership changes everything. My current church greatly values children, youth, and families. More adults are inspired to volunteer weekly to invest in relationships with our youth, thus, more students' lives are forever changed.

Being able to identify the specific needs of individual teens and knowing how to address them in relationship can be a difficult and overwhelming task at times. I'm excited to have this resource to give to our adult leaders to further educate them in the best ways to identify relational needs, and properly initiate and subsequently cultivate healthy Christ-centered relationships!

Tim Degelman, Middle School Pastor,
Highland Park Community Church, Casper, Wyoming

YOUTH LEADER ATTACHMENT STYLE

Diverging priorities alone may be making or breaking one's ministry effectiveness and leading to positive or negative consequences felt by one's entire family. By now, due to assorted personal experiences, many readers are wondering about their own attachment alignments. Those who aren't wondering either have experienced such secure childhood attachments that no doubts exist or may have already addressed these issues. Those who are possibly insecurely attached? This chapter and chapter 12 may help you personally before professionally. The truly curious can find a validated attachment assessment at: www.web-research-design.net/cgi-bin/crq/crq.pl.[2] Whatever one's style, it influences the shaping and potential success of one's ministry. Keep in mind though, attachment figures don't have to be perfect for secure attachments to occur; those trying hard under God's guidance probably provide what most Insecure teens need.

Regardless of attachment style, anyone can effectively lead in ministry. I tell my students all the time that some of them are biologically more intellectually capable than others, yet everyone can succeed in my classes. Those with less intellectual gifting just have to work twice as hard. Some have to work three times as hard. As I have no intentions to assume responsibility for or placate the less able, I tell them, "Know who you are, and study accordingly." God demands much from those who have agreed to teach His flock, especially professionally.

Youth ministry = teaching adolescents, sometimes in a classroom, but also while playing games, hiking, praying, or retreating (Deut 6:7). Those with insecure attachments have to lead, teach, and love, working harder than those with secure attachments. (Curiosity question for the secure—Do you sometimes wish you had a more dramatic conversion story? Never ever undervalue the testimony of strong Christian heritage. Curiosity question for the insecure—Do you realize the trial becomes gift in having to work twice as hard in ministry?) I have some drama in my story and am frequently tempted to wish I didn't, but I'm grateful anyway, trusting His blessings through what I sometimes know and sometimes don't. "The rich and the poor have a common bond, The Lord is the maker of them all" (Prov 22:2).

Working hard on intrapersonal issues saves valuable interpersonal working time, minimizing relational mistakes and ensuing predicaments.

2. See Chris Fraley's website for the full ECR-R questionnaire.

As has been emphasized, adolescence offers the best chance at altering problematic attachment orientations, but not one's last chance. One current youth ministry leader recently asked, "If I'm depressed can I help adolescents suffering from depression"? Yes. Actually helping others contributes to one coming out of severe or moderate depression. Our moods and personality snags may reflect our attachment styles, cultural circumstances, or poor sleep patterns. If they do suggest attachment difficulties, don't panic. Bowlby theorized that styles are set by age three, and with no assistance or introspective effort, they will always function as one's relational gatekeeper. But while they're locked in, deliberate and Spirit led adults can pick the lock. Styles may be set, but more in thick mud than in concrete. It's not easy, and it will be a lifelong battle, but it's doable, and worth it. If it weren't, I wouldn't be able to write this book. God provides for everyone, not just children.

Developing a relationship with God seriously attacks unhealthy attachment alignments. That is why youth leaders must seriously reflect on their representation of God, trusting God, even relative to some of the conditions He has allowed. When my wife tells me how I can show her I love her and I ignore what she says, she can't help but wonder why. Especially if I've told her how I want to be loved and she obliges with great care, effort, and joy. We're both supposed to be enjoying the benefits of relationship. Ultimately, when I love her the way she desires, our relationship quality improves. Interpersonal successes with her enhance my own intrapersonal thoughts and moods, consequentially improving my relational interaction with everyone. Now imagine how all this can go, if I love God the way He desires and deserves to be loved.

> Developing a relationship with God seriously attacks unhealthy attachment alignments.

Securely attached youth workers may minister to youth with less emotional baggage and interference, but they also may be the more likely to minister from the hip, so to speak. Such a person, must actually work hard to make sure that the insecure are not forgotten. Insecure leaders must make sure not to violate a cardinal youth ministry rule, the youth are not there to give the youth worker friends or to make him or her feel better about one's personal importance. Insecure leaders must avoid taking fluctuating attendance and commitment of youth personally. Teens have enough to worry about without having to be responsible for the emotional needs of their "leader(s)."

LEADERSHIP ABILITY AND COMMITMENT

Underestimating the difficulty of youth ministry overwhelms all new youth leaders, especially underprepared ones. They discover their leadership teams need more attention than the youth demand. Some have been poorly taught or lack a background of training. This impacts the budgeting of their time, making life especially difficult for the person who agreed to volunteer or work in a part time position. For some it's like trying to buy groceries for a family for the week with $50.00. What to buy, what not to buy? In ministry, what to do, what not to do?

So many expect full time work for part time pay. Some try to run youth ministries through volunteers alone, which amounts to asking one to put out a forest fire with a bucket of water. Others familiar with a church's philosophy, yet educationally not equipped, only realize the lack of equipping after taking a position. Life's pressures make or break relationships; this common adage proves true relative to one's relationship with God. If one is not securely attached to God, all other relationships falter. This means one's ministry falters.

Multiple factors play a role in a youth leader's ability to lead. Time demands by a flock of teens often don't match the arbitrary number of hours some churches identify when hiring a youth worker. They'll calculate time needed to lead the youth ministry as one night a week (two hours), one weekend night a month (three hours), and one morning every week (one hour), factor in travel, preparation, hanging out, and miscellaneous (three hours) and feel generous paying someone for ten hours per week. I get requests for "interns" regularly that reflect such a reality (these are some of the better ones). Many parachurch organizations hire folks with no training other than participation in the program. They often neglect to weigh the importance of education until the lack of results in a Christian participant espousing a heretical theology at home. Those hiring youth leaders do all of this while expecting tremendous commitment on the part of a young adult; organization commitment levels not matching up. Who wants to marry someone who demands 100 percent commitment and offers only 25 percent commitment back?

Full Time, Part Time, and Volunteer Considerations

How much time is necessary? GROUP's May 2014 issue focused on the notion that churches are pulling back from offering full time youth ministry positions. Praise God that many full-time positions are available, in fact more are looking for full-time help in youth ministry than I have graduating students to provide. As I've received phone calls from multiple Youth Ministry faculty on other campuses who have great positions available but not enough graduates, this seems to be a common problem. At the same time more part time positions are being offered too. Youth ministry requires at least one person's full time attention, no matter how small a church youth group or parachurch ministry currently stands. Note Schnitker's research findings in the quote at the beginning of this chapter, the only youth leader characteristic found significantly altering likelihood of a teen's conversion was time together. Volunteers running youth ministries, God bless you. I don't know how you do all that is asked of you. Youth Pastors and parachurch ministry directors need to treasure their volunteers. Youth Pastors and directors deserve compensation equal to their pastoral tasks, skills, and experience.

Churches need to respect and provide packages to Youth Pastors comparable to that given to other Pastors. I worked for a large church who hired me part time initially, as per their and my desires. As response and related strains to an effective ministry occurred fairly quickly, demands grew rapidly too. Essentially working fulltime, I asked for full pay and was told there wasn't room in the budget. After several more similar exchanges over two years I said I'd have to resign. Wow. Who could have imagined? All of a sudden the church could afford fulltime pay. Sadly, church families will love us, take every minute we have, and give as little back as possible. I've heard this story repeated so many times over the years it angers me. Churches treating any and all Pastors with the respect due all Elders benefit more from giving faithfully than holding back fearfully.

If churches decide to not call youth leaders Pastors, fine, but this should relate more to expected responsibility than to convenience. I know too many Youth "Directors" named today, in a day when "program" has a bad name, so churches can avoid the dilemma of affording all Pastors Elder roles. Where is the integrity of the church? The title relates to the differences in how one prioritizes his or her calendar and energy. Church—do you want someone to supervise and run a program? Or to lead and minister to a people? If the answer is, "minister to people," that position describes a Pastor.

Full time youth workers must more responsibly limit their average work week to fifty hours, forty for pay, and ten to out-volunteer all volunteers. As I became wiser, and some of those seventy hour weeks were unavoidable, I compensated myself and my family with ten hours from the previous or next week. Take days off, off. The older my family became I tried to limit weekend activities on my or any other adult associated with the youth ministry to two nights or days per month. We had more activity than that, but all leaders shared the load. Limit nights out to a maximum of three per week. It's not just about how much time one gives, it's also about the quality of that time. The more inordinate amount of time away from family, the less the quality of time at home. This threatens the quality of time a youth worker puts into the job.

Education and Training

With so many colleges and seminaries offering programs and courses in youth ministry and adolescent development today, it's sad that ministry organizations continue to hire those with no youth ministry educational background. It's unfair to those they hire and to the youth and families to whom they're supposed to minister. Things may have worked well enough that way when the profession of youth ministry was just starting, but so did flannelgraph boards and movie film projectors. What's worse is that yester year's teen culture issues pale in comparison to those of today. Consider the rapid deterioration of morality and its consequential impact on the family, education, and entertainment. Couple that with the rapid growth of technology and social media. How can those demeaning the need for and value of youth ministry face children and youth without shame? How can the church throw the untrained into this fire storm with no or very little training?

Some churches today prefer to hire youth workers from within, more concerned with them knowing a church's protocol than ministry and adolescent expertise. Familiarity with a system proves helpful, but not at the expense of deeper level training. Today's youth ministry demands so much expertise from its leaders. Some hiring from within hire preferring strong character to experience and education too, not realizing that the neglect of education and experience only increases the likelihood of a leader's moral failure. Who pays the price for youth ministry leaders lacking proper educational and experiential training?

Exactly how are many churches ensuring that the teens of their ministries are led by those understanding youth culture and possessing skills to interpret, understand, and apply Biblical truth? Many send their workers to the next large publisher generated, youth ministry conference. I'm sure some youth workers benefit somewhat from this intermittent teaching-learning method. But enough? And always? I personally know, like, and trust some common speakers. No doubt that attendees learn how to build the kingdom in their seminars. And there are others I personally know, like, and distrust. No doubt that attendees learn how to distract the building of the kingdom in their seminars. Amidst the technological pizazz, big names, packed rooms, late nights, fantastic entertainment, and plethora of eager, likeminded colleagues, how does an untrained youth worker discern the speaker who informs from the speaker who misinforms?

> how does an untrained youth worker discern the speaker who informs from the speaker who misinforms?

Especially when they're all only together for a weekend? Those who speak, write, and those who write, speak.

I replaced a Youth Director who had purchased and read almost every youth ministry book written in the five year period prior to and during his three year tenure. He had a great heart but was entirely stunned by church politics, behavior issues, power parents, vision casting, team leadership, budgeting, group management, small group leader training, and more. The longer he led the less confidence he had. His training? Attendance at ministry conferences, his extensive library and a bachelor's degree not in ministry. I was so jealous of his library, but all of those books didn't help him to lead well. His method to filter good resources from bad ones was based on whether or not he liked someone. He wasn't fired, he just opted out, broken.

Typically, the more youth workers like a resource, the better they presume it is. Many books my friend liked represented the generic youth ministry book, written by a big name at an eighth grade reading level with one good idea expanded into a hundred pages full of quips, quotes, and discussion questions. Liking something doesn't make it eternally beneficial. If I only have time and money for one meal today, should I eat broccoli or a pop tart? Ignoring careful and proven educational steps only increases the chances of developing the entertainment oriented ministries we're accused of offering. "Reaching the New Generation" reigns supreme as a hip speaking topic. It always has and always will. Most youth leaders would attend the seminar. That's good because Gen Alpha is here and Gen Beta is on the way, and everything we know or just learned about real ministry with Gen Z should be flushed. We already have descriptors of Gen Alpha despite the fact that most of them have yet to be born.[3] While I advocate for noticing cultural trends, volunteers and impressionable leaders with little study time or background

> volunteers and impressionable leaders with little study time or background knowledge need meaty and true more than trendy and woo.

knowledge need meaty and true more than trendy and woo.
Who woos?

Consider *The Huffington Post* and *The Atlantic*, simultaneously describe the millennial generation as both the generation that "doesn't believe in settling down" and the "stuck, go-nowhere-generation."[4] Which one of these potential speaking "experts," based on being *authors* for reputed purveyors of culture and news, do we listen to? Folks, this is real. Ten years ago I attended a seminar on, *How to Counsel Depressed Teens*, at a major conference. The woman speaking interviewed a therapist and wrote an article on the topic. She possessed zilch counseling background. Her answers proved as much. Some *experts* aren't. Youth leaders require better training.

Youth workers who can't attend a course somewhere, fare best when trained by personally and carefully selected teachers and books, using the sole authority of Scripture as one's main filter. Conferences should act as a condiment to training efforts, providing some extra zest and a new consideration here and there but not replacing the main meat. Who wants to eat a bun with nothing but condiments on it? Youth workers must steep themselves in God's word to be able to discern the good from the bad. Training should not be sought intermittently or at the mercy of a conference leader's inclinations. Churches who hire youth workers with no training and then send them to this training have created some of the situations that people are complaining about. One should take one's training into his/her own hands, personally budgeting time to train regularly. Such efforts might include:

3. Williams, "Meet Alpha," lines 17–39.

4. Braun, "This is Why Our Generation Doesn't Believe in Settling Down," lines 16–20; Thompson, "Generation Stuck," lines 1–14.

1. An intentional, hermeneutically sound study of a book in God's word[5]

2. Reading classic Christian authors and texts

3. Prayer saturated observations of culture, considering varied sources.

4. Careful selection of a wise, trusted, youth ministry mentor, who can suggest solid youth ministry resources and caution against others

5. Regularly meeting with observed, relationally successful other youth leaders

6. Reading in varied fields of disciplines related to youth ministry (psychology, sociology, science, education, technology)

7. Knowing one's Attachment Style and working to correct insecure styles

SPIRITUAL MATURITY AND INTENTIONAL RELATIONAL PRIORITY

Not all ministry leaders have deep relationships with Jesus Christ themselves, making the possibility of loving others out of His overflowing love impossible. Some want them but find little time to cultivate them. Many of our responsibilities end up relating more to a to-do list than because we've felt convicted or encouraged by the whisper of the Holy Spirit. If we're truthful with ourselves this problem reflects our priorities more than our crowded schedules. While we may try to love our flock authentically, devoid of the sustenance of God, our love will not be pure, will not last, and may lead to catastrophic results. Caught more in a cycle of program than in the true wind of the Holy Spirit, our teaching and leading depend more on our own inclinations.

Others might know everything there is to know about Christ but don't know Him. They're studied up from the past but expressing Him from the fumes of faint recall rather than on a new filling. The details of what they know may be accurate, but they struggle to communicate the peace, joy, and compassion of Christ. If one is not intentional about reading God's word on a regular basis, cultivating one's vertical relationship with Christ, he won't be able to convey God's thoughts clearly in any horizontal relationships. Who we are in today's moment is the same person we've been in yesterdays' and this morning's spiritual discipline.

5. See Duvall and Hayes, *Grasping God's Word.*

Apart From the Lord, No One Will Help You

By the way, it may not just be our work and supervisors who will interfere in our relational time with the Lord. Those who most need us to relate His love to them will interfere. Everyone in the church or para-church family will tell us they want us to have a good relationship with God first and our family second. Most of them forget, however, to acknowledge out loud–"as long as that time you spend with the Lord or your family conflicts with others' needs, not mine"! If we're not prioritizing God, we begin relating to everyone from a joyless position, not as a joy-full person. Those under our care notice the lack of passion and compassion.

When one's relational priorities fail beyond our relationship with God, it may be that our spouses take Christ's seat of influence. Often, however, they take the seat behind everyone else. Despite Jacob like wrestling with God (I did not want to have a family interfering with ministry and God knew it would be the strength of my ministry), and my ensuing notice to God that my family would take priority over my ministry, I started to fail God, my wife, and those under my care by allowing my wife to slip in relational priority.

My expressed thinking was that she was the only one who could/ would graciously understand all of the demands on my time (children, ministry, classes, counseling hours, teaching schedule and research). One day she approached me and told me that she would always love me, but no longer understood why she was the first and last one to always have to sacrifice relational time. She didn't understand. She was lonely. She was right.

The next day I came home at lunch and told her that my Lead Pastor assigned me a task on the upcoming Saturday, dismissing my plans with my wife.[6] When she heard I told him "no," she pleaded with me to comply. She feared my repercussions. She needed me and yet she was willing to sacrifice what she had just said she no longer could sacrifice— my misplacing her as a priority. Because of her own love for me, not even my own wife who desperately needed me to make her a priority would help me.

The Holy Spirit is our most dependable ally. If one's most important relationship is not prioritized as first in intent, time, and focus, then no

---

6. Giving me last minute assignments was typical for the Lead Pastor. This particular assignment was already scheduled on the year two different times. And the schedule had been set for a year.

other relationships will succeed as they should. It's impossible to be a good parent if one is not a good spouse. Parents love their children most effectively by loving the other parent as a priority. Children raised in the context of stable love attach securely to parents. It's extremely difficult to care for and lead others with integrity when one's home is not in order. We need to be both intentionally teaching about and modeling healthy marriage to our young people. "Faith communities that develop viable strategies at multiple levels are most likely to empower and support coming generations."[7]

By the way, I did not cave to my Pastor's continued demands. My wife and I had a great time together that day. I also got rid of cable [baseball/sports had become my addictive release], stopped counseling, and stopped aiming for "A's" in my graduate studies. I also started taking days off, holiday time off, and holding to a date night with my wife every week. Gratefully, God blessed her [us] with refreshed feelings for me.

Biblical Priority

Youth leaders ignoring deeper level personal and professional Bible study do not represent Jesus Christ or mimic the first disciples. Many dismiss Jesus' wielding of Scripture as impressive, essentially denying the reality of His human state. What about His disciples? As an uneducated fisherman, I'm astounded at how much Scripture Peter quotes at the beginning of the book of Acts.

Not immersing oneself into God's word makes sense if a leader's academic perspective minimizes the value of the historical reliability and authority of His word. Perhaps a leader has no perspective on these matters because he doesn't worry about theology. Prepared curriculums seem to work fine. Clearly some churches are not overly concerned with a potential leader's scriptural incompetence. God definitely cares. Opinion sharing Bible studies make human opinions more important than God's. I wish I had studied the competency one has with God's word when I studied how frequently one teaches from His word. If requiring youth to engage Scriptures frequently facilitated secure attachment relationships, just imagine how powerful competency with the word would show to contribute. Nevertheless, I do not doubt that incompetency with God's word or irreverence for it inhibits attachment relationships.

7. Silliman, "Building Healthy Marriages," 278.

YOUTH MINISTRY SYSTEMS ORIENTATION

Follow the same recommendations in the earlier section under "*Organizational Philosophy*," applying them to one's youth ministry setting. All leaders and leading teams should be analyzed for the same reasons and in the same ways. Discrepancies must be addressed by either recasting a new vision and mission or restating the old and aligning all youth ministry subsystems (small groups, worship team). Each subsystem should operationally be consistent with a balanced and universal youth ministry system, unless leaders intentionally want subsystems to function differently (see Figure 2, ch. 5).

The Youth Pastor must have clear understanding as to his own system preferences. Recall that differences in desires and relational efforts do not necessarily suggest that one way works better than other ways. But if a Youth Pastor's own system preference suggests an extreme approach, chances are that such a leader leads the ministry with unhealthy interactions and unhealthy expectations.

Volunteer leaders help in youth ministry to make a difference in the lives of teenagers not to stroke the ego of a leader. Too many volunteers quit helping because of disorganized structures and roles. Many volunteers need at least some guidance from a leader who prefers to offer more "freedom" (chaos) in ministry than "direction" (effort). Youth Pastors must tweak communications each year, relative to the varying system personalities of the rest of the leadership team(s), and with the idea in mind of allowing and empowering volunteer leaders to hold a Youth Pastor accountable.

DURATION OF RELATIONSHIP

"Over time, repeated interactions with an attachment figure lead to the development of mental representations of others and the self," fostering positive views of others and self as worthy of love, resulting in attachment security.[8] In research assessing teen attachment relationships with Youth Pastors, duration of time with a youth leader showed significant association with the development of attachment relationships in youth ministry.[9] Relationships with four years together showed greater likelihood for

8. Canterberry and Gillath, "Attachment and Caregiving," 208.

9. Belsterling, "Mentoring Approach," 77–92.

developing the strongest attachments, significantly differing from those who had two years or less together. Results indicated that even one year relationships showed association, but the longer time together clearly implied better prospects for attachments to take root. Adolescents with the strongest attachments also measured as less lonely than all others. With more relational confidence they explored and participated in new relationships between themselves and others, not just with the adult youth leader(s).

Four years together provides the possibilities for relationships to grow through two key adolescent developmental stages. Teens facing multiple identity issues fare better with an adult who represents both God and parents in tangible and non-threatening ways. Stability in relationship itself provides many teens with an immeasurable gift.

I encourage all of my graduating students to try to commit to five years in their first position. Many will face multiple dilemmas, but for those who persevere, they and their teens profit greatly. It would be helpful if churches and parachurch organizations demonstrated patience and support during one's early ministry years, anticipating the time to plant and cultivate before fruit becomes visible. Initially, in two of my ministries more youth stopped participating than started. After six months both started growing.

CONCLUSION

Staying close to God's word and spending guarded time with Him in prayer, assures the greater influence of the Holy Spirit on our life and work. He convicts us and guides us. He enables the unseen to be seen, relative to the eternal, the personal, and the relational. As a leader, try to be as consistent as possible between desires for self and others and practices taken to facilitate the development of those desires.

Secure attachment relationships require more work than relationships with no such results. Define as much as can be defined, from roles to rules, from expectations to methods of enforcement, both personally and communally. Maintain a right priority of relationship to ensure that ministry reflects God's nature more than one's own. Youth ministry today demands leaders who live in integrity, commit to stable availability, and know their Bibles, themselves, and how to converse with adolescents.

PERSONAL CHALLENGE AND DISCUSSION QUESTIONS
FOR LEADERSHIP TEAMS

1. Explain organizational and personal system similarities and differences.

2. Name some unwritten rules of one's organization. Name some unwritten rules of one's youth ministry setting. How can the productive ones become written and clarified, and the interfering ones be addressed? By whom? When?

3. Identify ministry leaders in your organization who would benefit most by reading this book. Why will or will you not suggest they read it?

CHAPTER 12

Individual Adolescent Issues Influencing ARM

"The problem with being terrified of an attachment figure is that it activates two different circuits in your brain that just don't work together. One is the attachment brainstem circuit that . . . gets you to flee. . . . The second circuit is the limbic-based attachment system that motivates you toward your attachment figure. The problem is that you cannot go both toward and away from the same person." (Siegel, *Brainstorm*, p. 154)

"When (cultural) war is declared, truth is the first casualty. . . . The greater legacy of the last century is a consequent casualty, namely, trust. . . . We live in a wilderness of mirrors now. . . . There can be no liberty for a community that lacks the information to detect lies."(Meynell, *A Wilderness of Mirrors*, pp. 17, 92–93)[1]

"While there are implications for an adolescent who experiences parental divorce, insecure attachments are not always the result. . . . Ongoing relational experiences in adolescence offer an adolescent chances at increasing or decreasing social and emotional competence." (Underwood and Dailey, *Counseling Adolescents Competently*, pp. 311–12)

---

1. Mark Meynell quoting Arthur Ponsonby, Jesus Angleton, and Walter Lippman.

MULTIPLE TEEN AND ADOLESCENT culture factors might interfere with or interrupt secure child to parent attachments, child/adolescent to God attachments, or adolescent to youth worker attachments. Sin nature chief among them. Teens make their own individual life decisions, some opting not only for developmental rebellion, but also for life long hedonism. Today's cultural immoral milieu greatly tempts and tests teens wanting to or trying to live holy lives. Our culture also breeds perverts who, taking advantage of affiliative attachments[2] or a child's isolated desperation, abuse children and teens at alarming rates. The developmental phase of adolescence itself ranks high as a potential problem factor, where teens make impulsive decisions, many resulting in short term or lifelong consequences. Some of these lead to more impulsive bad decisions. Peer pressure intensifies these problems, especially for those with passive or people-pleasing personalities, even the secure. We all know life isn't easy. While secure attachments will protect and guide many adolescents through these challenging times, individuals still make their own life decisions amidst the depravity of humanity.

TRAUMA AND ABUSE

Depending on when, how extensive, and by whom, trauma and abuse lead to disorganized insecure attachments or subvert secure attachments. If occurring during the first several years of one's life, traumatic loss through death of a parent or divorce may prevent secure feelings from establishing. These children learn not to trust availability, likely developing avoidant personalities as a defense mechanism. Unpredictability due to the extremes of availability or nature of interactions in divorced situations may lead to disorganized, insecure attachments. Even in unbroken family structures, if consistent unpredictability occurs on the extremes of a parent doting on a child one minute, and neglecting or abusing the child the next, disorganized attachments form. Children don't know whether to run to or away from a caregiver. According to Bowlby, while all forms of attachment form by the age of three, early traumatic violation may upset or interfere with further development of one's attachment.

---

2. People who are trusted, basically on the coat-tails of a child's secure attachment to a parent, and the parent's seeming trust in that person. This is typically described as secondary attachment. I say "affiliative" to convey my belief that it's not really as strong or potentially permanent as secondary attachments.

When a child trusts the primary caregiver, secure attachment forms. This means that a child believes the world to be safe and predictable. Attachments extend vicariously to other adults who appear to be trustworthy to a child and who the child perceives to be trusted by the primary care giver.

If an adult abuses a child emotionally, physically or sexually, a signal of distrust spreads throughout the whole universe of the child's attachments with other attachment figures. One horrific encounter undermines belief that relationships are predictable. A child stalls in seeking help from his/her primary caregiver, feeling doubtful in his/her ability to protect. Intrusive flash-backs and/or repeated experiences disorganize secure feelings, thinking patterns, and moods, with avoidant compulsions. Violation of trust by any adult in the trusted network, at any point in a child's developmental journey, strains all previously secure attachment relationships. Disorganized teens may personally avoid a youth worker for a month, while texting nonstop. Youth workers can only try their best to love the erratic teen. Such behavior clues a youth worker into the possibility of past and/or present abuse. If a youth worker is suspicious, he/she should always gently ask. Do not accuse anyone by including any names in the appeal. Immediately seek professional guidance if discovering the occurrence of abuse.

INDIVIDUAL SIN NATURE

"For all have sinned and fall short of the glory of God."[3] I grew up in a semi-psychotic environment, which was abusive. Being conflict-centered, my mother constantly initiated dramatic turmoil. When I was a child, I had contempt for her. In fourth grade, three male fifth grade teachers, whom I had never met before, called me out of line and surrounded me, taking turns telling me in various ways they didn't like the way I laughed. After some silence, as I didn't know what to say, one grabbed me and slammed me high against a wall, and sticking his face in mine, sneered, "You better not crack a smile." At the end of middle school, a teacher told me she sent all of the high school teachers a list with the six worst students they

---

3. Rom 3:23.

could expect, and I was first on the list. I despised teachers. My Pastor at church failed me in Confirmation class. *No one* fails Confirmation class. I resented him. As a teenager I had several interactions with police officers who, without provocation, accused me of selling drugs, flipping them off, and more. One walked up to me, glared, and poked me in the chest, saying, "We don't want your kind in this town."

I loathed cops. I hated adults. I despised authority. I hated hypocrisy. At an early age I determined to get everyone back. And, in many ways, I did. Guilty people suffered. But a lot of innocent people paid undeserved consequences too. Looking back, I realize I also paid consequences related more to my bad decisions than to what anyone had done to me. Sadly, masses of people experience unfortunate life circumstances. We can't use these to justify selfish behavior. When we do, we're just like the ones we deplore.

My mother succeeded as well as one could expect, considering her abusive past, psychological illness, and my father's alcoholism. My social behavior only increased her stress. I now empathize with her and appreciate what she accomplished despite her life issues. Some teachers tried hard to be kind to me, especially my third grade teacher. Those fifth grade teachers were likely friends with her and saw her upset by me more than once. The Pastor I resented tried to build relationship with me, and was one of the few adults in my life who humbly modeled the love of Christ completely, in mercy and justice.[4] Honestly, I made life difficult for police before and more than they did for me. And in truth, I had several encounters with police officers who were friendly.

Our teens need to assume responsibility for their own current and eternal life decisions. We need to listen to them in their pain, but we should try to stop them from ruining their own lives because of it. We rebel against God and each other just like Adam and Eve did. With God's help and compassion, we must also provide accountability—at the right time, after relationship has been established.

Ironically, one's pride and denial of unworthiness before God, actually leads to feeling unworthy and blaming others for that feeling. My problems had more to do with my own pride, poor decisions, behavior, occasional self-pity and selfishness than with anything or anyone else. More angry teens today are in the same boat. Did I have an easy life? Compared to whom? Insecure childhood attachments happen because

4. Mic 6:8.

parents have their own trials, dysfunctional pasts, insecurities, temptations, mistakes, life consequences, and sinful struggles. Teenagers can either make healthy or unhealthy efforts related to their insecurities. Either they perpetuate cycles of dysfunction or they stop them. Historical facts can't change, current decisions can. Sometimes a Youth Pastor might do absolutely everything right trying to assist an insecure teenager, but ultimately every teen decides whether to spread, wallow in, or grow from pain. There are no other options. We need to be sensitive,

> We need to be sensitive, compassionate, encouraging, guiding, available, and convicting. We can't, however, assume responsibility for another's choices, sinful or God-honoring.

compassionate, encouraging, guiding, available, and convicting. We can't, however, assume responsibility for another's choices, sinful or God-honoring.

GLOCAL YOUTH CULTURE

Uri Bronfenbrenner created a model which explains relationships between humans and environments (human ecology), and human development, changes through one's life span.[5] By framing culture's influence on today's teen through this model, one sees fairly quickly that teens grow up in a world where one's local life seamlessly connects to global life. Global culture first sways American culture, which in turn affects regional, state, and geographical cultures. Significant examples of the global world's impact, streaming through the country's impact, on a teen's local microsystems, include the following ways. America revered and opened itself to Asia's and Africa's fondness for many gods. America listened to and applied Europe's theological passion to reduce Jesus Christ and God to mythological, but not historical, importance. America envied and mimicked Japan's obsession with hyper-technological advance. America admired and adopted Sweden's penchant for daycare. These are but a few examples of macro issues crippling the micro system community of the average American teenager.

My primary concern with the last twenty years of glocalization is that global and local politicians, educators, and media outlets have joined forces to launch an intolerant attack on the Judeo-Christian values of the

5. Erwin, *Critical Approach to Youth Culture*, 107–16.

United States. Paradoxically, this crusade advances this agenda through supposed concern for social justice, advocating tolerance for diverse beliefs.

As most U.S. systems embraced this major movement, the last few generations have come to believe enlightened people reject Christianity's exclusive claim to knowing God through Jesus Christ. Today's new generations learn that all claims to truth are equally valid, pressuring impressionable minds to reject their own spiritual inclinations of right and wrong. Due to societal teaching and growing concerns to be culturally popular, most Christian adolescents grow more accepting of immorality, less religious, and further away from God as they just move through adolescence alone.[6]

Thus, many Christian teens today believe themselves to be more loving by not believing that Jesus Christ is the only way to know God. They embrace a "gentle" mindset, which deemphasizes biblical doctrine and obedience, while overemphasizing feeling good, being happy and worshipping God however one pleases as opposed to however God desires.[7] Even Byron Spradlin, a gifted artist, national speaker, and advocate of "imaginative expression" in worship, bemoans stylish and creative worship experiences not being steeped in "the objective truth of Scripture."[8] It's no longer the truth of Scripture that determines the validity of one's experiences, it's the truth of one's experiences which determines the validity of Scripture. Sociological sensitivity breeds theological conviction instead of the reverse. Youth Pastors fight against not only a culture hostile to Christianity, but also the effects on deceived generations of young people, believing that a more open theology means more sincere and compassionate Christianity.

Open theologies lead to multiple spiritual and practical problems, not benefits. "Why is there a constant stream of people searching for a 'new age,' for 'medicine men' and powwows and traditional ceremonies and Highland games? I think it is because there is a hole in modern culture, where the truly important spiritual and humane parts of life used to

---

6. Denton et al., "Religion and Spirituality," 22–23; Murphy, "Most Christian Groups Grow More Accepting of Homosexuality."

7. See Christian Smith's beliefs and work relative to describing today's religious teen, summarized as Moral Therapeutic Deism. When choosing a church, freedom to drink coffee during worship in God's sanctuary matters more to many Millennials, Gen Xers, and Gen Zers than what is being preached and taught in God's sanctuary.

8. Spradlin, "Art in Ministry."

be."[9] Teens today seek spiritual realities and influence beyond just being open to them. No one can develop a successful secure and guiding relationship with a god that one creates. Trust in that god can go no further than trust in oneself. Attachments to the real God empowers people, resulting in confident wisdom. Contrived attachments to contrived gods fail people, resulting in cocky foolishness. Cocky masks insecurity. Reasons for such dramatic increases in adolescent depression and institutionalization relate very much to societal success in removing God from the mainstream of life.[10]

Divorce

"Family life is changing. Two-parent households are on the decline in the United States as divorce, remarriage and cohabitation are on the rise. And families are smaller now, both due to the growth of single-parent households and the drop in fertility."[11] In many single parent homes, children experience loss without ever getting the chance to know life otherwise. For those raised in homes where divorce occurs, consequences arise on multiple levels. "Families are the cells which make up the body of society, if the cells are unhealthy and undernourished, or at worse cancerous and growing haphazard and out of control, in the end the body succumbs," says Justice Coleridge, senior judge in charge of family courts across Southwest England for the past eight years.[12] Families form society. The main indication of the body succumbing being the insecurely attached children who never develop trusting relationships with anyone.

Related frustrations show most during one's adolescence. Long term issues don't go away with divorce. Insecure teens might feel better due to no longer playing a role in fake family happiness or relief from constantly present tensions. But the elimination of some stresses simply breed others. Social and financial burdens increase. If one or both parents immediately begin new romantic relationships, subsystem tensions potentially

---

9. Knick, "Traditional Culture and Modern Culture."

10. Mojtabai et al., "National Trends in Treatment of Depression in Adolescents and Young Adults," 110.

11. Anthony and Anthony, *Theology for Family Ministries*, 11; Pew Research Center, "American Family Today."

12. Doughty, "Family Life Is in 'Meltdown.'"

increase in number and variety. Divorce creates many other stressors for adolescents.[13]

How does divorce impact youth relative to original attachment relationships? If the parental support pillar crash in divorce during early adolescent years, it might be IGSP youth who crack the hardest, followed by SGSP youth. For many IP youth, loss or parental absence has been a way of life. Not that we shouldn't help IP youth too, it's just that our help might not be needed as urgently. IGSP youth crack hardest because they don't have God to fall back on and parental absence has not been a way of life. SGSP youth generally have God and other adults of faith present in their lives for assistance. These teens may also fall lower into despair and struggle more with identity achievement than insecure youth, as their sense of security feels fraudulent. Trying to adapt during the turbulent emotional period of adolescence proves too difficult for many, often resulting in delinquent social behaviors. More like IGIP youth now, those engaging in such activities initially need warmth more than warning, patience more than expressed disappointment, and availability when feeling lonely or suffering from the thorns of loss and bad decisions.

Socioeconomic Conditions

The divide between the haves and have nots clearly grows larger today than ever.[14] Research indicates that during times of economic growth in our country's history, growth occurred fairly evenly for those across the economic spectrum from poor to wealthy. In the last thirty-five years, however, that pattern stopped.[15] Those considered to be wealthy have experienced about 20 percent increases in income, while the poor about 3.5 percent increases. Indications as to why, point to increased demand in the new era for more specialized skills, dependent on more carefully tailored educational success. This matters for several related reasons.

---

13. Leopold, "Gender Differences in the Consequences of Divorce," 769–97.

14. Abadi, "Income Inequality."

15. Kearney, "Income Inequality in the United States,."

Youth raised in impoverished communities possess less assets, less hope, and more inclination toward internalizing and externalizing, delinquent behaviors.[16] In the many homes where parents struggle to pay the bills, both parents work and some have to work more than one job. This means less physical availability to children and less mental availability and patience when parents are present.[17] Socioeconomic disadvantages consistently relate to harsh or unresponsive parenting, which relates to depression, self-injury, worse academic and psychosocial competence and deviant peer affiliations. Due to these factors, those living in poverty possess greater potential for developing insecure attachment relationships. Youth leaders in impoverished communities should consult the work of multiple successful urban youth ministries built on addressing multiple socio-cultural present and future concerns and needs of impoverished teenagers.[18]

> Socioeconomic disadvantages consistently relate to harsh or unresponsive parenting, which relates to depression, self-injury, worse academic and psychosocial competence and deviant peer affiliations. Due to these factors, those living in poverty possess greater potential for developing insecure attachment relationships.

The Forty Developmental Assets

Merton Strommen, a Lutheran Youth Director, started Search Institute more than fifty years ago.[19] Over the years their research has evolved into the Developmental Assets Framework, with their key position asserting the more of the forty developmental assets teens have, the more healthy they're likely to be, and the fewer they have, the less healthy they're likely to be.[20] They suggest that obtaining thirty-one assets will typically ensure success for most teens, but that also only 11 percent of teens have that many, with more than half of all teens having twenty or fewer.[21] This

16. DiClemente et al., *Adolescent Health*, 400.

17. DiClemente et al., *Adolescent Health*, 400.

18. Urban Promise in Camden, New Jersey, and Urban Impact in Pittsburgh, Pennsylvania, are two prime examples.

19. Search Institute, "Developmental Assets Framework," 14.

20. Forty Assets: twenty internal (values, emotional strengths) and twenty external (communities, schools, families).

21. Search Institute, "Developmental Assets Framework," 14.

research meshes well with systems and attachment theories and Search produces a plethora of findings which support their conclusions. Many of the suggestions given to implement ARM overlap with what Search Institute says youth need internally and externally.

Youth workers using ARM and the 40 Developmental Assets together have a micro (zoomed all the way in on ARM) and macro (zoomed all the way out on the 40 Assets) view of teen needs and can use each to identify, shape, and evaluate ministry action steps relative to the other. By considering the forty competencies, these Developmental Assets expand the four primary needs of every teen into an identifiable forty practical needs of every teen. With both models in mind, twenty-first century youth workers may be able to address some of the glocal cultural problems and develop some of today's cultural strengths more precisely, thoroughly, and preventatively.

Leadership team brainstorming sessions could really cultivate or enhance a ministry's vision and planning. Some ministries will find such efforts to bring more balance to a ministry philosophy and program. From my perspective, it seems that utilizing these will enable leaders to help SG teens assist IP teens specifically. This is especially true for those ministering in impoverished communities. These ideas support a lot of one's "do" with quality "think" in the background. Even if only a few actual action steps result, such an approach represents working smarter, not just harder.

Teen Rebellion

Society has removed all boundaries from what is acceptable behavior and any stigmas attached to those boundaries. During adolescence, humans fight to obtain an identity by individuating or rebelling against blind adoption of familial and social values, with the hope of arriving at an owned identity. Today, society gives adolescents an identity achieving quandary, how to rebel?

Rebellion used to be hanging with the wrong crowd. Participating in social causes. Smoking. Skipping church. Drinking a beer. Heterosexual interaction. Immodest dress. Then smoking marijuana. Then joining extremist groups. Then men piercing their ears. Then homosexual interaction. Then a tattoo. Then dropping out of school. Then body and face piercings. Then doing a little coke here and there. Then covering one's body with tattoos. Then huffing and dusting. Then sexual paraphilic behavior. Now? Dying of heroin addiction. Identifying as the opposite gender of one's biological design. Self-mutilation. Shooting other kids at school. What other options do they have? Society endorses and even encourages essentially every known behavior as acceptable.

How does the average teen who doesn't want to maim oneself, die, kill someone, or change gender, rebel? Educational programs exist to help teens participate at school as minimally as possible. Parents take children to clothing stores to buy clothes with less material than

> How does the average teen who doesn't want to maim oneself, die, kill someone, or change gender, rebel?

what used to be people's underwear. They also host teen drinking parties. Hookah lounges and vape cafes populate small town main street shops. What or who isn't tolerated today? Conservative, evangelical Christians. Maybe there is a way for teens to rebel.

ADULT ATTACHMENT ALTERNATIVES

Clearly with many microsystems surrounding youth, they have access to many other potential adults who would be able to convey loving care and availability, such as extended family, teachers, coaches, neighbors, scout leaders, program directors, music instructors, and more. Within the ranks mentioned, many of those folks are Christians, operating more covertly in youth ministry than overtly as a Youth Pastor. They also include those whose hearts are attuned to God's leading, but whose intellectual acknowledgment and consistent moral example is not. Praise God for the work of all of these allies.

Through conversations with one's teen community, wise leaders figure out who these allies are and intentionally connect. In Syracuse, guidance counselors in the Christian school and in one of the city schools and I worked together through several situations covering issues like abuse, truancy, anorexia, and delinquency. Judges allowed troubled youth to avoid going to juvenile detention centers under the condition of meeting with me for so many hours. These things happen when a youth leader travels outside of the Christian world of our teens and into their whole world, not just to visit with them on their space, but to also meet other teen influencers. Our potential teams extend beyond the walls of our organizations.

GENDER OF YOUTH AND ATTACHMENT TO YOUTH LEADERS

Some research indicates females develop insecure anxious attachments while boys adopt insecure avoidant styles more typically.[22] Study also confirms that preadolescent teens use insecure attachment strategies which they believe to be more gender normal and consistent with their own gender identities. Differences in attachment styles adopted by children based on gender suggests that aspects of both the parent, unavailable or unpredictable, and the child, male or female, contribute to the developing of particular insecure attachment styles. Adolescents also prefer to address their own attachment needs with adults of the same gender.[23]

Ministry Leader Response

Ron, by now you've seen 3 different generations of students go through our ranks, from Gen X to Millennials to Gen Z. One battle faced by me through these generations, in my 20 plus years of ministry, is the influence of different authorities in their lives. From God to parents to peers, these important relationships shape students. One truth remains, adolescents need the right relationships in their lives.

I appreciate the success of the ARM model and that you saw the need for secure relationships that give youth health and stability, which points them in the right direction. Bottom line is that those with good relationship with authorities in their lives go on to do well. Those without, in my experience, still struggle into their adult lives. And many leave the church.

I have always seen you Ron as a "peacemaker" as defined by Jesus in Matthew 5. A true son of God fighting to see the world of youth ministry, families, and the church in a growing partnership, successful in the discipling of teens and leaders. I hope this book is seen for what it is, an intense look at needs and means of reaching and leading the next generation.

Dale Patrick, Sr. High Ministry Pastor, Grace Church, Middleburg Heights, Ohio

---

In my research I found that girls prefer relationships with adult females, but will attach to either male or female leaders. Boys, on the other hand, develop attachment relationships with male youth workers, but generally not with female leaders. More research is needed in this area, but there seem to be some obvious reasons why these differences exist.

22. Pauletti et al., "Sex Differences in Pre-Adolescent Attachment," 390–404.

23. Belsterling, "Adolescent Attachment," 337–52.

In single-parent homes or divorced situations, mothers are the ones who most often stay committed to their children. In other words, many youth today lack positive adult male guidance.[24] Young ladies crave appropriate fatherly affirmation. Young men crave male role models. Teen girls also develop cognitively more quickly than boys, allowing them to mature and communicate more competently, therefore not feeling as awkward as boys in cross gender relationships. Lastly, it seems that more males minister through youth ministry than females, leaving girls with fewer options.

These points suggest that a smart Youth Pastor or Director will find adults of the opposite gender to assist in leading youth ministries. Gender variance in leadership, however, benefits youth ministries in more ways than just available adults for same gender youth. First, God thought the family system benefitted most by male and female leadership, suggesting that youth ministry cultures would also benefit most with such structure. Second, men and women think, communicate, create, and perceive differently; therefore, vision, structure, and communication aspects of youth ministry would all benefit. Ultimately, we want to meet teens where they are addressing their deepest level needs more successfully. By making male and female adult leaders available, we should.

CONCLUSION

These are difficult times. Statistics of those who are abused are mind-numbing. Children are being raised in homes where there never was any intent to have two parents and oftentimes with strangers living there. Cultural forces driven by exploiting children for the sake of financial and political gain abound. Too many teens lack too many assets. Traumatic loss of parental presence or ability to trust because of abuse, greatly interrupts secure attachment maturation, which only means adult relational struggles will mimic teen struggles.

Due to individual sin nature, spiritual decision making, and the world's catering to self-centered indulgence, youth workers show up at a pivotal developmental stage. And while we can't undo people's poverty, or divorced parents, or abusive histories, we can make huge differences in

---

24. DiClemente et al., *Adolescent Health*, 398: According to multiple research efforts, fatherless homes impact teenagers in the following ways: lower levels of cognitive development, less expression of empathy, more behavioral problems, worse social skills, and worse school performance.

other's lives in consistent and considerate ways. As the world clamors for adolescent attention and surrender, we can stand in between the youth and the world. We can pick them up and encourage them when they're feeling defeated. We can offer them hope in Jesus Christ for personal life peace and joy, and opportunity to inspire others with the same.

I hope we're not the only options for teens to develop adolescent attachment relationships. Whether we are or not, we can value the liberty of sharing Jesus Christ with them. We can stoke the fires of rebellion within them in positive ways which will bring glory to God. Because we live in such an immoral culture, opportunity to rebel as Christ did should be easier now in this country than ever before. We can pray for and offer assistance to teens who dream the impossible, turning a teen's moment's decision into a movement of the Holy Spirit.

For an encouraging, real life story of this in action see *Grain of Hope*, an international ministry providing resources to impoverished communities around the world, building churches in Muslim villages, and more. All because one Youth Pastor, Chris Coakley, listened to and helped a group of nineteen adolescents run with an idea to send grain and water to a third world country.[25] Chris would be the first person to tell you of his imperfections as a Youth Pastor, but he didn't let that stop God from using him and his youth group in powerful, global changing ways. This story illustrates what so many do on an everyday level. Some of you will change the world simply through truly loving one teen who never had that before or by supporting a teen who did, but needed a pillar to lean on at a crucial time. I praise God when I see allies believing in His ability to love and shine through them and modeling to the rest of us in ministry that God will use the imperfect, if we believe He can.

PERSONAL CHALLENGE AND DISCUSSION QUESTIONS FOR LEADERSHIP TEAMS

1. Have you allowed yourself to feel and verbally express the pain of any early life losses? Have you offered your losses on the altar, forgiving those who hurt you, surrendering your pain to Jesus Christ to use in your life to make others' lives better? If not, pray for His leading and

25. See Grain of Hope: https://www.grainofhope.org/

talk with someone privately. If so, share from His strength in you to encourage others.

2. Name some social problems in your community. Choose one to address and identify practical steps you can take through the youth ministry to do so. How and when will you implement them?

3. What are two or three key take-a-ways from reading this chapter?

CHAPTER 13

Conclusion: Biblical Approach Influencing ARM

THIS CHAPTER SERVES SEVERAL purposes. First, to conclude this book directing readers' attention to the best content in it—the Scripture. Second, in concluding, to highlight the incredible way that God's word transforms lives. If His people would just read it, they would find and live in the freedom of Christ, and so would their followers.[1] See later what I mean by "read it" and "live in freedom." It's incredible how God communicates, encourages, and guides through His Word no matter how many times one reads it. He is the Master Author.

READ, PRAY, AND LIVE GOD'S WORD

Whether raised in the church or knowing Christ apart from the church, God can bless. I envy those with strong Christian heritage who have parents and grandparents who consistently, though probably imperfectly, modeled the importance of standing in relationship with Christ. Because of them, some not have experienced the worst "fun" that life has to offer. Be thankful for not having the baggage, stronger temptations, and real life emotional and physical consequences. Never dismiss or neglect the value of strong Christian heritage. Also, no one has to live up to their

---

1. This bears uncanny resemblance to a line in *Braveheart*, where William Wallace says something similar to Robert the Bruce.

parents' or grandparents' faiths (or Job's for that matter), they simply need to broaden God's reach through the family in their own personal ways. That makes one a true teammate of all past and future Christian generations.

I found blessing in learning how to read the Bible apart from within the context of a church. Yes, I went to church as a child and finished confirmation classes and am grateful for the work on me that God did through some of those experiences, even though I couldn't see it at the time. But separating from the church during early adolescence, I never became churchified. I never felt secure in any of the motions that so many churchgoers go through. I never read God's word compelled to make someone else happy. As an older teen, I started reading the Bible because I wanted to see why I should. God captivated me. I led and lead my youth ministries through traditional approaches, but under spiritual leading and verbal and nonverbal trust. With the influence of His Word, God blesses me, blesses through me, and blesses despite me.

Reading the Bible has always meant praying the Bible has always meant living the Bible. If I read it and felt convicted by something, I prayed it. If I prayed it, I did it. When I read, "What must I do to be saved?" my decision to trust Christ as a child resonated in my spirit, spurring me onto a renewed confession of my need for Christ as my Savior.[2] My enthusiasm to live freely is now based on a strong sense of trust in God, a trustworthy secure base, not my recanted trust in myself or anyone else. Live to please God not man. Feel your freedom. Pleasing God means trusting in the consistency of God's words, expectations, and promises.

When I read about Gideon asking for a sign to confirm his call into a ministry situation,[3] I went out one night and did the same thing. When God provided a sign, I felt free to ask Him to provide another, just like Gideon. When He did, I broke. I was unleashed into a whole new lifestyle. When the Ethiopian eunuch asked, "What prevents me from being baptized?" and Philip took him to the water to baptize him, I said, "Why not me?"[4] I was convicted that my "infant baptism" wasn't a baptism upon confession, so I asked a Christian friend at college to baptize me in a local pond (she ended up becoming my wife). When I read that we

---

2. Acts 16:30.

3. Judges 6:36–40.

4. Acts 8:36.

need to seek the lost,[5] a friend of mine and I organized some trips down to Liberty Ave. in Pittsburgh, Pennsylvania, notorious for the presence of drug dealers and prostitutes. We had many successful interactions on those trips. (The women focused on the prostitutes, men on those dealing with drugs.) I also spent time at college with partyers as though they were my brothers and sisters. I intentionally cultivated friendship with some who clearly struggled with their sexual identities. When I pondered Paul's missionary journeys, under the conviction of Jesus' statement that He lost not one,[6] I asked God to help me to share the gospel with every person I spoke with on my own "missionary journey" to Alaska when I graduated from college. As far as I recall, I regretfully did lose one, a woman in Seattle, but she has been prayed over many times since.

Along life's way, we (my family and I) have quit jobs and sold our homes several times before attaining new jobs when God convicted me it was time to move onward. These decisions were not made flippantly, but in faith after prayer and fasting, which Julie, my wife, and I adopted into decision making after reading and realizing Jesus' expectation that we would be fasting.[7] (I fast for other reasons as well.) One time, with my position and time in our parsonage soon ending, God led us to reject a solid ministry opportunity, with no others looming. While friends and family were often nervous and we had stretching moments, God blessed our faithful trust, just as He has always promised.[8] The stretching added vitality to our lives. Stretching added more opportunity for us to watch God's loving hand at work over and over. Taking responsibility to cooperate with Holy Spirit nudges, we have tried to believe without seeing.[9] Each time our faith has been strengthened and our decisions have been confirmed. God calls us to certain places, people, and circumstances, of that I am now sure. My children grew up seeing their parents risk in trusting God prove to not be risky at all. The more you trust, the easier living freely becomes. "It was for freedom that Christ set us free" (Gal 5:1). We lead others as we live.

I hear so many stories today from youth workers living and loving as Jesus did, and I praise God. You are my heroes, partners, and you inspire

---

5. Luke 15; 19:10.

6. John 18:9.

7. Matt 6:16.

8. Josh 1:89; Jas 4:2; Matt 7:7.

9. John 20:29.

me. "If our security is in Christ, we can do anything" should not be a cliché. We lose dependency on the things of this world, which includes far more than we acknowledge, when we believe in both our minds and actions. We show and lead others to join us on the adventure this life offers. They'll see through us that the thrill of eternity has already started. God gives us eternal privilege and responsibility. That might sound overwhelming, but He knows we can rise to that expectation. He trusts Himself and us. I trust Him. I pray that we all do. We need to, making the most of our time, for the days are evil.[10]

STAND FIRM

Youth workers reinforce or show for the first time that authority can be trusted. Or they advance beliefs that it can't be trusted. For youth leaders who genuinely care and communicate their care in action, they'll do the first. For those who talk the talk more than walk the walk, they may distort the potential of the rest of a person's life. If one person, then probably many lives. As has been emphasized in this book, Christ's ARM warriors have won many battles, praise God. But there are many yet to come and for those beside us who have been playing the role, please, for the sake of today's adolescents and our credibility, pray and adjust. For those who work in the trenches, thank you. You have it hard and I pray for you.

Spend more time with Jesus to stay in His vision. Listen to young people and cry, laugh, and study with them. Help them to thrive not survive in this world. Thank you for reading this book. I know for many with big hearts that some of the reading took extra effort. May God bless all of you with His victories, one teen and relationship at a time.

---

10. Eph 5:16.

Spread Sheet and Blank Template for the ARM Model

There is a blank template after this one for those who wish to recreate or revise it relative to personal differences of opinion or specific contexts.	_Attachment Relationship Ministry model_	
	SGSP (1)	_IGSP (2)_
	SGIP (3)	_IGIP (4)_
Typical/Possible Program Element	_Put in order of which group needs what ministry most initially, and perhaps indefinitely._	
One-on-one time: youth-worker and 1 or 2 youth.	_4, 3 and 2, 1_	
	Meet practical relational needs first—(care, concern, being loved, belonging, etc.) 3 needs YW representing Christ, 2 needs YW representing parents [see text for explanations], 1 needs this too—more as a mentor, allowing vulnerability to express doubts and fears	
Youth Group Leader Talks	_1, 2, 3, 4 Of course volunteers and youth themselves can lead these talks. All benefit from sound, Spirit led, diligently studied and prepared messages. Youth leaders should do most of these, displaying exhortations of God as a trustworthy and loving rep of His authority. Insecure youth NEED trustworthy adult authority figures._	
Large Youth Group Discussions	_1–4_	

Adult Mentors	*3 first and foremost, 4, 2 and 1 Volunteer adult mentors with time and trust-worthy maturity are rare. Have them interact first as Parent Representatives with those needing them most—(listening, having fun together, talking through problems, teaching decision making skills, sharing stories with consequences and blessings).*
Hospitality Team	*4, 3 and 2, 1 Most secure people who trust relatively easily do not need to be welcomed to the same degree as those who are more insecure—though everyone wants to feel welcome.*
Missions Trips	*1 and 3 Mission Trips are for those who wish to share the love of Jesus Christ, most often the filling of the Holy Spirit is needed for the sake of authentic witness and witness in/ by community.*
Service Projects	*4 and 2, 3, 1 This might mean a 1 day experience, it might mean a week-long experience. Its healthy to differentiate this from a Mission Trip-Primary goal are for participants to learn the joy that one can have in serving/difficult circumstances. Group works together, not for purposes of observation by whoever is being served. If Christian, those being served have responsibility to love, encourage, and edify those serving.*
Parent Meetings	*1 and 2, 3, 4 Parents of those who are insecure are not likely to show up. It is hoped that non-Christian, good parents (and even not-so-good parents) who show up find interaction with the Christian parents refreshing, encouraging and the topics of conversation personally helpful in maturing as a parent and advocate of the ministry.*
Coffee Shop Chats	*See One-on-one time. Note—when meeting with the opposite gender, meet with at least 2, never just 1. Also, I often met with 3–5 box 1 youth together, who were often experiencing similar doubts, fears, etc but who could also speak to one another regarding such feelings, etc.*
Showing up at games, concerts, etc.	*4 and 3, 2, 1 All youth enjoy your acknowledging their importance to you at events important to them. Again, some parents won't or can't (many IPs come from single parent homes). I always made it a point to not only go to these events but to also try to connect with kids either directly after the event or discuss it with them later.*
Bible Studies	*1–4; 1 and 3 for discipleship purposes, 2 and 4 for gospel purposes.*

Worship and Praise Time	*1 and 3, 2 and 4, Those who know Christ interact with the Holy Spirit in ways that bring glory to God and to those worshipping (see Acts). They also experience leadership opportunity. While those who don't trust God may not fully participate, worship time gives them an opportunity to watch God's family together. Many unsaved youth will find this compelling.*
Corporate Prayer Time	*1 and 3, 2 and 4. Ditto much of that said in Worship time. Those not trusting God are not so inclined to pray to Him, but they do find it attractive and hopeful to participate with those praying who do trust God.*
Small Groups	*1–4 But for varying reasons. 1 for leadership opportunity, nurturing 3 into such. 2 and 4 to learn positive social interaction skills (not dominating, not withdrawing— small groups make it difficult for withdrawers. SG need relational-leadership responsibility. IG—need responsibility via "mastery" etc more relative to task leadership.*
Worship Team Responsibilities	*1 and 3 One may find those who are insecure with parents being rougher around the edges when leading worship than those secure with parents. Those who have not committed to Christ ought not to be leading others in (particularly believers) worship of Him. It makes a mockery of worship.*
Small Group Leader Responsibilities	*1 Discipleship or Community Developing Youth led small groups should always have 1–2 identified leaders, with 1–2 apprentices.*
Youth-Group Family Time (Outreach Not Allowed)	*1–4 of those who regularly participate in the youth ministry (they are encouraged to invite friends to almost everything else, this time together is just for FELLOWSHIP in Christ purposes ALONE).*
Prayer Team	*4 and 3, 2, 1* *Christian parents pray for their children more than anyone. While not all youth who have secure relationships with parents come from Christian homes, those who have both secure relationships are more likely.*

Blank Template	Attachment Relationship Ministry model	
	SGSP (1)	IGSP (2) (IW, IA)
Typical/Possible Program Element	SGIP (3) (IW, IA)	IGIP (4)
	Order Which Relational-Need Population Needs Most Initially	
One-on-one time: youth worker and 1 or 2 youth		
Youth Group Leader Talks		
Large Youth Group Discussions		
Adult Mentors		
Hospitality Team		
Missions Trips		
Service Projects		
Parent Meetings		
Coffee Shop Chats		
Showing up at games, concerts, etc.		
Bible Studies		
Worship and Praise Time		
Corporate Prayer Time		
Small Groups		
Small Group Discussions		
Worship Team Responsibilities		
Small Group Leader Responsibilities		
Youth-Group Family Time (Outreach Not Allowed)		
Prayer Team		

Bibliography

Abadi, Mark. "Income Inequality." *Time* (March 21, 2018.) http://time.com/money/5207987/income-inequality-every-state/.

Ainsworth, Mary D. Salter, et al. *Patterns of Attachment: A Psychological Study of the Strange Situation.* New York: Psychology, 2015.

Alupoaicei, Marla, and Dillon Burroughs. *Generation Hex: Understanding the Subtle Dangers of Wicca.* Eugene, OR: Harvest House, 2008.

Anthony, Michael, and Michelle Anthony. *A Theology for Family Ministries.* Nashville, TN: B&H Academic, 2011.

Anthony, Michelle, and Megan Marshman. *7 Family Ministry Essentials: A Strategy for Culture Change in Children's and Student Ministries.* Colorado Springs, CO: David C. Cook, 2015.

Arain, M., et al. "Maturation of the Adolescent Brain." *Neuropsychiatry, Disease and Treatment* 9 (2013) 449–61.

Arbinger Institute. *Leadership and Self-Deception: Getting Out of the Box.* San Francisco: Barrett-Koehler, 2009.

Arzola, Fernando, Jr. *Towards a Prophetic Youth Ministry.* Downers Grove, IL: InterVarsity, 2008.

Barglow, P., et al. "Effects of Maternal Absence Due to Employment on the Quality of Infant-Mother Attachment in a Low-Risk Sample." *Child Development* 58 (1987) 945–54.

Barna. "Evangelism is Most Effective Among Kids." https://www.barna.com/research/evangelism-is-most-effective-among-kids/.

————. "Gen Z: Your Questions Answered." https://www.barna.com/research/gen-z-questions-answered/.

Belnap, W. Dean. "Current Trends in the Diagnosis and Treatment of the Emotionally Disturbed Child and Adolescent." *Child and Adolescent Psychotherapy* 2 (1985) 179–86.

Belsky, Jay. "Early Day Care and Infant Attachment Security." In *Encyclopedia on Early Childhood Development*, edited by Tremblay RE, Boivin M, Peters RDeV, 1–4. London, UK: Centre of Excellence for Early Childhood Development, 2009. http://www.child-encyclopedia.com/sites/default/files/textes-experts/en/567/early-day-care-and-infant-mother-attachment-security.pdf.

————. "Infant Day Care: A Cause for Concern." *Zero to Three* 6 (1986) 1–7.

————. "A Nation (Still) at Risk"? *National Forum* 75 (1995) 36–38.

Belsterling, Ron. "Adolescent Attachment, Christian Youth Workers, & the Frequency of Bible Study." *Christian Education Journal* 6 (2009) 337–52.

———. *"Follow Me,* by David Platt." *Journal of Youth Ministry* 13 (2014) 140–42.

———. "Golfing with the Senior Pastor." In *Don't Do This,* edited by Len Kageler and Jonathan Hobbs, 144–46. San Diego: Youth Cartel, 2016.

———. "The Mentoring Approach of Jesus as Demonstrated in John 13." *Journal of Youth Ministry* 5 (2006) 77–92.

———. "Screwed Up: Making the Most of Your Ministry Mistakes." *Group* 40 (2014) 31-3.

———. "A Scriptural Basis for Teaching." In *Teaching the Next Generations,* edited by Terry Linhart, 25–33. Grand Rapids, MI: Baker Academic, 2016.

———. "Youth Work, Qualities of an Adult's Mentoring Approach and Adolescent Attachment: A New Construct for Measuring Effective Mentoring Characteristics in Ministry." *Journal of Youth Ministry,* 14 (2016) 31–47.

Belsterling, Ron, et al. "Religious Lives of Alliance Youth: A Survey of 1,600 Alliance Youth and 400 Youth Workers." 2013. Unpublished.

Blackaby, Henry T., and Claude King. *Experiencing God.* Nashville, TN: Broadman & Holman, 1994.

Blanks, Andy. "Five Fatal Youth Ministry Flaws." https://youthministry360.com/blogs/all/five-fatal-youth-ministry-flaws.

Bolman, Lee G., and Terrence E. Deal. *Reframing Organizations.* San Francisco: John Wiley, 2013.

Bolsinger, Tod. *Canoeing the Mountains.* Downers Grove, IL: InterVarsity, 2015.

Borgman, Dean. *Hear My Story: Understanding the Cries of Troubled Youth.* Peabody, MA: Hendrickson, 2003.

Boshers, Bo, and Judson Poling. *The Be-With Factor: Mentoring Students.* Grand Rapids, MI: Zondervan, 2006.

Bowlby, John. *Attachment: Attachment and Loss.* New York: Basic, 1983.

Bradshaw, Matt, et al. "Attachment to God, Images of God, and Psychological Distress." *International Journal for the Psychology of Religion* 20 (2010) 130–47.

Braun, Allie. "This Is Why Our Generation Doesn't Believe in Settling Down." *Huffington Post* (April 5, 2017). https://www.huffingtonpost.com/entry/this-is-why-our-generation-doesnt-believe-in-settling_us_58e534a2e4b00ea3841db52d.

Breakey, Caleb. "Divided: Should Youth Ministry Go Away?" *Christian Broadcasting Network* (2018). http://www1.cbn.com/spirituallife/divided-should-youth-ministry-go-away.

Brion-Meisels, Gretchen, et al. "Not Anyone Can Do This Work." In *The Changing Landscape of Youth Work,* edited by Kristen Pozzoboni and Ben Krishner, 71–91. Charlotte, NC: Information Age, 2016.

Brown, Douglas. "United Families Dividing Churches: An Assessment of the FICM." https://www.faith.edu/2012/01/united-families-dividing-churches-an-assessment of-the-family-integrated-church-movement/.

Brown, Scott. *A Weed in the Church.* Wake Forest, NC: Merchant Adventures, 2011.

Burns, Jim, and Mark Devries. *Partnering with Parents in Youth Ministry.* Colorado Springs, CO: Gospel Light, 2003.

Canterberry, Melanie, and Omri Gillath. "Attachment and Caregiving." In *Sharing Risk in Meeting the Responsibilities of Ministry, the Wiley-Blackwell Handbook of*

Couples and Family Relationships, edited by Patricia Noller and Gery C. Karantzas, 207–19. West Sussex, UK: Blackwell, 2012.

Capuzzi, David, and Douglas R. Gross. *Youth at Risk: A Prevention Resource.* Alexandria, VA: American Counseling Association, 2014.

Chamorro-Premuzic, Thomas. "Why Are Religious People Generally Less Intelligent? Understanding the Negative Relationship Between IQ and Religiosity." *Psychology Today* (December 26, 2013). https://www.psychologytoday.com/us/blog/mr personality/201312/why-are-religious-people-generally-less-intelligent.

Clark, Chap. *Adoptive Youth Ministry: Integrating Emerging Generations.* Grand Rapids, MI: Baker Academic, 2016.

————. *Hurt, 2.0: Inside the World of Today's Teenagers.* Grand Rapids, MI: Baker Academic, 2011.

Clinton, Tim, and Joshua Straub. *God Attachment: Why You Believe, Act, and Feel the Way You Do About God.* Brentwood, TN: Howard, 2014.

Collins, Suzanne. *Catching Fire.* New York: Scholastic, 2009.

Columbus, Chris, dir. *Home Alone 1.* 1990; Hughes Entertainment; distributed by 20th Century Fox.

Crouch, Andy. *Culture Making: Recovering Our Creative Calling.* Downers Grove, IL: InterVarsity, 2008.

Curtis, Chris, and Martin Saunders. "Rethinking Youth Work." *Youth and Children's Work* (October 2017). https://www.youthandchildrens.work/Youth-Work/Read/Features/Rethinking-youth-work.

Davis, Glyn, and Kay Dickinson. *Teen TV: Genre, Consumption, and Identity.* London: British Film Institute, 2011.

Dean, Jamie. "What Went Wrong? An In-depth Report on the Vision Forum Scandal." *Christian Headlines* (March 25, 2014). https://www.christianheadlines.com/news/biblical-patriarch-doug-phillips-found-unfaithful-closes-ministry.html.

Denton, Melinda Lundquist, et al. "Religion and Spirituality on the Path through Adolescence, Research Report Number 8." https://youthandreligion.nd.edu/assets/102568/religion_and_spirituality_on_the_path_though_adolescence.pdf.

Deutsch, Nancy, and Renee Spencer. "Capturing the Magic: Assessing the Quality of Youth Mentoring Relationships." *New Directions for Youth Development* 121 (2009) 47–70.

DeVries, Mark. "The End of Paid Youth Ministry." *Group* 40 (2014) 26–27.

————. *Family Based Youth Ministry.* Downers Grove, IL: InterVarsity, 1994

————. *Family Based Youth Ministry.* Downers Grove, IL: InterVarsity, 2004.

————. *Sustainable Youth Ministry.* Downers Grove, IL: InterVarsity, 2008.

Diamond, Guy, et al. "Attachment-Based Family Therapy." *Family Process* 55 (2016) 595–610.

Diaz, April. *Redefining the Role of the Youth Worker: A Manifesto of Integration.* San Diego: Youth Cartel, 2013.

DiClemente, Ralph J., et al., eds. *Adolescent Health: Understanding and Preventing Risk Behaviors.* San Francisco: Jossey-Bass, 2009.

Doughty, Steve. "Family Life Is in 'Meltdown': Judge Launches Devastating Attack on Our Fractured Society." *Daily Mail* (May 30, 2009). http://www.parents4protest.co.uk/justice_coleridge.htm.

Dunn, Richard R. *Shaping the Spiritual Life of Students.* Downers Grove, IL: InterVarsity, 2001.

Dunnington, Kent. *Addiction and Virtue*. Downers Grove, IL: InterVarsity, 2011.

Duvall, J. Scott, and J. Daniel Hays. *Grasping God's Word*. Grand Rapids, MI: Zondervan, 2012.

Elliott, Mark W. *Isaiah 40–66*. Downers Grove, IL: InterVarsity, 2007.

Ellison, Christopher G., et al. "Prayer, Attachment to God and Symptoms of Anxiety." *Sociology of Religion* 75 (2014) 208–33.

Erikson, Eric. *Childhood and Society*. New York: W. W. Norton, 1963.

Erwin, Pam. *A Critical Approach to Youth Culture*. Grand Rapids, MI: Zondervan/YS, 2010.

Escobar, Maria Josephina, et al. "Brain Signatures of Moral Sensitivity in Adolescents with Early Social Deprivation." *Scientific Reports* 4 (June 19, 2014). https://www.nature.com/articles/srep05354.

Evans, Craig. *God Speaks: What He Says, What He Means*. Franklin, TN: Worthy, 2015.

Feucht, Oscar. *Helping Families through the Church*. St. Louis: Concordia, 1971.

Folmsbee, Chris. *Gladhearted Disciples*. Nashville, TN: Abingdon, 2015.

———. *A New Kind of Youth Ministry*. Grand Rapids, MI: Zondervan/YS, 2007.

Freeze, Tracy A., and Enrico DiTommaso. "An Examination of Attachment, Religiousness, Spirituality, and Well-Being in a Baptist Faith Sample." *Mental Health, Religion & Culture* 17 (2014) 690–702.

Freudenberg, Ben, and Rick Lawrence. *The Family Friendly Church*. Loveland, CO: Vital Ministry, 1998.

Fritz, Everett. *The Art of Forming Young Disciples: Why Youth Ministries Aren't Working*. Manchester, NH: Sophia Institute Press, 2018.

———. "The Problem With the Youth Group Mentality." n.d. http://everettfritz.com/the-problem-with-the-youth-group-mentality/.

Geisler, Norman L., and Douglas E. Potter. *The Doctrine of Christ*. CreateSpace, 2016.

Gerali, Steve. "Seeing Clearly: Community Context." In *Starting Right: Thinking Theologically about Youth Ministry*, edited by Kenda Creasy Dean, Chap Clark, and Dave Rahn, 285–95. Grand Rapids, MI: Zondervan/YS, 2001.

Gilbert, Roberta M. *Extraordinary Relationships*. Toronto, Canada: John Wiley, 1992.

Ginsburg, Kenneth. "The Importance of Play." *Pediatrics* 119 (2007) 182–91. http://pediatrics.aappublications.org/content/119/1/182.

Gray, Derwin. "Transformation Church-Teens-Events." http://transformationchurch.tc/events/.

Gray, P. "The Decline of Play and the Rise of Psychopathology in Children and Adolescents." *American Journal of Play* 3 (2011) 443–63.

Grimes, C. "God Image Research." *Journal of Spirituality in Mental Health* 9 (2008) 11–32.

Haddock, Laura, and Jennie Falkner. "Who Am I? Unique Issues for Multiracial Youth." In *Youth at Risk: A Prevention Resource*, edited by David Capuzzi and Douglas R. Gross, 169–96. Alexandria, VA: American Counseling Association, 2014.

Haley, Melinda, et al. "A Future in Jeopardy." In *Youth at Risk: A Prevention Resource*, edited by David Capuzzi and Douglas R. Gross, 265–90. Alexandria, VA: American Counseling Association, 2014.

Hampton, James, et al. "Survey of Youth Ministry Degrees." *Journal of Youth Ministry* 15 (2018) 8–33.

Harris, Sam. *The End of Faith*. New York: W. W. Norton, 2004.

Hartley, Fred. *Holy Spirit Fill Me*. Camp Hill, PA: Christian Publications, 1992.

Heffelfinger, Katie M., and Patrick G. McGlinchey. *Atonement as Gift: Reimagining the Cross*. Carlisle, UK: Paternoster, 2014.

Heschmeyer, Joe. "Neurology and C. S. Lewis' Argument from Desire." https://strangenotions.com/neurology-and-c-s-lewis-argument-from.

Honig, Alice. *Risk Factors in Infancy*. New York: Gordon and Beach Science, 1986.

Hughes, Daniel A. *8 Keys to Building Your Best Relationships*. New York: W. W. Norton, 2013.

Hummel, Charles. *Tyranny of the Urgent*. Downers Grove, IL: InterVarsity, 1994.

Hunt, Stephen, ed. *New Religions and Spiritualities*. New York: Routledge, 2010.

Issler, Klaus. *Wasting Time with God: A Christian Spirituality of Friendship with God*. Downers Grove, IL: InterVarsity, 2001.

Jacober, Amy E. *The Adolescent Journey*. Downers Grove, IL: InterVarsity, 2011.

Jones, Timothy Paul. *Family Ministry Field Guide*. Indianapolis: Wesleyan, 2011.

Jones, Timothy Paul, and John David Trentham. *Practical Family Ministry*. Nashville, TN: Randall, 2015.

Jones, Tony. *Postmodern Youth Ministry*. Grand Rapids, MI: Zondervan/YS, 2001.

Kageler, Len, and Jonathan Hobbs, eds. *Don't Do This: Learning from the Screw-Ups of Youth Ministry Leaders*. San Diego: Youth Cartel, 2016.

Kaplan, Sarah. "The Rise and Fall of Abercrombie's 'Look Policy.'" *The Washington Post* (June 2, 2015). https://www.washingtonpost.com/news/morning-mix/wp/2015/06/02/the-rise-and-fall-of-abercrombies-look-policy/.

Kearney, Melissa. "Income Inequality in the United States." https://www.brookings.edu/testimonies/income-inequality-in-the-united-states/.

Keener, Craig. "Jesus's Disciples Were Teenagers." http://www.craigkeener.com/jesuss-disciples-were-teenagers/.

Keller, Tim. "The Insistence that Doctrine Does Not Matter Is Itself a Doctrine." September 1, 2017, 3:01 p.m. https://twitter.com/timkellernyc/status/903686426679705600.

Kelley, M. M., and K. T. Chan. "Assessing the Role of Attachment to God, Meaning, and Religious Coping as Mediators in the Grief Experience." *Death Studies* 36 (2012) 199–227.

Keuss, Jeffrey. *Blur: A New Paradigm for Understanding Youth Culture*. Grand Rapids, MI: Zondervan, 2014.

Kimball, Dan. *The Emerging Church*. Grand Rapids, MI: Zondervan, 2003.

———. *They Like Jesus but Not the Church*. Grand Rapids, MI: Zondervan, 2007.

King, Mike. *Presence-Centered Youth Ministry*. Downers Grove, IL: InterVarsity, 2006.

Kirk, Brian, and Jacob Thorne. *Missional Youth Ministry*. Grand Rapids, MI: Zondervan/YS, 2011.

Knabb, Joshua J., and Matthew Y. Emerson. "Attachment Theory and the Grand Metanarrative of Scripture." *Pastoral Psychology* 62 (2013) 827–41.

Knick, Stanley. "Traditional Culture and Modern Culture: Man's Fall from Grace." *Huffington Post* (May 25, 2011). https://www.huffingtonpost.com/entry/traditional-culture-and m_b_655992.html.

Kostenberger, Andreas J. *God, Marriage and Family*. Wheaton, IL: Crossway, 2010.

Kricher, Lee D. *For a New Generation: A Practical Guide for Revitalizing Your Church*. Grand Rapids, MI: Zondervan, 2016.

Lanker, Jason, and Klaus Issler. "The Relationship Between Natural Mentoring and Spirituality in Christian Adolescents." *Journal of Youth Ministry* 9 (2010) 93–109.

Larson, Scott. *At Risk*. Loveland, CO: Group, 1999.

Lawrence, Rick. *Jesus Centered Youth Ministry*. Loveland, CO: Group, 2007.

Leopold, Thomas. "Gender Differences in the Consequences of Divorce." *Demography* 55 (2018) 769–97.

Lester, Stuart, and Wendy Russell. "Turning the World Upside Down: Playing as the Deliberate Creation of Uncertainty." In *The Role of Play in Children's Health and Development*, edited by Ute Navidi, 14–20. Basel, Switzerland: MDPI, 2016.

Lewis, C. S. *The Abolition of Man*. New York: HarperOne, 2015.

———. *The Four Loves*. Orlando: Harcourt Brace, 1960.

———. *Mere Christianity*. San Francisco: HarperCollins, 1980.

———. *The Voyage of the Dawn Treader*. San Francisco: HarperCollins, 2008.

Lewis, Gordon R., and Bruce A. Demarest. *Integrative Theology*. Grand Rapids, MI: Zondervan, 1996.

Lifeway Research. "American Millennials Prefer Experience Over Expertise." https://lifewayresearch.com/2010/11/03/lifeway-research-finds-american-millennials-prefer-experience-over-expertise/.

Lipka, Michael. "Millennials Increasingly Are Driving Growth of 'Nones.'" *Pew Research* (May 12, 2015). http://www.pewresearch.org/fact-tank/2015/05/12/millennials-increasingly-aredriving-growth-of-nones/.

MacDonald, James. *Vertical Church: What Every Heart Longs For*. Colorado Springs, CO: David C. Cook, 2015.

Marino, Matt. "Is the Way We Are Doing Youth Ministry Emptying the Church?" October 3, 2012. https://thegospelside.com/2012/10/03/is-the-way-we-are-doing-youth-ministry-emptying-the-church/.

Maxwell, John. "9 Ways to Lead Your Leader." http://www.johnmaxwell.com/blog/9-ways-to-lead-your-leader.

McKee, Jonathan. *Connect: Real Relationships in a World of Isolation*. Grand Rapids, MI: Zondervan/YS, 2009.

———. "When Did Programming Become the P-Word"? *Youth Specialities* (February 7, 2012). https://youthspecialties.com/blog/when-did-programming-become-the-p-word/.

Meynell, Mark. *A Wilderness of Mirrors*. Grand Rapids, MI: Zondervan, 2015.

Michelson, Paul E. "Of Urban Blockheads and Trousered Apes: C. S. Lewis and the Challenge of Education." *Inklings Forever* 4 (2004). http://library.taylor.edu/cslewis/colloquium/2004/michelson.shtml.

Mojtabi, Ramin, et al. "National Trends in the Prevalence and Treatment of Depression in Adolescents and Young Adults." *American Academy of Pediatrics* (October 31, 2017). http://pediatrics.aappublications.org/content/early/2016/11/10/peds.2016-1878.

Moore, Cassie. *Authentic Youth Ministry*. St. Louis, MO: Concordia, 2016.

Moore, Lucy, and Jane Leadbetter. *Messy Church*. Downers Grove, IL: InterVarsity, 2017.

Moreland, J. P. *Kingdom Triangle*. Grand Rapids, MI: Zondervan, 2007.

Morgan, Brock. *Youth Ministry 2027: A New Vision for Youth Ministry*. San Diego: Youth Cartel, 2017.

Moriarity, Glendon L., et al. "Understanding the God Image through Attachment Theory." *Journal of Spirituality in Mental Health* 9 (2006) 43–56.

Murphy, Caryle. "Most Christian Groups Grow More Accepting of Homosexuality." *Pew Research* (December 18, 2015). http://www.pewresearch.org/fact-tank/2015/12/18/most-u-s-christian-groups-grow-more-accepting-of-homosexuality/.

Nathanson, Ariel. "Embracing Darkness: Adolescents and Young Adults Addicted to Sexual Enactments." *Journal of Child Psychotherapy* 42 (2016) 272–84.

National Association of Evangelicals. "When Americans Become Christians." https://www.nae.net/when-americans-become-christians/.

Natterson-Horowitz, Barbara, and Kathryn Bowers. *Zoobiquity*. New York: Vintage, 2013.

Noffke, Jacquelin L., and Todd W. Hall. "Attachment, Psychotherapy, and God Image." *Journal of Spirituality in Mental Health* 9 (2007) 57–78.

Olson, David. *Circumplex Model: Systemic Assessment and Treatment of Families*. New York: Routledge, 1989.

Ortlund, Dane C. *Zeal without Knowledge: The Concept of Zeal in Romans 10*. New York: Bloomsbury, 2014.

———. "Zeal without Knowledge: For What did Paul Criticize His Fellow Jews in Romans 10:2–3." *Westminster Theological Journal* 73 (2011) 23–37.

Osmer, Richard R. *Practical Theology: An Introduction*. Grand Rapids, MI: Eerdmans, 2008.

Ostreicher, Mark. *Youth Ministry 3.0: A Manifesto of Where We've Been, Where We Are, and Where We Need to Go*. Grand Rapids, MI: Zondervan/YS, 2008.

Parrett, Gary. "Toward What End? A Response to Chap Clark's Youth Ministry as Practical Theology." *The Journal of Youth Ministry* 7 (2008) 59–65.

Parsley, Ross. *Messy Church*. Colorado Springs, CO: David C. Cook, 2012.

Pauletti, Rachel E., et al. "Sex Differences in Pre-Adolescent Attachment Strategies." *Social Development* 25 (2016) 390–404.

Pearce, Lisa D., and Melinda Lundquist Denton. *A Faith of Their Own*. New York: Oxford University Press, 2011.

Pearson, Jo. "Inappropriate Sexuality? Theology and Sexuality." In *New Religions and Spiritualities*, edited by Stephen Hunt, 291–304. New York: Routledge, 2010.

Pew Research Center. "The American Family Today." http://www.pewsocialtrends.org/2015/12/17/1-the-american-family-today/.

———. "Atheists." http://www.pewforum.org/religious-landscape-study/religious-family/atheist/.

———. "The Rise in Dual Income Households." http://www.pewresearch.org/ft_dual-income-households-1960-2012-2/.

Platt, David. *Follow Me*. Carol Stream, IL: Tyndale, 2013.

Powell, Kara, et al. *Growing Young: 6 Essential Strategies*. Grand Rapids, MI: Baker, 2016.

Pozzoboni, Kristen, and Ben Krishner, eds. *The Changing Landscape of Youth Work: Theory and Practice for an Evolving Field*. Charlotte, NC: Information Age, 2016.

Quintana, Heather. *Momentum: Moving in the Right Direction*. Hagerstown, MD: Review and Herald, 2012.

Rainer, Thom. *The Bridger Generation*. Nashville, TN: B&H, 2006.

———. *I Am a Church Member*. Nashville, TN: B&H, 2013.

Rambo, Lewis R., and Steven C. Bauman. "Psychology of Conversion and Spiritual Transformation." *Pastoral Psychology* 61 (2012) 879–94.

Ramirez, Eddie. "More High School Students Take College Classes." *U.S. News* (June 26, 2008). https://www.usnews.com/education/articles/2008/06/26/more-high-school-kids-takecollege-classes.

Renfro, Paul, et al. *Perspectives on Family Ministry*. Nashville, TN: B&H, 2009.

Robbins, Duffy. "Teaching the Bible so Young People Will Learn." In *Teaching the Next Generations*, edited by Terry Linhart, 211–28. Grand Rapids, MI: Baker Academic, 2016.

———. *Youth Ministry Nuts & Bolts*. Grand Rapids, MI: Zondervan, 2010.

Root, Andrew. *Exploding Stars, Dead Dinosaurs, and Zombies: Youth Ministry in the Age of Science*. Minneapolis: Fortress, 2018.

———. *Faith Formation in a Secular Age*. Grand Rapids, MI: Baker Academic, 2017.

———. *Relationships Unfiltered*. Grand Rapids, MI: Zondervan/YS, 2009.

———. *Revisiting Relational Youth Ministry*. Downers Grove, IL: InterVarsity, 2007.

———. *Taking Theology to Youth Ministry*. Grand Rapids, MI: Zondervan, 2012.

Rowatt, Wade, and Lee A. Kirkpatrick. "Dimensions of Attachment to God." *Journal for the Scientific Study of Religion* 41 (2002) 637–51.

Ryken, Leland, et al., eds. "Right, Right Hand." In *Dictionary of Biblical Imagery*, 727–28. Downers Grove, IL: InterVarsity, 1998.

Schaeffer, Francis. *A Christian Manifesto*. Westchester, IL: Crossway, 1981.

Schnitker, Sarah A., et al. "Attachment Predicts Adolescent Conversions at Young Life Religious Summer Camps." *The International Journal for the Psychology of Religion* 22 (2012) 198–215.

Search Institute. "The Developmental Assets Framework." https://www.search-institute.org/ourresearch/development-assets/developmental-assets-framework/.

Sell, Charles. *Family Ministry*. Grand Rapids, MI: Zondervan, 1995.

Senter, Mark, III, et al. *Four Views of Youth Ministry and the Church*. Grand Rapids, MI: Zondervan, 2001.

Siegel, Dan. *Brainstorm*. New York: Penguin, 2013.

———. *Pocket Guide to Interpersonal Neurobiology*. New York: W. W. Norton, 2012.

Silliman, Benjamin. "Building Healthy Marriages through Early and Extended Outreach with Youth." *Journal of Psychology and Theology* 31 (2003) 270–82.

Sim, Tick Ngee, and Amanda Shixian Yow. "God Attachment, Mother Attachment, and Father Attachment in Early and Mid-Adolescence." *Journal of Religious Health* 50 (2011) 264–78.

Smith, Christian. "The National Study of Youth and Religion." https://youthandreligion.nd.edu/.

Smith, Christian, and Melina Lundquist Denton. *Soul Searching: The Religious and Spiritual Lives of American Teenagers*. New York: Oxford University Press, 2009.

"Sonlife." https://www.sonlife.com/.

Spradlin, Byron. "Art in Ministry." Paper presented at Youth Ministry Executive Council. San Diego, May 2015.

Steinberg, Laurence, and Kathryn C. Monahan. "Age Differences in Resistance to Peer Influence." *Developmental Psychology* 43 (2007) 1531–43.

Stetzer, Ed. "Evangelism and Youth." Paper presented at Youth Ministry Executive Council. San Diego, May 2015.

Stier, Greg. "The Hidden Danger in Dropping Youth Ministry for a Family Ministry Approach." http://gregstier.dare2share.org/the-hidden-danger-in-dropping-youth-ministry-for-a-family-ministry-approach.

Stollar, R. L. "6 Things You Should Know about Voddie Baucham." https://homeschoolersanonymous.org/2014/12/01/6-things-you-should-know-about-voddie-baucham/.

Strommen, Merton, et al. *Youth Ministry that Transforms*. Grand Rapids, MI: Zondervan/YS, 2001.

Svboda, Greg. "Re-thinking Incarnational Ministry." http://gregsvoboda.com/re-thinking-incarnational-ministry/.

Talbot, Christopher. *ReModeling Youth Ministry*. Gallatin, TN: Welch College Press, 2017.

Thomas, Robert L. *New American Standard Exhaustive Concordance of the Bible*. Nashville, TN: Holman Bible, 1981.

Thompson, Derek. "Generation Stuck." *The Atlantic* (March 12, 2012). https://www.theatlantic.com/business/archive/2012/03/generation-stuck-why-dont-young-people-move-anymore/254349/.

Turner, Steve. *Popcultured: Thinking Christianly about Style, Media, and Entertainment*. Downers Grove, IL: InterVarsity, 2013.

Twenge, Jean M. *iGen*. New York: Atria, 2017.

Underwood, Lee A., and Frances L. L. Dailey. *Counseling Adolescents Competently*. Thousand Oaks, CA: SAGE, 2017.

Urban, Hugh B. *New Age, Neopagan, and New Religious Movements: Alternative Spirituality in Contemporary America*. Oakland: University of California Press, 2015.

Vandegriff, Steve. "Family Ministry in the Midst of a Cataclysmic Culture Shift in Sexuality." *D6, Family Ministry Journal* 1 (2016) 119–32.

Vander Laan, Ray. "Follow the Rabbi Lectures." http://oneinjesus.info/2008/10/ray-vander-laans-follow-the-rabbi-lectures/.

Vaz, Kim Marie. "A Woman in the Grip of the Archetype of the Sexual Priestess." In *New Religions and Spiritualities*, edited by Stephen Hunt, 277–90. New York: Routledge, 2010.

Wells, Samuel. *Incarnational Ministry: Being with the Church*. Grand Rapids, MI: Eerdmans, 2017.

Whitbeck, Les B., and Viktor Gecas. "Value Attributions and Value Transmission Between Parents and Children." *Journal of Marriage and Family* 50 (1988) 829–40.

Williams, Alex. "Meet Alpha: The 'Next Generation.'" *New York Times* (September 19, 2015). https://www.nytimes.com/2015/09/19/fashion/meet-alpha-the-next-next-generation.html.

Woodward, J. R., and Dan White Jr. *The Church as Movement*. Downers Grove, IL: InterVarsity, 2016.

Wright, Dave, and Dixon Kinser. "Post-Relational Youth Ministry." http://aidanslegacy.typepad.com/lillylewin/files/articles_postrelational_youth_ministry_beyond_youth_work_as_we_know_it_youthworker_journal.html.

Wright, H. Norman. *Marriage and Family Enrichment Resource Manual*. Tustin, CA: Christian Marriage Enrichment, 1979.

Yaconelli, Mark. *Contemplative Youth Ministry*. Grand Rapids, MI: Zondervan/YS, 2006.

———. "The Failure of Youth Ministry." https://donbryant.wordpress.com/2008/02/14/the-failure-of-youth-ministry/.

———. *Messy Spirituality*. Grand Rapids, MI: Zondervan/YS, 2015.

Yarhouse, Mark A. *Understanding Sexual Identity*. Grand Rapids, MI: Zondervan/YS, 2013.

Zahl, Bonnie Poon, and Nicholas J. S. Gibson. "God Representations, Attachment to God, and Satisfaction with Life." *The International Journal for the Psychology of Religion* 22 (2012) 216–30.

Zemple, Heather. *Community Is Messy: The Perils and Promise of Small Group Ministry.* Downers Grove, IL: InterVarsity, 2012.

Zuckerman, M., J. Silberman, and J. A. Hall. "The Relation Between Intelligence and Religiosity: A Meta-Analysis." *Personality and Social Psychology Review* 17 (2013) 325–54.

Index

Made in the USA
Middletown, DE
10 February 2021

33460634R00155